# Corporate Liability for Insider Trading

*Corporate Liability for Insider Trading* examines the reasons why there have been no successful criminal prosecutions, or successful contested civil proceedings, against corporations for insider trading, and analyses the various rationales for prohibiting insider trading. It reviews the insider trading regulatory regime and describes its key features, using both national and international examples. The book inspects a variety of criminal and civil models of corporate liability and considers the historical and theoretical basis on which corporations are subject to insider trading laws.

The specific elements of the insider trading offence and the manner in which they are attributed to corporations are analysed in detail. Defences available to corporations, such as Chinese Walls, are explored, and the obligations that are imposed on businesses as a result of insider trading regulation – security trading policies and notifications, continuous disclosure obligations, and duties concerning conflicts of interest – are detailed and examined. The book concludes with reform proposals intended to remedy the many legal and commercial difficulties identified, in order that a new regulatory regime might be adopted to better serve regulators, businesses, investors, and the broader market.

This volume addresses these corporate law topics and will be of interest to researchers, academics, financial institution compliance officers, investment bankers, corporate and comparative lawyers, and students and scholars in the fields of commercial law, corporate law, financial crime, company law, and white-collar crime.

**Dr Juliette Overland** is an Associate Professor at the University of Sydney Business School, Australia.

# The Law of Financial Crime

Series Editor: Nicholas Ryder

Available titles in this series include:

**Fighting Financial Crime in the Global Economic Crisis**
*Nicholas Ryder, Umut Turksen and Sabine Hassler*

**The Financial War on Terror**
A Review of Counter-Terrorist Financing Strategies Since 2001
*Nicholas Ryder*

**The Financial Crisis and White Collar Crime – Legislative and Policy Responses**
A Critical Assessment
*Edited by Nicholas Ryder, Jon Tucker and Umut Turksen*

**Countering Economic Crime**
A Comparative Analysis
*Axel Palmer*

**The Global Anti-Corruption Regime**
The Case of Papua New Guinea
*Hannah Harris*

**Financial Crime and Corporate Misconduct**
A Critical Evaluation of Fraud Legislation
*Edited by Chris Monaghan and Nicola Monaghan*

**Corporate Liability for Insider Trading**
*Juliette Overland*

For more information about this series, please visit: www.routledge.com/The-Law-of-Financial-Crime/book-series/FINCRIME

# Corporate Liability for Insider Trading

Juliette Overland

Routledge
Taylor & Francis Group

LONDON AND NEW YORK

First published 2019
by Routledge
2 Park Square, Milton Park, Abingdon, Oxon OX14 4RN

and by Routledge
52 Vanderbilt Avenue, New York, NY 10017

First issued in paperback 2020

*Routledge is an imprint of the Taylor & Francis Group, an informa business*

*British Library Cataloguing-in-Publication Data*
A catalogue record for this book is available from the British Library

*Library of Congress Cataloging-in-Publication Data*
Names: Overland, Juliette, author.
Title: Corporate liability for insider trading / Juliette Overland.
Description: New York, NY : Routledge, 2019. | Series: The law of
    financial crime | Includes bibliographical references.
Identifiers: LCCN 2018051916 | ISBN 9781138299023 (hardback)
Subjects: LCSH: Insider trading in securities—Law and legislation—
    Australia. | Insider trading in securities—Law and legislation. | Tort
    liability of corporations—Australia. | Tort liability of corporations.
Classification: LCC KU894.4.I57 O94 2019 | DDC 346.9403—dc23
LC record available at https://lccn.loc.gov/2018051916

ISBN 13: 978-0-367-66032-1 (pbk)
ISBN 13: 978-1-138-29902-3 (hbk)

Typeset in Galliard
by Apex CoVantage, LLC

To Ben, Imogen and Xavier

# Contents

*Acknowledgements*                                                          xi
*Abbreviations*                                                            xii

**1   Corporate liability for insider trading: an introduction**             1
*Background to the prohibition of insider trading  2*
*The rationale for the prohibition of insider trading  6*

**2   The regulation of insider trading**                                   13
*The key features of Australian insider trading laws  13*
*The possession of information  16*
  *The nature of information  16*
  *The nature of possession  20*
*Information which is not generally available  24*
  *Readily observable information  25*
  *Publishable information  26*
  *Deductions, conclusions and inferences  28*
*Material information  28*
*Knowledge that information is inside information  34*
*Trading, procuring and tipping in relevant financial
   products  37*
*Contentious aspects of insider trading  38*

**3   The application of insider trading laws to corporations**             39
*A corporation as a 'person' caught by the prohibition of insider
   trading  39*
*International comparisons  41*
*The history and theory of the application of Australian insider
   trading laws to corporations  44*
*Why corporations should be liable for insider trading  51*

**4    Corporate criminal and civil liability**                              55

*Models of corporate criminal liability 55*
*Vicarious liability 57*
*Direct liability 58*
*Aggregation doctrine 64*
*Organisational fault 66*
*Statutory principles of corporate criminal liability 66*
*Civil liability for insider trading 69*
*A model of corporate liability for insider trading in
    Australia 71*

**5    Attributing the elements of insider trading to corporations**         73

*The relevant elements of insider trading 73*
*Attributing the possession element to corporations 75*
    *Statutory mechanisms 82*
    *General law agency rules 90*
    *Identification doctrine 91*
    *Collective knowledge 93*
    *Relationship with continuous disclosure obligations 94*
    *Different mechanisms for determining when a corporation
        possesses information 95*
*Attributing the knowledge element to corporations 99*
    *Statutory mechanisms 100*
    *General law principles 103*
    *Identification doctrine 104*
    *Agency principles 105*
    *Different mechanisms for establishing the knowledge of
        corporations 105*
    *Demonstrating that a corporation 'ought reasonably' to have
        certain knowledge 107*
    *International comparisons 108*
*Attributing the trading element to corporations 110*
    *Statutory mechanisms 111*
    *Identification doctrine 115*
    *Different mechanisms for establishing the conduct of
        corporations 116*
*Preliminary conclusions and recommended reforms 117*

**6    The Chinese Wall defence to insider trading**                         119

*The nature of the Chinese Wall defence 120*
*The origins of Chinese Walls 122*

*The necessity for Chinese Walls 125*

*Requirements for reliance on the Chinese Wall defence 126*

    *The person deciding to trade in relevant financial products did not possess inside information 126*

    *A sufficient Chinese Wall was in place 130*

    *Cases concerning Chinese Walls and insider trading 131*

    *Market rules and accepted industry practices 133*

    *Cases concerning Chinese Walls in other contexts 136*

    *The inside information was not communicated and no advice was given 139*

    *International comparisons 140*

*Preliminary conclusions and recommended reforms 146*

**7 Insider trading and business obligations**    148

*Continuous disclosure regime 148*

*Securities trading policies 151*

*Insider trading notifications 152*

*Notification of directors' securities trading 153*

*Directors' duties and conflicts of interest 154*

*Concluding comments on business obligations 155*

**8 Corporate liability for insider trading: reform proposals**    156

*Flaws in the current regime 157*

*Proposed new provisions 161*

*Nature of the proposed reforms 164*

    *Exclusion of the general law 164*

    *Continued exclusion of the Criminal Code 165*

    *Exclusion of section 769B of the Corporations Act 166*

    *No requirement for nexus with role or position for information or knowledge 166*

    *Attribution is possible for all officers, employees and agents of a corporation 167*

    *Conduct must occur within the scope of authority or with authorisation of a person with authority, on behalf of corporation 167*

    *Link between the possession of information, knowledge and conduct 168*

    *Direct model of corporate liability for insider trading 168*

    *Redrafting of the Chinese Wall defence 169*

    *Amendments concerning section 1043M of the Corporations Act 169*

**9   Conclusions**                                                           171


*Appendix*                                                                   173
*Bibliography*                                                               175
*Index*                                                                      187

# Acknowledgements

This book had its origin in my PhD thesis, which I undertook at the Australian National University. I am very grateful to my supervisors, Professor Stephen Bottomley and Professor Alex Steel, for their invaluable guidance, constructive criticisms and insightful suggestions over many years of research and writing.

Some of the material included in this book has also been published in journal articles appearing in the *Australian Journal of Corporate Law*, the *Company and Securities Law Journal* and the *Australian Business Law Review*. In particular, the key research and recommendations underlying this book featured as a two-part article published in the *Australian Journal of Corporate Law*. The publishers of these journals have generously granted permission for material from those journal articles to be included in this book, as set out in the Appendix.

Any errors or omissions are my responsibility.

# Abbreviations

| | |
|---|---|
| ASIC | Australian Securities and Investments Commission |
| ASX | Australian Securities Exchange Limited |
| CAMAC | Corporations and Markets Advisory Committee |
| *Corporations Act* | *Corporations Act 2001* (Cth) |
| *Criminal Code* | *Criminal Code Act 1995* (Cth) |
| SEC | Securities Exchange Commission |

# 1 Corporate liability for insider trading

## An introduction

The regulation of insider trading is a controversial and complex area of corporate law. In essence, insider trading is the act of trading in financial products (such as shares or other securities) while in possession of relevant non-public, price-sensitive information.

Insider trading is generally acknowledged, if not universally accepted, as a significant threat to market integrity, which is widely regarded as an essential requirement for the proper, efficient functioning of securities markets.[1] Indeed, the accepted rationale for prohibiting insider trading in Australia is to protect and maintain market integrity.[2] However, regulators are regularly criticised for a perceived lack of enforcement action in relation to insider trading. Indeed, although there has been a marked increase in the number of individual offenders convicted of insider trading in recent years, there has never been a successful criminal prosecution of a corporation for insider trading in Australia, and just one successful set of civil penalty proceedings, in which liability for insider trading was admitted.[3]

While commonly referred to as 'insider' trading, the prohibition under Australian law is not limited to those who might generally be classified as corporate insiders – such as directors, senior executives or other officers – and it is not limited to direct trading by the relevant person, but also encompasses the related conduct of the procuring of trading, and tipping. The term 'insider trading' is used in this context throughout this book. Additionally, the inclusive term 'corporation' is used, rather than 'company' or 'body corporate'.[4]

---

1   See, for example, ASIC, *Consultation Paper 68, Competition for Market Services – Trading in Listed Securities and Related Data*, 2007; Utpal Bhattacharya and Hazem Daouk, 'The World Price of Insider Trading' (2002) 57 *Journal of Finance* 75; Laura Nyantung Beny, 'Insider Trading Laws and Stock Markets Around the World: An Empirical Contribution to the Theoretical Law and Economics Debate' (2007) 32 *Journal of Corporation Law* 237.

2   This rationale was confirmed by the majority of the High Court of Australia in *Mansfield and Kizon v R* (2012) 87 ALJR 20. A detailed analysis of the various rationales for prohibiting insider trading is set out later in this chapter.

3   *ASIC v Hochtief* [2016] FCA 1489.

4   The definition of 'corporation' in s 57A of the *Corporations Act* includes a company and other forms of body corporate.

## Background to the prohibition of insider trading

Insider trading has been the subject of significant international attention and scrutiny over recent decades. The United States was the first country to formally prohibit insider trading.[5] After the Second World War, Japan was pressured to adopt insider trading regulations modelled on the laws of the United States.[6] Other countries gradually began to adopt laws regulating insider trading – in Australia, insider trading was first prohibited under statute in the 1970s[7] – and the vast majority of countries with securities markets now have legislation which prohibits insider trading.[8] There appear to be a number of reasons for the rapid increase in the enactment of laws prohibiting insider trading. Countries within the European Union were obliged to adopt insider trading laws as a result of a binding directive of the European Council issued in 1989.[9] Other countries enacted insider trading laws as they sought to make their stock exchanges more competitive internationally, often in response to the enactment of similar laws in other jurisdictions.[10] Although the insider trading regimes of different countries do not have the same characteristics, and the underlying reasons for the prohibition of insider trading vary, more than 90 countries prohibit insider trading,[11] with all developed nations and 80 per cent of nations with emerging securities markets

---

5  Franklin A Gevurtz, 'The Globalisation of Insider Trading Prohibitions' (2002) 15 *Transnational Lawyer* 63, 64. SEC rule 10b5–1 is the basis for the prohibition of insider trading in the United States and was first adopted in 1942 pursuant to rule 10(b) of the *Securities Exchange Act of 1934*, 15 USC § 78a (1934).

6  Lori Semaan, Mark Freeman and Michael Adams, 'Is Insider Trading a Necessary Evil for Efficient Markets? An International Comparative Analysis' (1999) 17 *Company and Securities Law Journal* 220, 228.

7  Insider trading was first prohibited by statute in Australia under amendments made in 1975 to the uniform *Securities Industry Acts* previously adopted by four States: *Securities Industry Act 1970* (Qld); *Securities Industry Act 1970* (NSW); *Securities Industry Act 1970* (WA); *Securities Industry Act 1970* (Vic), as noted in Gregory Lyon and Jean J du Plessis, *The Law of Insider Trading in Australia* (Federation Press, Sydney, 2005) 5.

8  Gevurtz, above n 5, 65.

9  *Council Directive 89/592/EEC of 13 November 1989 Coordinating Regulations on Insider Dealing*, OJ 1989 L 334/30. This directive was later superseded by the *Directive 2003/6/EC of the European Parliament and of the Council of 28 January 2003 on Insider Dealing and Market Abuse*, OJ 2003 I 96/16, which has now been replaced by the *Regulation (EU) 596/2014 of the European Parliament and of the Council of 16 April 2014 on Market Abuse* (Market Abuse Regulation), and the *Directive 2014/57/EU of the European Parliament and of the Council of 16 April 2014 on Criminal Sanctions for Market Abuse*, OJ 2014 L 173.179 (Market Abuse Directive).

10  Gevurtz, above n 5, 67.

11  Laura Nyantung Beny, 'The Political Economy of Insider Trading Laws and Enforcement: Law vs. Politics? International Evidence', in Stephen M Bainbridge (ed), *Research Handbook on Insider Trading* (Edward Elgar, Cheltenham, 2013) 266, 287; Bhattacharya and Daouk, above n 1, 77; Gordon R Walker and Andrew F Simpson, 'Insider Conduct Regulation in New Zealand: Exploring the Enforcement Deficit' (2013) *New Zealand Law Review* 521, 521–522.

regulating this form of conduct.[12] Additionally, the International Organisation of Securities Commissions views the regulation of insider trading as a 'cornerstone of securities trading laws'.[13]

Despite the widespread adoption of insider trading laws internationally, insider trading has a reputation as a notoriously difficult offence to successfully detect and prosecute, and the regulation of insider trading continues to be the subject of ongoing debate. Some members of the financial services industry openly state that they believe insider trading is both rife and increasing, particularly when markets are volatile,[14] and some commentators consider insider trading to be unavoidable and endemic to securities markets.[15] Indeed, some anecdotal evidence appears to indicate that insider trading in shares in the period immediately prior to takeover announcements causes rises in share prices of, on average, 10 per cent.[16] Empirical evidence, both within Australia and overseas, seems to indicate that corporate insiders are able to earn abnormal profits and avoid abnormal losses through share trading.[17]

12  Gevurtz, above n 5, 67; CAMAC, *Insider Trading Discussion Paper*, 2001, [1.4]. Australia's insider trading regime is compared with those of other jurisdictions in chapter 2.

13  Paul Latimer and Philipp Maume, *Promoting Information in the Marketplace for Financial Services – Financial Market Regulation and International Standards* (Springer, Cham, 2014) 68. Of the 38 principles developed by the International Organisations of Securities Commissions to achieve its key objectives of securities regulation, principle 36 is that 'regulation should be designed to detect and deter manipulation and other unfair market practices': International Organisations of Securities Commissions, *Objectives and Principles of Securities Regulation*, 2010.

14  See, for example, Peter Hunt, Chairman of Caliburn Partnership, as reported in Michael West, 'Insider Trading Still on the Rise: Banker', *The Sydney Morning Herald* (Sydney), 20 February 2008; Professor Ian Ramsay, Director of the Centre for Corporate Law and Securities Regulation, University of Melbourne, as reported in Vanessa Burrow, 'ASIC on Insider Trading Hunt', *The Age* (Melbourne), 21 March 2008.

15  Leo Herzel and Leo Katz, 'Insider Trading: Who Loses?' (1987) *Lloyds Bank Review* 15; Phillip Anthony O'Hara, 'Insider Trading in Financial Markets: Legality, Ethics, Efficiency' (2001) 28 *International Journal of Social Economics* 1046, 1048; Stanislav Dolgopolov, 'Risks and Hedges of Providing Liquidity in Complex Securities: The Impact of Insider Trading on Options Market Makers' (2010) 15 *Fordham Journal of Corporate and Financial Law* 387.

16  See, for example, Michael Sainsbury, 'Insider Trading Rife in Australia', *The Australian* (Sydney), 20 February 2008.

17  See, for example, H Negat Seyhun, 'Insider Profits, Costs of Trading and Market Efficiency' (1986) 16 *Journal of Financial Economics* 189; Laura Nyantung Beny and H Nejat Seyhun, 'Has Illegal Insider Trading Become More Rampant in the United States? Empirical Evidence from Takeovers', in Stephen M Bainbridge (ed), *Research Handbook on Insider Trading* (Edward Elgar, Cheltenham, 2013) 211; Mark A Freeman and Michael A Adams, 'Australian Insiders' Views on Insider Trading' (1999) 10 *Australian Journal of Corporate Law* 148; Arturo Bris, 'Do Insider Trading Laws Work' (2005) 11 *European Financial Management* 267; Philip Brown, Mark Foo and Iain Watson, 'Trading by Insiders in Australia: Evidence on the Profitability of Directors' Trades' (2003) 21 *Company and Securities Law Journal* 248, 260.

The first conviction for insider trading in Australia did not occur until 1991,[18] and further convictions were obtained intermittently, with only four additional convictions for insider trading in the following ten years. Since that time, the frequency and number of insider trading prosecutions and convictions has significantly increased, and greater enforcement action has been taken, particularly in recent years. However, there have been no successful criminal proceedings brought against a corporation for insider trading in Australia, or a successful set of contested civil penalty proceedings. In 2007, ASIC, the local regulator, brought civil penalty proceedings for insider trading against a corporation, the Australian subsidiary of the global investment bank, Citigroup, but those proceedings were unsuccessful.[19] A set of civil penalty proceedings brought against Hochtief Actiengesellschaft by ASIC in 2016, in which liability for insider trading was admitted, was the first Australian case in which a corporation has been found liable for insider trading.[20]

As insider trading has the potential to create major negative impacts on global securities markets, the application of insider trading laws to corporations is a significant issue warranting further research and attention, because of the potential to reduce insider trading and improve the ability of regulators to take appropriate enforcement action. The reform of insider trading laws as they apply to corporations offers Australia the opportunity to adopt laws of international significance, and which would enable Australia's securities markets to remain globally competitive.

There may be a number of possible reasons why there has never been a successful prosecution or successful set of contested civil penalty proceedings for insider trading brought against a corporation: (i) corporations may not engage in insider trading – insider trading may only be engaged in by individuals in circumstances that would not result in a corporation having any liability for insider trading; (ii) corporations may engage in insider trading, but prosecutors and regulators may be reluctant to pursue insider trading cases against corporations due to uncertainties in the law and difficulties in applying insider trading laws to corporations; or (iii) corporations may engage in insider trading, but in circumstances where individuals associated with the relevant corporations may also have liability for insider trading, so that prosecutors and regulators elect to take action against those individuals, rather than to pursue the corporation.

Although it might technically be possible that corporations do not engage in insider trading, the idea that insider trading is only engaged in by individuals in circumstances that would not result in a corporation having any liability is less than compelling. Why would it be the case that individuals engage in insider trading and not corporations? The majority of Australian insider trading cases have involved conduct which occurred in a corporate context and the admissions of insider trading by Hochtief Aktiengesellschaft refute the suggestion that corporations do not engage in insider trading. It can also be observed that in certain circumstances

18  *R v Teh* (District Court of Victoria, Kelly DCJ, 2 September 1991).
19  *ASIC v Citigroup Global Markets Australia Pty Ltd* (2007) 160 FCR 35.
20  *ASIC v Hochtief* [2016] FCA 1489.

where an individual has been successfully prosecuted for insider trading, a corporation may also have had potential liability for the offence.[21] Insider trading may occur in circumstances where a corporation could be found to have engaged in that conduct, but prosecutors and regulators may be reluctant to take enforcement action, or may prefer to take action against individual offenders instead. Indeed, ASIC has noted, in the context of the general enforcement of corporate crime:

> We may take action against corporations, individuals, or both, depending on the circumstances of the case. For example, taking action against individuals who are directly responsible or in charge, instead of corporations, may reduce the incentive for those individuals and others in similar positions to engage in like misconduct given the potential impact on their reputation and livelihood. This approach is likely to have a greater deterrent effect.[22]

However, if difficulties in the application of insider trading laws to corporations can be identified and resolved, appropriate insider trading enforcement action could be more effectively brought against corporations, increasing the general deterrent effect for all potential offenders.

Even though the majority of jurisdictions with insider trading laws also apply those laws to corporations, there are no recorded instances worldwide of a corporation being convicted in a criminal prosecution, with only a small number of successful civil proceedings for insider trading. Accordingly, while this book focuses upon the position under Australian law, the application of insider trading laws to corporations is a global issue. With insider trading acknowledged as a global problem with the potential to affect all securities markets, there is regular co-operation between the various international regulators responsible for insider trading enforcement to confront issues in detecting and prosecuting insider trading in their respective jurisdictions. As a result, there is the potential for any reforms in the application of insider trading laws to corporations to have great international relevance and significance, particularly in jurisdictions which prohibit insider trading on the basis of the same rationale as Australia – the protection and maintenance of market integrity.

When corporations are bound by laws prohibiting insider trading, they must carry on business and conduct their activities within the ambit of that regulation. When this occurs, all participants in securities markets must have confidence that the application of those laws is appropriate, that the system of regulation is neither unnecessarily burdensome nor inappropriately lax, that there is certainty in the operation and application of those laws and that those laws give effect to their stated aims.

---

21  For example, in *R v Rivkin* (2004) 184 FLR 365, Mr Rene Rivkin purchased and sold shares in Qantas through a private corporation which he controlled – it could be argued that the corporation, Rivkin Investments Pty Ltd, also engaged in insider trading but no action was taken against it.

22  ASIC, *Report 387, Penalties for Corporate Wrongdoing*, 2014, 9.

As insider trading is prohibited in Australia in order to protect and maintain market integrity,[23] all investors and market participants must have confidence that those who might otherwise gain an unfair informational advantage from insider trading are identified and appropriately sanctioned. However, in order for such confidence to exist and for market integrity to be maintained, corporate insider traders must also be detected, not just individual offenders, and corporations found to have engaged in insider trading must be the subject of appropriate enforcement action. Market integrity requires legislative certainty for regulators, market participants, potential investors in securities markets, and all corporations. Therefore, current uncertainties as to the operation of insider trading laws and their application to corporations threaten market confidence and, as a result, market integrity. This problem could be addressed through the reform of the application of insider trading laws to corporations.

## The rationale for the prohibition of insider trading

An understanding of the basis on which insider trading is prohibited is crucial to an evaluation of the relevant laws as they apply to corporations, so that any resulting reform proposals can be crafted appropriately. Despite the fact that the vast majority of countries with securities markets prohibit insider trading, the underlying rationale for such regulation differs between nations. In order to understand the intended operation of insider trading laws, the reasons for its prohibition must also be considered. There are four primary reasons variously identified as the possible bases for the prohibition of insider trading: (i) market fairness; (ii) market efficiency; (iii) fiduciary duty; and (iv) misappropriation.

The 'market fairness' rationale, also referred to as an 'equal access' rationale, is based on the premise that it is not fair for some market participants to have access to price-sensitive information, and to be able to trade on the basis of that information, if it is not also available to all other market participants.[24] Ideally, all market participants should have equal access to relevant information when making trading decisions and therefore be exposed to the same trading risks, but insiders with an 'unerodable informational advantage' are able to trade with a reduced risk, or almost no risk at all.[25] Investor confidence in securities markets is reduced if some investors are believed to have the ability to use information which is not readily available.[26] For this reason, market fairness requires insider

---

23 The majority of the High Court of Australia in *Mansfield and Kizon v R* (2012) 87 ALJR 20 [45].
24 O'Hara, above n 15, 1053.
25 Victor Brudney, 'Insiders, Outsiders and Informational Advantages under the Federal Securities Laws' (1979) 93 *Harvard Law Review* 322, 346.
26 See, for example, ASIC, *Consultation Paper 68*, above n 1; Bhattacharya and Daouk, above n 1; Beny, above n 1.

trading to be prohibited to prevent those with access to inside information from exploiting that unfair advantage.[27]

In circumstances where price-sensitive information is not released to the market in a timely manner, the prices of financial products cannot be said to accurately represent their true value, and therefore market inefficiencies exist.[28] If those with access to price-sensitive information delay its release to the market to allow themselves time to trade, the efficiency of the market is eroded.[29] Additionally, the participation of some investors in the market may be reduced, if those who hold and have access to price-sensitive information are perceived to have a trading advantage.[30] Without confidence in the efficiency of the market, investors may choose alternative investments or demand a premium for assuming higher risks, which in turn increases the cost of capital for corporations.[31] Thus, the 'market efficiency' rationale, first promoted by the work of Fama,[32] requires insider trading to be prohibited in order to maintain an efficient, effective market with the maximum possible participation.

According to the 'fiduciary duty' rationale, a person who is in a legal relationship which imposes obligations of trust and confidence must not profit from that relationship or allow a conflict of interest to arise. If a person who owes a corporation a fiduciary duty derives a personal benefit by using that corporation's confidential information to trade, or if a person owes a fiduciary duty to the counterparty to a trade and does not disclose to that counterparty price-sensitive information which they possess, the fiduciary duty is breached and for that reason insider trading should be prohibited.[33] This reasoning is only applicable where

---

27  CAMAC, *Insider Trading Discussion Paper*, above n 12, [1.20]; Semaan, Freeman and Adams, above n 6, 222. Green takes another view and suggests that insider trading is in fact a form of cheating, noting that the 'stock market is viewed as a highly formalized, rule-governed game. Confidence in the market depends on investors feeling that the game is being played fairly. . . . Market participants who trade on undisclosed inside information . . . [are] cheaters': Stuart P Green, *Lying, Cheating and Stealing: A Moral Theory of White-Collar Crime* (Oxford University Press, 2006) 235.

28  Eugene F Fama, 'Efficient Capital Markets: A Review of Theory and Empirical Work' (1970) 25 *Journal of Finance* 383.

29  Keith Kendall, 'The Need to Prohibit Insider Trading' (2008) 25 *Law in Context* 106.

30  Bhattacharya and Daouk, above n 1; CAMAC, *Insider Trading Discussion Paper*, above n 12, [1.22]. It is also worth noting that some commentators consider that insider trading creates an efficient market by providing a mechanism for the distribution of information: see, for example, Michael Whincop, 'The Political Economy of Corporate Law Reform in Australia' (1999) 27 *Federal Law Review* 77; Michael Whincop, 'Towards a Property Rights and Market Microstructural Theory of Insider Trading Regulation – The Case of Primary Securities Markets Transactions' (1996) 7 *Journal of Banking and Finance Law and Practice* 212.

31  Ashley Black, 'The Reform of Insider Trading Law in Australia' (1992) 15 *University of New South Wales Law Journal* 214, 220.

32  Fama, above n 28.

33  CAMAC, *Insider Trading Discussion Paper*, above n 12, [1.14]; Semaan, Freeman and Adams, above n 6, 222.

the insider trading prohibition applies to those who owe a fiduciary relationship to the corporation which 'owns' the relevant information, or to their trading counterparty, and not where there is no such relationship in existence.[34]

The 'misappropriation' rationale is an extension of the 'fiduciary duty' rationale, being predicated on the basis that using confidential information to trade amounts to a misuse that is inconsistent with the proprietary rights of the true 'owner' of that information.[35] Where the owner of the confidential information is the corporation to which the information relates, the use of that information to trade for personal profit amounts to a theft or misappropriation of that information, and for that reason insider trading should be prohibited.[36]

In this context, it must also be noted that, although the vast majority of countries with established securities exchanges have chosen to prohibit insider trading, a number of commentators consider that insider trading should not be regulated. Manne[37] took the view that insider trading actually allows economic efficiencies, by moving the price of securities towards their real value more quickly. This position was further advanced by those who argue that insider trading most efficiently enables share prices to reflect relevant information, that the prohibition of insider trading decreases the flow of information, and that securities prices are more likely to be accurate when insider trading is permitted.[38] These views support an 'efficient markets hypothesis', which suggests that if insiders can trade on inside information, price signalling will occur, causing the relevant share price to move more quickly towards equilibrium, and creating a more accurate and efficient securities market.[39] Manne has also argued that insider trading rewards innovation by allowing entrepreneurs to make additional profits on top of their ordinary salary and remuneration arrangements.[40] However, other notable commentators, such as Bainbridge, argue that insider

---

34  Jennifer Moore, 'What Is Really Unethical About Insider Trading?' (1990) 9 *Journal of Business Ethics* 171, 174.

35  Lawrence E Mitchell, 'The Jurisprudence of the Misappropriation Theory and the New Insider Trading Legislation: From Fairness to Efficiency and Back' (1988) 52 *Albany Law Review* 775; Stephen M Bainbridge, 'Insider Trading Regulation: The Path Dependent Choice Between Property Rights and Securities Fraud' (1999) 52 *Southern Methodist University Law Review* 1589.

36  CAMAC, *Insider Trading Discussion Paper*, above n 12, [1.18]; Alan Strudler and Eric W Orts, 'Moral Principle in the Law of Insider Trading' (1999) 78 *Texas Law Review* 375; Semaan, Freeman and Adams, above n 6, 222; Moore, above n 34, 175.

37  Henry G Manne, *Insider Trading and the Stock Market* (The Free Press, New York, 1966); Henry G Manne, 'In Defence of Insider Trading' (1966) 43 *Harvard Business Review* 113; Henry G Manne, 'Insider Trading: Hayek, Virtual Markets, and the Dog that Did Not Bark' (2005) 31 *Journal of Corporation Law* 167.

38  See, for example, Hayne E Leland, 'Insider Trading: Should It Be Prohibited?' (1992) 100 *Journal of Political Economy* 859; Javier Estrada, 'Insider Trading: Regulation, Deregulation and Taxation' (1994) 5 *Swiss Review of Business Law* 209.

39  Semaan, Freeman and Adams, above n 6, 225.

40  Manne, *Insider Trading and the Stock Market*, above n 37, 131; Henry G Manne, 'Entrepreneurship, Compensation, and the Corporation', in Stephen M Bainbridge (ed), *Research Handbook on Insider Trading* (Edward Elgar, Cheltenham, 2013) 67.

trading should be prohibited in order to properly protect the property rights in inside information.[41] Securities markets are also considered to be more liquid in jurisdictions where insider trading laws are more stringent,[42] and while the mere adoption of insider trading laws appears to have no effect on securities markets and the cost of equity, the cost of capital decreases when insider trading enforcement action is taken.[43]

The reform proposals contained in this book are predicated on the basis that insider trading is a form of conduct that should be prohibited – regardless of the various underlying rationales – and that the law should be aimed at ensuring that the manner in which insider trading laws apply to corporations reflects the 'mischief' which those laws are intended to remedy which, in Australia, is market fairness and market efficiency,[44] since both are considered necessary to maintain market integrity.[45] In 1981 it was stated in the report of the 'Campbell Inquiry' that insider trading should be prohibited in Australia:

> to ensure that the securities market operates freely and fairly, with all participants having equal access to information. Investor confidence . . . depends importantly on the prevention of the improper use of inside information.[46]

A similar position was taken by the 'Griffiths Committee' in 1989, when it was stated that:

> insider trading damages an essential component in the proper functioning of the securities markets, that is investor confidence.[47]

When the *Corporations Law* was amended by the *Corporations Legislation Amendment Act 1991* (Cth), the Explanatory Memorandum specifically stated that:

> the Government's policy view is . . . that it is necessary to control insider trading to protect investors and make it attractive for them to provide funds to the issuers of securities.[48]

---

41 Bainbridge, above n 35; Stephen M Bainbridge, 'Regulating Insider Trading in the Post-Fiduciary Duty Era: Equal Access or Property Rights?', in Stephen M Bainbridge (ed), *Research Handbook on Insider Trading* (Edward Elgar, Cheltenham, 2013) 80.
42 See, for example, Beny, above n 1; Laura Nyantung Beny, 'Do Insider Trading Laws Matter? Some Preliminary Comparative Evidence' (2005) 7 *American Law and Economics Review* 144.
43 See, for example, Bhattacharya and Daouk, above n 1.
44 Standing Committee on Legal and Constitutional Affairs, House of Representatives, *Fair Shares for All: Insider Trading in Australia* (Australian Government Publishing Service, Canberra, 1989), [3.34] to [3.36].
45 CAMAC, *Insider Trading Discussion Paper*, above n 12, [0.20].
46 Committee of Inquiry into the Australian Financial System, *Australian Financial System: Final Report* (Australian Government Publishing Service, Canberra, 1981) 382.
47 Standing Committee on Legal and Constitutional Affairs, above n 44, 17.
48 Explanatory Memorandum, Corporations Legislation Amendment Bill 1991 (Cth), [307].

The underlying rationale for prohibiting insider trading has also been discussed in a number of Australian cases. In *Hooker Investments Pty Ltd v Baring Bros Halkerston & Partners Securities Ltd*,[49] Young J stated that the prohibition of insider trading[50] was 'to prevent one person having an unfair advantage from another',[51] and the Court of Appeal endorsed this comment on appeal.[52] In *Exicom Pty Ltd v Futuris Corporation Ltd*,[53] Young J again commented on the rationale for prohibiting insider trading and determined that it was only relevant where 'an insider [was] making use of information in a market to gain an advantage over another'.[54] In *R v Firns*,[55] Mason P noted the various theories which have been offered as reasons for prohibiting insider trading, as well as arguments that insider trading is beneficial.[56] His Honour stated that 'market fairness . . . cannot be invoked as the sole basis'[57] for prohibiting insider trading and confirmed that the current Australian system of regulation embodies both market fairness and market efficiency theories.[58] In the first appeal in *R v Mansfield and Kizon*,[59] Buss JA also noted and discussed the four policy rationales which may underlie the insider trading prohibition[60] and confirmed that the market fairness and market efficiency theories underlie Australia's insider trading laws.[61] Then, in 2012, the majority of the High Court of Australia confirmed that the prohibition of insider trading exists to protect and maintain market integrity, stating that the laws were intended to ensure that:

> the securities market operates freely and fairly, with all participants having equal access to relevant information.[62]

---

49  *Hooker Investments Pty Ltd v Baring Bros Halkerston & Partners Securities Ltd* (1986) 10 ACLR 462.
50  At that time contained in s 128 of the *Securities Industry Code*.
51  *Hooker Investments Pty Ltd v Baring Bros Halkerston & Partners Securities Ltd* (1986) 10 ACLR 462, 464.
52  *Hooker Investments Pty Ltd v Baring Bros Halkerston & Partners Securities Ltd* (1986) 5 NSWLR 157, 163.
53  *Exicom Pty Ltd v Futuris Corporation Ltd* (1995) 18 ACSR 404.
54  Ibid 410.
55  *R v Firns* (2001) 19 ACLC 1495.
56  Ibid 1501.
57  Ibid 1503.
58  Ibid 1502.
59  *R v Mansfield and Kizon* (2011) 251 FLR 286.
60  Ibid 296–298.
61  Ibid 312.
62  *Mansfield and Kizon v R* (2012) 87 ALJR 20, [45], referring to statements in the Committee of Inquiry into the Australian Financial System, above n 46, 382, and the Standing Committee on Legal and Constitutional Affairs, above n 44, 17. See further, Juliette Overland, 'What Is Inside "Information"? Clarifying the Ambit of Insider Trading Laws' (2013) 31 *Company and Securities Law Journal* 189.

Thus, a market integrity rationale, premised on a need for both market fairness and market efficiency, has clearly been accepted as the basis for prohibiting insider trading in Australia.[63]

Many other jurisdictions also base their insider trading laws on market fairness and market efficiency rationales. In the European Union, the 'Market Abuse Directive',[64] which sets out the legal framework for insider trading and market misconduct to be adopted in local legislation by the Member States of the European Union, specifically states that:

> An integrated and efficient financial market requires market integrity. The smooth functioning of securities markets and public confidence in markets are prerequisites for economic growth and wealth. Market abuse harms the integrity of financial markets and public confidence in securities, derivatives and benchmarks.[65]

Market fairness and market efficiency rationales are also accepted as the basis for prohibiting insider trading in the United Kingdom,[66] Germany,[67] Singapore[68] and New Zealand.[69]

By contrast, in the United States, although concepts of market fairness and market efficiencies have previously been considered as appropriate bases for prohibiting insider trading,[70] the fiduciary duty and misappropriation rationales are now both accepted as the appropriate reasons for the prohibition.[71] This approach can be traced to the origin and source of the prohibition of insider trading in

---

63 See, for example, former ASIC Chairman, Tony D'Aloisio, *ASIC's Approach to Market Integrity* (speech delivered at the Monash Centre for Regulatory Studies and Clayton Utz Luncheon Lecture, Melbourne, 11 March 2010) 4; former ASIC Chairman Tony D'Aloisio, *Insider Trading and Market Manipulation* (speech delivered at the Supreme Court of Victoria Law Conference, Melbourne, 13 August 2010) 3–4; CAMAC, *Insider Trading Discussion Paper*, above n 12, [1.34]; CAMAC, *Insider Trading Report*, 2003, [1.4]; Commonwealth Treasury, *Insider Trading Position and Consultation Paper*, 2007, 1; Black, above n 31, 220; Lyon and du Plessis, above n 7, 9.
64 *Directive 2014/57/EU of the European Parliament and of the Council of 16 April 2014 on Criminal Sanctions for Market Abuse*, OJ 2014 L 173.179.
65 Ibid 1.
66 UK Financial Services Authority, Consultation Paper 59, *Market Abuse: A Draft Code of Market Conduct*, 2000, [1.6].
67 German Federal Ministry of Finance, *Our Stock Exchange and Securities System*, 2000, 39.
68 Monetary Authority of Singapore, *Insider Trading: Consultation Document*, 2001.
69 Walker and Simpson, above n 11, 388.
70 See, for example, *Securities and Exchange Commission v Texas Gulf Sulphur Co*, 401 F 2d 833 (1968); *Shapiro v Merrill Lynch*, 495 F 2D 228 (2d Cir 1974).
71 Whincop, 'Towards a Property Rights and Market Microstructural Theory of Insider Trading Regulation – The Case of Primary Securities Markets Transactions', above n 30; Justin J Mannolini, 'Insider Trading – The Need for Conceptual Clarity' (1996) 14 *Company and Securities Law Journal* 151; Strudler and Orts, above n 36.

the United States, which is founded on the 'anti-fraud' provisions of SEC Rule 10b5-1.[72]

Additionally, under the laws of the United States, a distinction is made between the liability of 'primary insiders' and 'secondary insiders', which focuses on the person's relationship with the relevant corporation and the source of the inside information.[73] Thus, primary liability is more easily attributed to those who are likely to owe duties to the relevant corporations, which makes the concepts of fiduciary relationships and misappropriation more relevant in these circumstances. Australian law no longer makes such a fine distinction between different types of insiders and applies the insider trading prohibition to all who trade on material information which is not generally available.

This book is comprised of nine chapters. In this first chapter, the topic of corporate liability for insider trading has been introduced, and the rationale for the prohibition of insider trading has been discussed. In the subsequent chapters, the necessary regulatory background is provided in order to understand the operation of Australian insider trading laws, the manner in which insider trading laws currently apply to corporations in Australia and the challenges in attributing criminal liability to corporations. The specific elements of insider trading, and relevant defences, are examined in order to demonstrate the manner in which they are currently attributed and applied to corporations, and to analyse the problems and difficulties which arise in that context. Business obligations placed on corporations arising from, or complementary to, insider trading regulation are also considered. This book concludes with law reform proposals designed to introduce legislative amendments, which are aimed at ensuring that insider trading laws can be better applied to corporations, in a manner consistent with the market integrity rationale for prohibiting insider trading, and to ensure that Australian law provides an effective regulatory model within the international sphere.

---

72  The SEC promulgated Rule 10b-5 pursuant to s 10(b) of the *Securities Exchange Act of 1934*, 15 USC § 78a (1934) and a variety of judicial decisions have interpreted that rule as prohibiting insider trading: Stephen M Bainbridge, 'An Overview of Insider Trading Law and Policy. An Introduction to the Research Handbook on Insider Trading', in Stephen M Bainbridge (ed), *Research Handbook on Insider Trading* (Edward Elgar, Cheltenham, 2013) 1–2.

73  *Dirks v Securities and Exchange Commission*, 463 US 646 (1983); *United States v O'Hagan*, 521 US 642 (1997); Marc I Steinberg, 'Insider Trading: A Comparative Perspective' (2003) 37(1) *The International Lawyer* 153, 156.

# 2 The regulation of insider trading

While this book focuses on the application of insider trading laws to corporations, in order to undertake such a review, it is necessary to first consider the key features of insider trading laws, so that the nature and scope of the relevant regulatory regime can be clearly understood. This chapter sets out an overview and analysis of the primary elements of Australian insider trading laws, in order to provide the necessary background and context for the central issues and arguments advanced in later chapters.

## The key features of Australian insider trading laws

It was noted by Jacobson J of the Federal Court of Australia in *ASIC v Citigroup Global Markets Australia Pty Ltd*[1] that the statutory offence of insider trading was first created in Australia under the uniform *Securities Industry Acts*, which provided that insider trading occurred:

> where a person, through his or her association with a corporation or body, had 'knowledge of specific information relating to the corporation' and acted on that information to the benefit of himself or herself or to enable another person to gain an advantage by using that information.[2]

Despite the passage of more than 40 years since insider trading was first prohibited under statute in Australia, the legislative framework which regulates insider trading is, unfortunately, regarded by many as particularly complex and unclear.[3] Indeed, when discussing the complexity of the insider trading regulatory regime,

---

1 *ASIC v Citigroup Global Markets Australia Pty Ltd* (2007) 160 FCR 35.
2 Ibid 104.
3 See, for example, Michael Whincop, 'Towards a Property Rights and Market Microstructural Theory of Insider Trading Regulation – The Case of Primary Securities Markets Transactions' (1996) 7 *Journal of Banking and Finance Law and Practice* 212; Roman Tomasic, 'Corporate Crime: Making the Law More Credible' (1990) 8 *Company and Securities Law Journal* 369, 380.

many commentators[4] have quoted Rolfe J's critical comments in *Ampolex Ltd v Perpetual Trustee Trading Co (Canberra) Ltd*:[5]

> [I]t is a matter of concern that legislative provisions, which create serious criminal offences . . . should provide not only difficulties of interpretation because of the language used, but because of apparent internal inconsistencies. I would respectfully suggest that reconsideration be given to these provisions. They are intended to have a beneficial commercial effect. It is unfortunate that they should be couched in language which is difficult of understanding and application.[6]

These sentiments were echoed by McLure P of the Court of Appeal of Western Australia in *R v Mansfield and Kizon*:[7]

> The insider trading provisions of the *Corporations Act 2001* (Cth) . . . are devilishly difficult to construe. It is difficult to discern an entirely coherent, internally consistent statutory framework. Thus, it is difficult to be entirely confident as to their proper construction.[8]

The present prohibition of insider trading is contained in s 1043A(1) of the *Corporations Act*, which provides as follows:

> Subject to this subsection, if:
>
> (a) a person (the insider) possesses inside information; and
> (b) the insider knows, or ought reasonably to know, that the matters specified in paragraphs (a) and (b) of the definition of inside information in section 1042A are satisfied in relation to the information;
>
> the insider must not (whether as principal or agent):
>
> (c) apply for, acquire, or dispose of, relevant Division 3 financial products, or enter into an agreement to apply for, acquire, or dispose of, relevant Division 3 financial products; or

---

4   See, for example, Robert P Austin and Ian M Ramsay, *Ford's Principles of Corporations Law* (LexisNexis Butterworths, Sydney, 2018) 9.860; Gil North, 'The Australian Insider Trading Regime: Workable or Hopelessly Complex?' (2009) 27 *Company and Securities Law Journal* 310, 311; Adam Jacobs, 'Time Is Money: Insider Trading from a Globalisation Perspective' (2005) 23 *Company and Securities Law Journal* 231, 236; Simon Rubenstein, 'The Regulation and Prosecution of Insider Trading in Australia: Towards Civil Penalty Sanctions for Insider Trading' (2002) 20 *Company and Securities Law Journal* 89, 105.
5   *Ampolex Ltd v Perpetual Trustee Trading Co (Canberra) Ltd* (1996) 20 ACSR 649.
6   Ibid 658.
7   *R v Mansfield and Kizon* (2011) 251 FLR 286.
8   Ibid 289. See further, Juliette Overland, 'What Is Inside "Information"? Clarifying the Ambit of Insider Trading Laws' (2013) 31 *Company and Securities Law Journal* 189.

(d)  proure another person to apply for, acquire, or dispose of, relevant Division 3 financial products, or enter into an agreement to apply for, acquire, or dispose of, relevant Division 3 financial products.

Section 1042A of the *Corporations Act* then defines 'inside information' to mean:

information in relation to which the following paragraphs are satisfied:

(a)  the information is not generally available; and
(b)  if the information were generally available, a reasonable person would expect it to have a material effect on the price or value of particular Division 3 financial products.

There is an additional prohibition in s 1043A(2) of the *Corporations Act*, which prohibits 'tipping' and which provides that an insider must not:

directly or indirectly, communicate the information, or cause the information to be communicated, to another person if the insider knows, or ought reasonably to know, that the other person would or would be likely to:

(d)  apply for, acquire, or dispose of, relevant Division 3 financial products, or enter into an agreement to apply for, acquire, or dispose of, relevant Division 3 financial products; or
(e)  procure another person to apply for, acquire, or dispose of, relevant Division 3 financial products, or enter into an agreement to apply for, acquire, or dispose of, relevant Division 3 financial products.

It is not easy at first glance to determine the precise meaning or operation of the prohibition, particularly as it is necessary to consider the definitions in a number of other sections of the *Corporations Act* in order to understand the content of several elements of the offence. However, in *Mansfield and Kizon v R*,[9] which is to date the only insider trading case to be considered by the High Court of Australia, the majority neatly summarised the nature of insider trading as follows:

The *Corporations Act* prohibits trading in securities by persons who possess information that is not generally available and know, or ought reasonably to know, that, if the information were generally available, a reasonable person would expect it to have a material effect on the price or value of the securities.[10]

Insider trading can therefore be broadly described as having the following elements: (i) a person possesses certain information; (ii) the information is not

---

9  *Mansfield and Kizon v R* (2012) 87 ALJR 20.
10  Ibid 21. See further, Overland, above n 8.

generally available; (iii) if the information were generally available, it would be material information; (iv) the person knows (or ought reasonably to know) that the information is not generally available and that, if it were, the information would be material information; and (v) while in possession of the information, the person trades in relevant financial products or procures another person to do so, or communicates the information to another person likely to do so.

## The possession of information

The first element of insider trading is that a person possesses certain information, which in turn must be 'inside information'. This element is derived from s 1043A(1)(a) of the *Corporations Act*, which requires that 'a person (the insider) possesses inside information'. Therefore, to understand the requirements of this element of the offence, two concepts need to be considered – what is meant by each of the terms 'information' and 'possesses'?

### *The nature of information*

Section 1042A of the *Corporations Act* defines 'information' to include:

(a)  matters of supposition and other matters that are insufficiently definite to warrant being made known to the public; and
(b)  matters relating to the intentions, or likely intentions, of a person.

This definition was first used in the *Corporations Law*[11] and was intentionally drafted to enable the word 'information' to be interpreted as broadly as possible.[12] It is clear that the information does not need to be specific or precise.[13] The absence of such a requirement means that rumours and speculation can amount to information caught by the insider trading prohibition,[14] as information 'may include a rumour that something has happened with respect to a corporation which a person neither believes nor disbelieves'.[15] In *Mansfield and Kizon v R*,[16]

11  This definition was inserted by the *Corporations Legislation Amendment Act 1991* (Cth) which contained many amendments resulting from the recommendations of the report of the Standing Committee on Legal and Constitutional Affairs, House of Representatives, *Fair Shares for All: Insider Trading in Australia* (Australian Government Publishing Service, Canberra, 1989).
12  Explanatory Memorandum, Corporations Legislation Amendment Bill 1991 (Cth), 90.
13  *Ampolex Ltd v Perpetual Trustee Trading Co (Canberra) Ltd* (1996) 20 ACSR 649, 658 (Rolfe J).
14  ASIC, *Consultation Paper 118: The Responsible Handling of Rumours*, 2009; CAMAC, *Insider Trading Report*, 2003, [3.7]; CAMAC, *Aspects of Market Integrity Report*, 2009, 116.
15  *Hooker Investments Pty Ltd v Baring Bros Halkerston & Partners Securities Ltd* (1986) 10 ACLR 462, 468 (Young J); *ASIC v Citigroup* (2007) 160 FCR 35, 105 (Jacobson J).
16  *Mansfield and Kizon v R* (2012) 87 ALJR 20.

it was made clear that information does not need to be 'truthful' or based on a 'factual reality'.[17]

Information can also include knowledge obtained from a hint or suggestion,[18] or a supposition made from non-specific information received from another person.[19] An inference drawn from words or conduct can also amount to information, so long as those words or conduct are communicated or observed in some way.[20]

*ASIC v Citigroup*[21] was a set of unsuccessful civil penalty proceedings brought against a corporation for insider trading, and in that case the issue arose as to whether an 'uncommunicated thought process' was a supposition that could amount to inside information. Toll Holdings Limited was proposing to takeover Patrick Corporation Limited and had retained executives within the Investment Banking Division of the investment bank, Citigroup, to provide it with advice on the takeover. ASIC had alleged that, on the day prior to the announcement of the takeover bid, Mr Manchee (a Citigroup employee who was engaged in proprietary share trading – that is, trading on Citigroup's own behalf rather than for its clients) purchased over one million Patrick shares. This trading was noticed by personnel within the Investment Banking Division. An executive from the division then asked Mr Manchee's manager, Mr Darwell, whether he knew who was undertaking the trading and, when told, stated words to the effect that 'we may have a problem with that'. Mr Darwell then took Mr Manchee outside and told him to stop buying Patrick shares. After that conversation, Mr Manchee returned to the office and began *selling* Patrick shares.

In the subsequent insider trading proceedings brought against Citigroup, ASIC alleged that the proprietary trader possessed inside information, being a supposition he allegedly made, when told to stop buying Patrick shares, that Citigroup must be acting on Toll's behalf in relation to a takeover of Patrick. In its defence, Citigroup argued that, as that supposition (if it had been made) had not actually been communicated to the proprietary trader but was simply a deduction he may have made, it was an 'uncommunicated thought process' and could not amount to information. Citigroup's arguments were not accepted by Jacobson J of the Federal Court, who determined that an uncommunicated supposition *could* amount to 'information', as can inferences or suppositions drawn from words or conduct.[22]

17 Ibid 25.
18 *Commissioner for Corporate Affairs v Green* [1978] VR 505, 511 (McInerney J); *ASIC v Citigroup* (2007) 160 FCR 35, 105 (Jacobson J); *Hannes v DPP* [2006] NSW CCA 373, [410] (Barr and Hall JJ).
19 *ASIC v Citigroup* (2007) 160 FCR 35, 105–106.
20 Ibid 105.
21 *ASIC v Citigroup* (2007) 160 FCR 35.
22 Ibid 106. However, on the facts, Jacobson J was not satisfied that the proprietary trader had in fact actually made such a supposition. See further, Juliette Overland and Katrina Li, 'Room for Improvement: Insider Trading and Chinese Walls' (2012) 40 *Australian Business Law Review* 223.

The year after the decision in *ASIC v Citigroup*, Mr Simon Hannes sought special leave to appeal to the High Court of Australia in relation to an earlier conviction for insider trading.[23] The argument underlying the application for special leave was that the information he had allegedly possessed about a proposed takeover was not 'information' as defined in the *Corporations Act* because it was only a supposition he had made, not information communicated to him. Although special leave to appeal was refused on the basis that there were insufficient prospects of success, Gummow ACJ did note that the question as to whether there are any limitations on the concept of 'information' for the purposes of s 1043A of the *Corporations Act* had not, at that time, been considered by the High Court and was a question of public importance.[24]

The meaning of the term 'information' in the context of insider trading did come before the High Court of Australia in 2012 in *Mansfield and Kizon v R*.[25] In that case, the High Court confirmed that information does not have to be true, it does not have to originate from the corporation to which it relates, and it need not be confidential information belonging to that corporation. *Mansfield and Kizon v R* concerned the purchase of shares in a listed corporation, where the corporation's managing director had made false, but positive, statements to prospective investors about the corporation's expected profits and turnover. When two of those investors were later charged with insider trading, they argued that a false statement could not properly amount to 'information' within the meaning used in the *Corporations Act*. However, the majority of the High Court[26] stated that the word 'information' should be interpreted in accordance with its ordinary meaning and in accordance with that meaning:

> the word 'information' . . . is not understood to be confined to knowledge communicated which constitutes or concerns objective truths. Knowledge can be conveyed about a subject-matter . . . and properly be described as 'information' whether the knowledge conveyed is wholly accurate, wholly false or a mixture of the two. The person conveying that knowledge may know or believe that what is conveyed is accurate or false, whether in whole or part, and yet, regardless of that person's state of mind, what is conveyed is properly described as 'information'.[27]

Although the provenance of information does not matter for the purposes of this element of the offence,[28] information may also include the source of the underlying state of affairs which has been communicated. For example, in *R v*

23 *Hannes v R* [2008] HCA 224.
24 Ibid.
25 *Mansfield and Kizon v R* (2012) 87 ALJR 20.
26 Hayne, Crennan, Kiefel and Bell JJ delivered a joint judgment, with a separate judgment from Haydon J.
27 *Mansfield and Kizon v R* (2012) 87 ALJR 20, 25. See further, Overland, above n 8.
28 Gregory Lyon and Jean J du Plessis, *The Law of Insider Trading in Australia* (Federation Press, Sydney, 2005) 19.

*Rivkin*,[29] the relevant information that Mr Rivkin possessed was that the executive chairman of Impulse Airlines had stated that there was a proposed 'merger' deal between Impulse Airlines and Qantas. Of course, vague or imprecise information may have little material value, but this consideration is more relevant to whether the information is likely to be material than whether it can be categorised as information.[30]

Thus, information may come in many forms, which can be variously described as facts, details, data or gossip. The manner in which they exist – whether in documentary form, electronic form or as a topic of conversation – has no bearing on their status as information and the form of the information is obviously of little consequence in that context.

The current position under Australian law, which does not require information to be specific or precise, can be contrasted with that of a number of overseas jurisdictions, which have laws providing that insider trading will only occur as a result of trading on specific or precise information.[31] It appears that the primary reason that such a position is adopted in some other countries is to exclude rumours from the definition of inside information, so that trading on the basis of rumours will not amount to insider trading in those jurisdictions.[32] CAMAC revisited this issue when undertaking its review of Australian insider trading laws in 2001–2003, but determined that it would not be appropriate to amend the law to impose a requirement that information be 'specific' because it would 'unduly narrow the application of the legislation and create artificial distinctions between what does and what does not constitute inside information'.[33] This view was confirmed again by CAMAC in the 2009 report on 'Aspects of Market Integrity'.[34] ASIC has also indicated in its consultation paper on the 'Responsible Handling of Rumours'[35] that it takes the view that trading on the basis of rumours can clearly amount to insider trading.[36] Despite this, almost all convicted insider traders in Australia have traded on the basis of information which appears to be quite specific. Two notable exceptions are Mr Rene Rivkin[37] and Mr Bart Doff[38]

---

29  *R v Rivkin* (2004) 184 FLR 365.
30  Ibid 389–390.
31  For example, in Germany, inside information must be 'specific information' – *Securities Trading Act (WpHG)*, s 13; in the European Union, inside information must be 'information of a precise nature' – chapter 2, Article 7.1 (a) of the *Regulation (EU) 596/2014 of the European Parliament and of the Council of 16 April 2014 on Market Abuse* (Market Abuse Regulation); in the United Kingdom, inside information must be 'information of a precise nature' – *Criminal Justice Act 1993* (UK) c 36, s 56(1)(b); and in Hong Kong, inside information must be 'specific information' – *Securities and Futures Ordinance* (Hong Kong) cap 571, s 245.
32  CAMAC, *Insider Trading Discussion Paper*, 2001, 45.
33  CAMAC, *Insider Trading Report*, above n 14, [3.7].
34  CAMAC, *Aspects of Market Integrity Report*, above n 14, 116.
35  ASIC, *Consultation Paper 118*, above n 14.
36  Ibid 10.
37  *R v Rivkin* (2003) 198 ALR 400.
38  *R v Doff* (2005) 23 ACLC 317.

who traded on the comparatively vague (and not quite correct) information that Qantas and Impulse Airlines were about to 'merge', as conveyed to them by the executive chairperson of Impulse Airlines. The definition of information, and whether or not it includes information that is not specific or precise, does not have any particular bearing on the application of insider trading laws to corporations, but it is clearly important that all market participants, investors and regulators understand the nature and scope of the forms of information which are caught by this term.

### The nature of possession

Part 7.10 of the *Corporations Act*,[39] which contains the prohibition of insider trading in s 1043A, does not contain a definition of the words 'possess' or 'possession'. However, s 86 of the *Corporations Act*, contained in Part 1.2,[40] does provide some guidance on the meaning of the term 'possession', as it states that:

> A thing that is in a person's custody or under a person's control is in the person's possession.

However, this definition is not particularly helpful in interpreting the elements of insider trading, as it is not clear if 'information' is intended to be a 'thing' and the definition of 'information' in s 1042A of the *Corporations Act* does not assist in this respect. The definition of possession in s 86 does not import any notion of awareness, and requires only custody or control. As Steel[41] notes in relation to the concept of 'possession':

> The legal meaning of possession is complex, largely due to its long use in the common law and its wide adoption in statutory offences. This means courts have felt compelled to caution that: 'the term "possession" . . . always giv[es] rise to trouble, and . . . in each case its meaning must depend on the context in which it was used'.[42]

In *He Kaw Teh v R*,[43] the High Court of Australia considered whether awareness was necessary in connection with criminal offences concerning the possession of prohibited drugs, and in doing so made pronouncements about the general

---

39  Part 7.10 is titled 'Market Misconduct and Other Prohibited Conduct Relating to Financial Products and Financial Services'.
40  Part 1.2 is titled 'Interpretation'.
41  Alex Steel, 'The True Identity of Australian Identity Theft Offences: A Measured Response or an Unjustified Status Offence?' (2010) 33 *University of New South Wales Law Journal* 503, 513–514.
42  *Warner v Commissioner of Police of the Metropolis* [1969] 2 AC 256, 304 (Lord Pearce) citing *Towers & Co Ltd v Gray* [1961] 2 QB 351, 361 (Lord Parker CJ).
43  *He Kaw Teh v R* (1985) 157 CLR 523.

nature of possession under the criminal law. In particular, Dawson J stated that the concept of possession would ordinarily import a notion of awareness but that 'the degree of knowledge required may vary according to context'.[44] It was also stated by Brennan J that possession is 'a state of affairs . . . proved by various acts varying with the nature of the subject matter'.[45]

Certainly, in respect of criminal offences which relate to tangible property, the element of possession is generally satisfied where a person has either physical control or custody of that property.[46] Within the *Corporations Act*, the concept of the possession of information for the purposes of the prohibition of insider trading is not the only context within which the notion of possession arises – for example, s 419 of the *Corporations Act* is concerned with controllers taking possession of a corporation's property. It is certainly conceivable that the s 86 definition, concerned with custody and control rather than awareness, is intended to relate to provisions such as s 419 and not necessarily s 1043A. However, without a separate definition of possession in Part 7.10 of the *Corporations Act*, this remains unclear.

The earlier discussion about the nature of information does indicate that it may come in a variety of forms. Those various forms of information could potentially be possessed in many different ways. For example: (i) information may be possessed in a *tangible, physical sense* – for example, information may be possessed by means of physical custody of the paper or documents on which the relevant information is contained in written form; (ii) information may be possessed in an *intermediate physical sense* – for example, information may be possessed by means of physical custody of equipment or devices which enable the information to be accessed electronically, such as via email; and (iii) information may be possessed in a *non-tangible, non-physical sense* – for example, information may be possessed by a person because they know or are aware of the information, without any physical evidence of such possession.

Only information possessed in a non-tangible, non-physical sense automatically requires actual knowledge of the content of the information by the person who possesses it. Where there is possession in a tangible, physical sense or an intermediate physical sense, the person may have physical custody or control of the information or the means by which the information can be accessed, but it is possible that they may not necessarily be aware of the actual existence of the relevant information or its content. Of course, knowledge and physical custody may exist simultaneously, but that is not necessarily the case. Is knowledge, or physical custody and control, or both, necessary for there to be 'possession' of information for the purposes of the prohibition of insider trading? This issue is of particular importance when considering the position of corporations as potential insider traders, and when determining how a corporation may possess

---

44  Ibid 601.
45  Ibid 564, citing Isaacs J in *Moors v Burke* (1919) 26 CLR 265, 271.
46  Steel, above n 40, 516.

inside information, as it is possible for one person within a corporation to have physical custody and control of information without awareness of the content of the information, for another person to have awareness without physical custody or control of the information, and for a third person within the corporation to engage in the act of trading in relevant shares without awareness or physical custody or control of the information. Accordingly, the definition of possession in this context will significantly impact on the circumstances in which a corporation might be considered to engage in insider trading.[47]

Fortunately, despite the lack of clarity existing under the provisions of the *Corporations Act*, case law provides useful guidance on this critical issue. In an appeal by Mr Simon Hannes to the New South Wales Court of Criminal Appeal over a conviction for insider trading,[48] one of the numerous grounds of appeal was that the trial judge erred when giving directions to the jury in relation to the requirement that the defendant 'possess' information. The defendant alleged that there was an error of law in that case in failing to distinguish between physical possession and awareness of information. Although the appeal was ultimately allowed and a direction given for a retrial, this particular ground of the appeal was rejected. In this context, Spigelman CJ confirmed in his judgment that, in order for information to be possessed, there must be 'an element of awareness'[49] of the relevant information.

This means that mere physical possession of documents or the means to access information electronically would not be sufficient to constitute possession without an awareness or knowledge of the content of the relevant information.[50] Steel notes that the result of such a decision is that ' . . . "possession" in this context approaches a synonym for knowledge'.[51] This position has also been implicitly confirmed by the New South Wales Court of Criminal Appeal in *Fysh v R*.[52] While the Court did not explicitly state that there is a requirement for actual awareness of information in order for there to be possession for the purposes of insider trading laws, when overturning Dr Fysh's conviction for insider trading, it was made clear that Dr Fysh could not be regarded as having possession of all the information alleged, due to the Crown's inability to prove that all the relevant information had been discussed with him or provided to him. Even though Dr Fysh might briefly have had physical possession or access to the information in written form, the Crown's inability to prove that he had an opportunity to examine that information also meant that he was not

---

47 See further, Juliette Overland, 'Re-Evaluating the Elements of the Insider Trading Offence: Should There Be a Requirement for the Possession of Inside Information?' (2016) 44 *Australian Business Law Review* 256.
48 *R v Hannes* (2000) 158 FLR 359.
49 Ibid 398.
50 See further, Overland, above n 47.
51 Steel, above n 41, 518.
52 *Fysh v R* [2013] NSWCCA 284 (20 November 2013).

considered to have possessed it for the purposes of Australian insider trading laws.[53]

Of course, if a person cannot be shown to have knowledge or awareness of information, it will likely be difficult to establish the other elements of insider trading, which will require proof that a person knew (or ought reasonably to have known) that the relevant information was not generally available and was likely to be material. However, that may only be the case for individual offenders. For corporations, the various elements of the insider trading may be attributed to a corporation as a result of the knowledge and conduct of different people within the organisation. So, depending on the applicable rules of attribution, it might be possible that the person who has possession of inside information is not the person who engages in the relevant trading in financial products. For this reason, it is particularly important in the context of corporate offenders to be able to understand the precise requirements of each of the elements of the offence.

There is no requirement that a person believe the relevant information to be true[54] or to have received the information in confidence.[55] There is also no need to prove that a person 'used' or relied on the information when deciding to engage in the prohibited conduct and it is no defence that the person did not rely on the inside information (for example, because they had already planned to trade prior to coming into possession of the information, or that they based their decision to trade on alternative information which was not inside information).[56] This position differs from that of many overseas jurisdictions, some of which either require that the 'use' of the relevant inside information be demonstrated, or have a defence of 'non-use' available, which requires the alleged offender to prove that he or she would still have engaged in the relevant conduct, with or without the information.[57] These differences could be explained in a number of ways. Jurisdictions

---

53 Commentators have offered some additional, if conflicting, assistance on this topic – Austin and Ramsay suggest that it is possible for a person to have possession of inside information, within the meaning of s 1043A of the *Corporations Act*, even if the person has temporarily forgotten it or has not read it: Austin and Ramsay, above n 4, [9.870]. However, Lyon and du Plessis state that a person cannot be considered to possess inside information without proof that the person knows and is aware of the information: Lyon and du Plessis, above n 27, 23. In this context, the view of Lyon and du Plessis appears to be more consistent with the judicial statements made in *R v Hannes* (2000) 158 FLR 359 and *Fysh v R* [2013] NSW-CCA 284 (20 November 2013). See further, Overland, above n 47.

54 *Hooker Investments Pty Ltd v Baring Bros Halkerston & Partners Securities Ltd* (1986) 10 ACLR 462.

55 *R v Rivkin* (2004) 184 FLR 365, 390.

56 CAMAC, *Insider Trading Report*, above n 14, [3.4].

57 For example, in Germany, it must be shown that an alleged insider trader 'made use' of the inside information: *Securities Trading Act (WpHG)*, s 14(1); in the European Union, it must be shown that an alleged insider trader 'used' the inside information: Article 8.1 of the *Regulation (EU) 596/2014 of the European Parliament and of the Council of 16 April 2014*

which prohibit insider trading on the basis of a 'breach of fiduciary duty' or 'misappropriation' rationale are essentially prohibiting the misuse of inside information. In that context, it would make sense that the actual use of the information must be demonstrated before there is liability. However, in jurisdictions relying on 'market efficiency' or 'market fairness' rationales, investor confidence requires that market participants with access to inside information should not have advantages over ordinary market participants, rendering them unable to trade in affected securities at any time when they possess inside information. When conducting its review of insider trading laws, CAMAC did consider whether it would be appropriate to introduce a 'use' requirement to Australian law, but determined that this would unnecessarily make the offence harder to prove and enable potential offenders to more easily offer plausible excuses for illegal activity.[58]

## Information which is not generally available

The second element of insider trading requires that the information the person possesses is not generally available. This element comes from the first limb of the definition of 'inside information' in s 1042A of the *Corporations Act*, which provides that 'inside information' means information in relation to which the following paragraphs are satisfied:

(a)  the information is not generally available; and
(b)  if the information were generally available, a reasonable person would expect it to have a material effect on the price or value of particular Division 3 financial products.

The term 'generally available' is then defined in s 1042C of the *Corporations Act*, which provides that information is generally available if:

(a)  it consists of readily observable matter; or
(b)  both of the following subparagraphs apply:

(i)  it has been made known in a manner that would, or would be likely to, bring it to the attention of persons who commonly invest in Division 3

---

on *Market Abuse* (Market Abuse Regulation), although there is a rebuttable presumption of use if the insider is in possession of inside information: Case C-45/08, *Spector Photo Group*, 2009 ECR I-12073, as noted in Katja Langenbucher, 'The "Use or Possession" Debate Revisited – Spector Photo Group and Insider Trading in Europe' (2010) 5 *Capital Markets Law Journal* 452, 466; in the United Kingdom, insider trading only occurs where it is 'on the basis of' the relevant inside information: *Criminal Justice Act 1993* (UK) c 36, s 53. In the United States, it must be shown that the alleged insider trading occurred 'on the basis of' the inside information. However, a person will be regarded as trading on the basis of information if the person 'was aware of the material, nonpublic information when the person made the purchase or sale': SEC, *Final Rule: Selective Disclosure and Insider Trading*, SEC Release No 33-7881, 23 October 2000.

58  CAMAC, *Insider Trading Discussion Paper*, above n 32, [2.150]-[2.152].

financial products of a kind whose price might be affected by the information; and

(ii) since it was made known, a reasonable period for it to be disseminated among such persons has elapsed; or

(c) it consists of deductions, conclusions or inferences made or drawn from either or both of the following:

(i) information referred to in paragraph (a);

(ii) information made known as mentioned in subparagraph (b)(i).

These three limbs of the definition can be classified as 'readily observable information', 'publishable information' and 'deductions, conclusions or inferences'.

### Readily observable information

The term 'readily observable' is not defined in the *Corporations Act* but, according to the Explanatory Memorandum to the Corporations Legislation Amendment Bill 1991 (Cth) which first inserted the term into the *Corporations Law*, 'readily observable' is intended to mean 'facts directly observable in the public arena'.[59] It appears that it does not matter how a person actually observes the information (or, indeed, if any person actually does so) so long as it would be possible for a person to observe it.[60] Observation can occur by various means – for example, with the use of the 'unaided human senses' or with the assistance of devices such as the 'telephone, telex, facsimile, television and the internet'.[61]

There was previously some confusion as to whether or not information must be readily observable *in Australia* or if it is sufficient if it is readily observable in an overseas jurisdiction. In *R v Firns*,[62] an employee of a mining corporation, Carpenter Pacific Resources NL, received notification in Australia that the corporation had been successful in proceedings brought in the Supreme Court of Papua New Guinea in relation to a mining licence dispute. The employee then telephoned his son and, after passing on the information, asked him to buy shares in the corporation, which his son then arranged. The issue arose as to whether the information about the judgment delivered in open court in Papua New Guinea was readily observable and therefore generally available. The trial judge, Sides J, stated that the relevant information was readily observable overseas but not in Australia so was therefore not 'generally available' and the defendant was convicted of insider trading.

There was, however, a different outcome in *R v Kruse*,[63] which resulted from a very similar set of facts. In that case, another employee of Carpenter Pacific

---

59  Explanatory Memorandum, Corporations Legislation Amendment Bill 1991 (Cth), [328].
60  *R v Firns* (2001) 19 ACLC 1495.
61  Ibid 1507 (Mason J).
62  *R v Firns* (District Court of New South Wales, Sides J, 4 November 1999).
63  *R v Kruse* (District Court of New South Wales, O'Reilly DCJ, 2 December 1999).

Resources NL, who was actually present in the Supreme Court of Papua New Guinea when the judgment about the mining licence was handed down, bought shares in the corporation just after the judgment was given, while still in Papua New Guinea. The trial judge, O'Reilly J, found that information can be generally available even if it is only readily observable overseas, and the defendant in that case was not convicted of insider trading.[64] The conviction in *R v Firns* was then overturned on appeal by the New South Wales Court of Appeal,[65] with the majority of the Court[66] finding that information need only to be readily observable in an overseas jurisdiction to be considered 'generally available'.

Accordingly, under Australian law, it appears that information that is readily observable will be considered to be generally available, including information that is only observable overseas. Of course, now that technology easily enables information to be communicated globally in an almost instantaneous manner, it is much less likely that information which is observable overseas would not also be considered to be observable in Australia.

### *Publishable information*

Information is also considered to be generally available if it has been made known in a manner that would, or would be likely to, bring it to the attention of persons who commonly invest in Division 3 financial products, and a reasonable period for it to be disseminated has elapsed, pursuant to paragraph (b) of the s 1042C definition of 'generally available' information. This limb of the definition is often referred to as the 'publishable information' test.[67]

This limb of the definition appears to apply to information that has been made available to those investors who would be likely to invest in the financial products to which the information relates. Section 1042A of the *Corporations Act* defines 'Division 3 Financial Products' very widely as:

(a)  securities; or
(b)  derivatives; or
(c)  interests in a managed investment scheme; or

---

64  The decisions of the trial judges in *R v Firns* and *R v Kruse* proved difficult to reconcile, although Walker was able to distinguish the two cases on their facts, effectively arguing that the relevant provisions providing for extra-territorial application of the laws meant that where the relevant conduct occurred overseas (as was the case in *R v Kruse*) the information need only be readily observable in that location, but where the relevant conduct occurred in Australia (as was the case in *R v Firns*) the information must be readily observable in Australia: Gordon Walker, 'Insider Trading in Australia: When is Information Readily Available?' (2000) 18 *Company and Securities Law Journal* 213, 215–216. The successful appeal in *R v Firns* (2001) 19 ACLC 1495 meant that this argument was not judicially tested.
65  *R v Firns* (2001) 19 ACLC 1495.
66  Carruthers AJ delivered a strong dissenting judgment.
67  Martin K Earp and Gai M McGrath, *Listed Companies – Law and Market Practice* (Lawbook, Sydney, 1996) 309.

(ca) debentures, stocks or bonds issued or proposed to be issued by a government; or

(d) superannuation products, other than those prescribed by regulations made for the purposes of this paragraph; or

(e) any other financial products that are able to be traded on a financial market.

The amendments made to the *Corporations Act* by the *Financial Services Reform Act 2001* (Cth) changed the nature of the relevant financial products caught by the insider trading prohibition. Prior to the implementation of the *Financial Services Reform Act*, insider trading was only prohibited in relation to 'securities'. Thus, certain 'financial products' which were not previously subject to insider trading laws have now been brought within the ambit of the prohibition. The reasoning behind this reform was the desire to ensure that conduct which amounts to an offence in relation to certain financial products should not, from a policy perspective, be permissible in relation to other financial products – especially given that it was an aim of the *Financial Services Reform Act* to regulate 'functionally similar' financial products in a similar manner.[68] All financial products which are tradable on a market (and some which are not) are now subject to the prohibition of insider trading.

It appears that the manner in which information would need to be disseminated in order to bring it to the attention of those likely to invest in the financial products has been intentionally left open.[69] Where the relevant financial products are listed on an exchange, information may be made known to those who invest via continuous disclosure mechanisms and the release of information to the exchange. This concept is more difficult to apply to non-listed entities. However, information is made known in a manner that would bring it to the attention of people who commonly invest in the relevant financial products if the information is admitted into evidence in open court.[70]

The intention of this requirement is to allow potential investors time to absorb the impact of the relevant information, so that someone who already possesses the information prior to its publication does not receive an unfair trading advantage.[71] There is no guidance given as to what amounts to a reasonable time, so it will necessarily depend on the circumstances as to how long must be allowed, which will also be influenced by the manner of dissemination of the information.[72]

---

68  Explanatory Memorandum, Financial Services Reform Bill 2001 (Cth), [2.76].

69  Keith Kendall and Gordon Walker, 'Insider Trading in Australia and New Zealand: Information that is Generally Available' (2006) 24 *Company and Securities Law Journal* 343, 349.

70  *ICAL Ltd v Country Natwest Securities Australia Ltd* (1988) 13 ACR 129.

71  Explanatory Memorandum, Corporations Legislation Amendment Bill 1991 (Cth), [328].

72  Michael Ziegelaar, 'Insider Trading Law in Australia', in Gordon Walker, Brent Fisse and Ian Ramsay (eds), *Securities Regulation in Australia and New Zealand* (Lawbook, 2nd ed, Sydney, 1998) 554, 573; Lyon and du Plessis, above n 28, 32; Kendall and Walker, above n 69, 348.

It is also apparent that, in this context, a class of investors who 'commonly invest' in securities is 'broader than current' shareholders and 'encompasses potential investors'.[73]

### Deductions, conclusions and inferences

The third limb of the definition of 'generally available information' enables a diligent researcher who is able to interpret other generally available information to act in accordance with the results of that research.[74] Information will be considered to be generally available if it consists of deductions, conclusions or inferences drawn from readily observable matter or publishable information. However, research which is based on non-public information will not be protected, even if it is obtained as a result of the researcher's own efforts.[75]

## Material information

The third element of insider trading requires that, if the relevant information were generally available, a reasonable person would expect it to have a material effect on the price or value of particular Division 3 financial products. This element comes from the second limb of the definition of 'inside information' in s 1042A of the *Corporations Act*. As noted earlier, s 1042A provides that 'inside information' means information in relation to which the following paragraphs are satisfied:

(a) the information is not generally available; and
(b) if the information were generally available, a reasonable person would expect it to have a material effect on the price or value of particular Division 3 financial products.

Section 1042D of the *Corporations Act* then sets out a test for determining when a reasonable person would have that expectation by providing that:

> a reasonable person would be taken to expect information to have a material effect on the price or value of Division 3 financial products if (and only if) the information would, or would be likely to, influence persons who commonly acquire Division 3 financial products in deciding whether or not to acquire or dispose of the first-mentioned financial products.

---

73 Kendall and Walker, above n 69, 348; Keith Kendall and Gordon Walker, 'Insider Trading in Australia', in Stephen M Bainbridge (ed), *Research Handbook on Insider Trading* (Edward Elgar, Cheltenham, 2013) 365, 375.
74 Explanatory Memorandum, Corporations Legislation Amendment Bill 1991 (Cth), [326].
75 CAMAC, *Insider Trading Report*, above n 14, 49; Lyon and du Plessis, above n 28, 54; Kendall and Walker, above n 69, 349; Michael Gething, 'Insider Trading Enforcement: Where Are We Now and Where Do We Go from Here?' (1998) 16 *Company and Securities Law Journal* 607, 613.

It is also useful to consider the provisions concerning continuous disclosure laws for listed corporations, as very similar concepts are used to determine when 'material' information concerning a corporation needs to be disclosed to an exchange. Austin and Ramsay note that '[t]he insider trading provisions dealing with materiality are in substance identical to the test for materiality [in relation to] continuous disclosure for listed entities'.[76] Section 674(2) of the *Corporations Act* provides as follows:

> If:
>
> (a) this subsection applies to a listed disclosing entity;
> (b) the entity has information that those provisions require the entity to notify to the market operator; and
> (c) that information:
>
>> (i) is not generally available; and
>> (ii) is information that a reasonable person would expect, if it were generally available, to have a material effect on the price or value of ED securities of the entity;[77]
>
> the entity must notify the market operator of that information in accordance with those provisions.

Section 677 of the *Corporations Act* then provides, in language that is almost identical to s 1042D of the *Corporations Act*, that:

> a reasonable person would be taken to expect information to have a material effect on the price or value of ED securities of a disclosing entity if the information would, or would be likely to, influence persons who commonly invest in securities in deciding whether to acquire or dispose of the ED securities.[78]

As was noted in *Hannes v DPP*:[79]

> materiality is concerned with investor conduct and . . . the capacity of information to influence investor behaviour which, in turn, has a material effect on price or value of securities. Accordingly, materiality is concerned with information which might be said to be price sensitive.[80]

---

76  Austin and Ramsay, above n 4, [9.870.18].
77  ED securities are "enhanced disclosure securities" under s 111 AD of the *Corporations Act*, to which the continuous disclosure rules apply.
78  The ASX considers that the reference in s 677 of the *Corporations Act* to 'persons who commonly invest in securities' means 'persons who commonly buy and hold securities for a period of time, based upon their view of the inherent value of the security', thereby excluding high-frequency traders seeking to take advantage of very short-term price fluctuations: ASX, Listing Rules, *Guidance Note 8, Continuous Disclosure: Listing Rules 3.1–3.1B*, 2018, 10.
79  *Hannes v DPP* (2006) 165 A Crim R 151.
80  Ibid 384.

The materiality of information may be demonstrated by the following methods: (i) expert evidence from financial specialists as to whether they would consider certain information to be likely to raise or lower the relevant share price once it becomes publicly known;[81] and (ii) tracking the actual movement in share prices once the relevant information does become generally available.[82]

Assessing the materiality of information solely by reference to its impact on short-term movements in a corporation's share price is generally considered to be a 'simplistic' approach.[83] In the context of continuous disclosure obligations, it has been stated that the materiality of information should be assessed on an 'ex ante' and not an 'ex post' approach – that is, the materiality of information is to be determined as a 'forward, not backward, looking exercise'.[84] However, the ability to later consider the ultimate effect of the release of certain information, such as a retrospective inquiry into movements in share prices, is certainly still considered useful to test the reasonableness of a determination that information was material.[85] Such 'ex post' enquiries are a common reference point for determining the materiality of information in Australian insider trading cases, as is demonstrated below.

In *R v Rivkin*,[86] it was argued on appeal, following a conviction for insider trading at first instance, that a reasonable person could not have considered the relevant information that Mr Rivkin received from the executive chairperson of Impulse Airlines about a proposed 'merger' with Qantas to be 'material' information, because its content was uncertain and indefinite, and a potential investor would have regarded the information as being unreliable. The Court of Criminal Appeal of New South Wales rejected this argument, although it did recognise that the source of information may have an impact on its materiality.[87] That is, the more reliable the source is considered to be, the more likely it is that the information may be considered to be reliable and therefore likely to have a material effect on the price or value of securities. The fact that the source of the information was the executive chairperson of Impulse Airlines might make the information more likely to be reliable than if the same information had been received from an unrelated source. Accordingly, the source of the information could affect the materiality of the information because investors might consider some sources to be more credible or reliable than others. In that case, an upward movement in

---

81  For example, *R v Rivkin* (2003) 198 ALR 400.
82  Gething, above n 74, 619–620. For example, *ASIC v Citigroup* (2007) 160 FCR 35.
83  See, for example, Gil North, 'The Insider Trading Generally Available and Materiality Carve-Outs: Are They Achieving Their Aims?' (2009) 27 *Company and Securities Law Journal* 234, 250–251; Gething, above n 75, 619; David Pompilio, 'On the Reach of Insider Trading Law' (2007) 25 *Company and Securities Law Journal* 467, 473.
84  *ASIC v Fortescue Metals Group Ltd* (2009) 264 ALR 201, [474]-[475].
85  *Rivkin Financial Services Ltd v Sofcom Ltd* (2004) 51 ACSR 486 [113]-[116]; *Jubilee Mines NL v Riley* (2009) 253 ALR 673 [33], [130], [134]; *ASIC v Macdonald (No 11)* (2009) 256 ALR 365 [1067]; *ASIC v Fortescue Metals Group Ltd* (2009) 264 ALR 201, [477].
86  *R v Rivkin* (2004) 184 FLR 365.
87  Ibid 390.

the price of Qantas Airways Limited shares, once it was publicly announced that Qantas was to acquire Impulse Airlines (after a period of speculation that the national airline industry could not support the four airlines operating at the time) was considered to assist in demonstrating the materiality of the information possessed by Mr Rivkin: 'the fact of the price rise, after the announcement, meant the market had not factored in the disappearance of one of the players'.[88]

In *R v Hannes*,[89] the New South Wales Court of Criminal Appeal considered the impact of a takeover announcement on the increase in the share price of the target corporation, TNT Limited. Mr Hannes had allegedly purchased options in TNT with knowledge that a takeover was proposed and, when the takeover was later formally announced, the TNT share price rose. Mr Hannes argued that it was not appropriate to regard the information he possessed when he purchased the TNT options as material because, at that time, the takeover was merely a 'prospect', whereas when the takeover was later announced it had become more certain. Spigelman CJ stated that 'no doubt the effect on the price of securities of a mere prospect was less than the actuality, but that does not mean that what actually happened was irrelevant to an assessment of the materiality of the prospect'.[90] Clearly, a certain event is more likely to affect a corporation's share price than an uncertain event, but the possibility of an uncertain event occurring may still have some effect.

In *Fysh v R*,[91] the question arose as to whether the materiality of information is a matter of fact to be determined by a jury or whether it must be the subject of expert evidence. In this case, the New South Wales Court of Criminal Appeal stated that 'the question of materiality must be measured against both reasonableness and some knowledge of the market',[92] as determining the materiality of information is partly a question of 'common sense' but 'could also be the subject of specialised knowledge'.[93] Accordingly, depending upon the particular circumstances of a case, a jury may be able to themselves determine whether information is likely to influence persons who commonly acquire the relevant financial products, or they may need to rely on expert evidence in order to make such an assessment. In *Fysh v R*, the increase in a corporation's share price was not in itself considered to be evidence of materiality of certain information because there were other factors which may also have contributed to the increase, including the release of another unrelated announcement.[94]

In *ASIC v Petsas & Miot*,[95] the relevant inside information concerned confidential merger negotiations between BRL Hardy Ltd and Constellation Brands. It was stated by Finkelstein J of the Federal Court that 'Mr Petsas and Mr Miot

---

88  Ibid 399.
89  *R v Hannes* (2000) 158 FLR 359.
90  Ibid 409.
91  *Fysh v R* [2013] NSWCCA 284 (20 November 2013).
92  Ibid 208.
93  Ibid.
94  Ibid 214.
95  *ASIC v Petsas & Miot* [2005] 23 ACLC 269.

knew that if the information about the merger discussions became public it would affect the price of BRL's shares'.[96] The materiality of the information was also determined by reference to a rise in the BRL share price when the merger was later announced.

In *ASIC v Citigroup*,[97] Jacobson J of the Federal Court found in relation to one charge of insider trading that, at the time Citigroup's proprietary trader traded in Patrick shares, the relevant information concerning the proposed takeover of Patrick Holdings Ltd by Toll Holdings Ltd was unlikely to be material because the 'share price had already moved to a price which reflected a substantial likelihood of a takeover'.[98] However, on a separate charge of insider trading, Jacobson J relied on an upward movement in the price of Patrick shares at an earlier time to demonstrate that information about the timing of the bid would have been material at that stage:

> It seems to me to be likely that information as to the timing of the bid would have been price sensitive within the test stated in s 1042D of the *Corporations Act*. This seems to me to be borne out by the fact that Patrick shares opened on the day of the announcement at AUD$7.15, being 10.9% above the closing price on Friday 19 August 2005, and, during the course of very heavy trading on 22 August 2005, rose to AUD$7.38.[99]

It can therefore be seen that, even though the legislation prescribes a test of the 'reasonable person' or 'reasonable investor' in order to determine the level of materiality of particular information, and the time for determining whether that information would be material to such an investor is the time at which the alleged insider trader trades in relevant financial products, courts regularly consider later movements in share price caused by the release of the information sometime after that relevant trading has occurred when determining whether the information was material at that earlier time.

When considering who the 'reasonable person' or 'reasonable investor' might be, the Court of Appeal of Western Australia in *Jubilee Mines v Riley*[100] found that 'persons who commonly invest in securities', in the context of continuous disclosure obligations, refers to persons who commonly invest in securities of the type in question, when stating that:

> [T]he effect of the section was to obviate the need to address the question of whether a reasonable person would be taken to expect a 'material' effect on price to be produced by deeming that question to be answered in the affirmative if the information would, or would be likely to, influence persons

---

96  Ibid 7.
97  *ASIC v Citigroup* (2007) 160 FCR 35.
98  Ibid 109.
99  Ibid 110. See further, Juliette Overland, 'The Possession and Materiality of Information in Insider Trading Cases' (2014) 32 *Company and Securities Law Journal* 353.
100  *Jubilee Mines v Riley* (2009) 53 ALR 67.

who commonly invest *in the relevant securities* in deciding whether or not to subscribe for, or buy or sell those securities.[101]

However, a decision of the Full Court of the Federal Court in *Grant-Taylor v Babcock & Brown*[102] has significantly altered this position, as the Court found that the expression in s 677, 'persons who commonly invest in securities', refers to a class of persons rather than individuals, thereby avoiding 'distinctions dealing with large or small, frequent or infrequent, sophisticated or unsophisticated individual investors'.[103] Accordingly, when considering the potential materiality of information, it must be determined whether it 'would or would be likely to influence a *hypothetical* class of persons namely "persons who commonly invest in securities"'.[104] It was also noted in *Grant-Taylor v Babcock & Brown* that:

> [i]n our view, as a matter of text and context, there is no reason to give 'securities' in that phrase any narrower meaning . . . 'securities' can embrace listed and unlisted shares, debentures, options, interests in managed investment schemes and the like. But what is apparent is that it is not confined to listed securities, securities of the same type or class of the ED securities or of the same sector as the entity that has issued the ED securities.[105]

Thus, the decision of the Full Court of the Federal Court in *Grant-Taylor v Babcock & Brown* leads to a different understanding of materiality, with the findings in *Jubilee Mines v Riley* being specifically rejected.[106] In particular, it was stated that:

> The phrase 'commonly invest in securities' in s 677 is not limited to shares in the type of company in question.[107]

Accordingly, the reference to securities is not restricted to listed securities, but refers to any securities (as broadly defined in s 92 of the *Corporations Act*).[108]

---

101 Ibid 34 (emphasis added). An application for special leave to appeal to the High Court of Australia was refused: *Riley v Jubilee Mines NL* [2009] HCA Trans 168 (31 July 2009).
102 *Grant-Taylor v Babcock & Brown Limited* [2016] FCAFC 60.
103 Ibid 115.
104 Ibid 116.
105 Ibid 99.
106 Ibid 130.
107 Ibid.
108 Section 92(1) of the *Corporations Act* provides that 'securities' means:

   (a) debentures, stocks or bonds issued or proposed to be issued by a government; or
   (b) shares in, or debentures of, a body; or
   (c) interests in a managed investment scheme; or
   (d) units of such shares;

   but does not include:

   (f) a derivative (as defined in Chapter 7), other than an option to acquire by way of transfer a security covered by paragraph (a), (b), (c) or (d); or
   (g) an excluded security.

Thus, for the purposes of the continuous disclosure obligations, when determining whether a reasonable person would consider certain information to be material, the question to be asked is whether the information would (or would be likely to) influence the class of persons who commonly invest in securities as broadly defined in s 92 of the *Corporations Act*, rather than persons who commonly invest in the particular type of securities in question, in deciding whether to acquire or dispose of the particular securities in question.

Due to the similarity of the language of the provisions relating to both continuous disclosure and insider trading, and the fact that the cases concerning continuous disclosure are readily applied to insider trading, the pronouncements of the Full Court of the Federal Court in *Grant-Taylor v Babcock & Brown* in relation to the meaning of 'material effect' are likely to be applied to the insider trading provisions as well. Of course, while the issue of materiality has been discussed in a number of insider trading cases, as noted earlier, it has not been the subject of detailed judicial pronouncement. Thus, the pronouncements in cases concerning materiality in the context of continuous disclosure are likely to be followed. Therefore, when determining whether or not a 'reasonable person' would consider certain information to be material for the purposes of the prohibition of insider trading, the question to be asked is whether the information would (or would be likely to) influence persons who commonly acquire Division 3 financial products (as defined in s 1042A of the *Corporations Act*) in deciding whether or not to acquire or dispose of the particular financial products in question.[109]

## Knowledge that information is inside information

The fourth element of insider trading is that the person knows, or ought reasonably to know, that the relevant information is not generally available and that, if it were generally available, it would be likely to be material. This element comes from the requirement in s 1043A(1)(b) of the *Corporations Act* that:

> the person knows or ought reasonably to know, that the matters specified in paragraphs (a) and (b) of the definition of inside information in s1042A are satisfied in relation to the information.

It has long been recognised that this 'knowledge element' of insider trading is the most difficult to prove, and that this difficulty appears to create one of the greatest obstacles to the successful prosecution of insider trading cases.[110]

---

109 See further, Juliette Overland, 'Insider Trading, Materiality and the Reasonable Person: Who Must Be Influenced for Information to have a "Material Effect"?' (2017) 45 *Australian Business Law Review* 213.

110 Explanatory Memorandum, Financial Services Bill 2001 (Cth), [2.78]-[2.79]; CAMAC, *Insider Trading Report*, above n 14, [2.139]; Roman Tomasic, *Casino Capitalism? Insider Trading in Australia* (Australian Institute of Criminology, Canberra, 1991) 115–126. As has been noted by the former Chair of ASIC, Alan Cameron, 'proving that a person had knowledge is often harder than it sounds unless there is smoking-gun type of evidence':

As noted earlier, the definition of inside information in s 1042A of the *Corporations Act* provides that 'inside information' means information in relation to which the following paragraphs are satisfied:

(a)  the information is not generally available; and
(b)  if the information were generally available, a reasonable person would expect it to have a material effect on the price or value of particular Division 3 financial products.

A careful examination of this element of insider trading reveals that it must be proved that either: (i) the alleged insider trader *knew* that the relevant information was not generally available and that a reasonable person would have expected the information to be material; *or* (ii) the alleged insider trader ought reasonably to have known that the relevant information was not generally available and that a reasonable person would have expected the information to be material.

It was stated by the New South Wales Court of Criminal Appeal in *R v Rivkin*[111] that, when considering what an alleged insider trader 'ought reasonably to have known', the question is subjective to the particular defendant, having regard to all of the relevant circumstances.[112] This means that one does not consider whether the theoretical *reasonable person* ought to have had certain knowledge, but whether *the particular defendant* in question ought to have had such knowledge, bearing in mind subjective factors such as his or her particular level of knowledge, experience, level of business and commercial expertise and any other relevant personal characteristics.

This means that it must be proved either that the alleged insider trader *knew* what a reasonable person would have expected, or *ought to have known* what a reasonable person would have expected, in relation to the materiality of the information. Of course, the effect of s 1042D of the *Corporations Act*, in providing when a reasonable person is taken to expect information to be material, is that the reasonable person in question is not necessarily taken to be in the position of the alleged insider trader. It must therefore be shown that the alleged insider trader knew, or ought reasonably to have known, that the 'information would, or would be likely to, influence persons who commonly acquire Division 3 financial products in deciding whether or not to acquire or dispose of' those products.[113] Accordingly, knowledge of what would be likely to influence the trading decisions of persons who commonly acquire the relevant financial products is necessary, resulting in a complicated set of tests.[114]

---

Alan Deans, 'The Fetter of the Law', *The Bulletin* (Sydney), 28 November 2000, 52; Rubenstein, above n 4, 106.
111  *R v Rivkin* (2004) 184 FLR 365 (Mason P, Wood CJ at CL and Sully J).
112  The New South Wales Court of Criminal Appeal cited the case of *Boughey v Queen* (1986) 161 CLR 10, 28–29, as authority for that proposition and noted that it was accepted by both counsel for Mr Rivkin and the Crown: *R v Rivkin* (2004) 184 FLR 365, 384.
113  *Corporations Act*, s 1042D.
114  See further, Overland, above n 98, and Juliette Overland, 'Corporate Liability for Insider Trading: How Does a Company Have the Necessary "Mens Rea"?' (2010) 24 *Australian Journal of Corporate Law* 266.

As this element of insider trading is recognised as one of the most difficult to prove, the introduction of civil penalty proceedings under the *Financial Services Reform Act 2001* (Cth), which came into effect on 11 March 2002, was much vaunted. The availability of civil penalty proceedings was intended to assist in overcoming perceived difficulties in prosecuting insider trading by providing an alternative regime with a lower standard of proof, based on the balance of probabilities and using civil rules of evidence. Indeed, it was stated in the Explanatory Memorandum to the Financial Services Reform Bill 2001 (Cth) that:

> [A] major problem that exists in relation to the market misconduct and insider trading provisions, is the difficulty ASIC has in successfully prosecuting a breach of the provisions. As the existing provisions are offence provisions, the criminal burden of proof (beyond reasonable doubt) applies. ASIC has found it difficult to prove elements of the offences beyond reasonable doubt, as many elements refer to the defendant's state of mind. This difficulty may result in cases not being pursued even where there has been a breach of the provisions. This is undesirable as it casts the law into disrepute, and also threatens the integrity of financial markets. It is therefore proposed to make the market misconduct and insider trading provisions civil penalty provisions. The application of the civil burden of proof (balance of probabilities) will facilitate the bringing of actions for breaches of the provisions. The application of civil penalties is likely to act as a deterrent to market misconduct.[115]

The elements of the offence remained unchanged under the introduction of the civil penalty regime to insider trading, but the standard of proof was lowered when civil penalty proceedings were utilised. However, there have been very few civil penalty proceedings for insider trading undertaken since they became available, largely due to the complexities and technicalities associated with pursuing alleged insider traders remaining – the challenges in detecting incidents of insider trading; the complexity of insider trading laws and resulting interpretational difficulties; the limited judicial consideration of insider trading laws; and, in particular, the obstacles to proving the knowledge element of the offence.[116]

The knowledge element is particularly contentious when considering the liability of corporations for insider trading, as the question of proving what a corporation knew, or ought reasonably to have known, is more complex than for a natural person.

---

115 Explanatory Memorandum, Financial Services Reform Bill 2001 (Cth), [2.78]-[2.79]; *Corporations Act*, ss 1317L and 1332.

116 See, for example, Rubenstein, above n 4; Roman Tomasic and Brendan Pentony, 'The Prosecution of Insider Trading; Obstacles to Enforcement' (1989) 22 *Australian and New Zealand Journal of Criminology* 65; Tomasic, above n 109, 115–126; Lyon and du Plessis, above n 28, 163–168.

# Trading, procuring and tipping in relevant financial products

The final 'trading element' of insider trading requires that the alleged insider trader, while in possession of information which they know or ought reasonably to know is inside information, either trades in the relevant financial products,[117] procures another person to do so,[118] or communicates the information to another person likely to either trade or procure trading in relevant financial products (commonly known as 'tipping').[119]

'Procure' is defined in s 1042F(1) of the *Corporations Act* as follows:

> For the purposes of this Division, but without limiting the meaning that the expression procure has apart from this section, if a person incites, induces, or encourages an act or omission by another person, the first-mentioned person is taken to procure the act or omission by the other person.

Section 9 of the *Corporations Act* also provides that ' "procure" includes cause'.

The 'tipping' aspect of the offence is satisfied where a person, while in possession of information which they know or ought reasonably to know is inside information, communicates the information, or causes it to be communicated to another person, when the insider knows, or ought reasonably to know, that the other person would or would be likely to trade in relevant securities, or procure another person to do so.

In general, the trading element is one of the least contentious of the elements of insider trading, and it will usually not be in doubt, if the other elements have been satisfied, whether or not a person has traded, or procured another to trade in financial products, or tipped. However, in *R v Evans and Doyle*,[120] charges of insider trading were dismissed due to a failure to make out this element. The defendants in that case had placed instructions with a broker to purchase securities prior to certain inside information becoming generally available. The trade was not actually effected by the broker until later that day, after a public release of the relevant information. The defendants were prosecuted for insider trading on the basis that they had 'entered into an agreement to purchase securities' while in possession of inside information. However, McDonald J determined that an agreement to purchase securities was not actually entered into until the broker had effected the trade, by which time the information had become generally available, so no offence was committed.[121] The *Corporations Act* has now been

---

117 That is, applies for, acquires, disposes of or enters into an agreement to apply for, acquire or dispose of the relevant securities: *Corporations Act*, s 1043A(1)(c). Previously, under the repealed s 1002G(2), the relevant conduct was subscribing for, purchasing, selling or entering into an agreement to subscribe for, purchase or sell the relevant securities.
118 *Corporations Act*, s 1043A(1)(d).
119 *Corporations Act*, s 1043A(2).
120 *R v Evans and Doyle* (Supreme Court of Victoria, McDonald J, 15 November 1999).
121 Ibid 51.

amended so that a similar result would not occur in the future, as the relevant conduct now includes applying for, acquiring and disposing of securities, *or entering into an agreement to do so*,[122] which would appear to include instructing a broker to buy (or sell) securities or other financial products.

No offence is committed if a person who had been intending to trade in securities comes into possession of 'inside information' and then, as a result, decides not to trade after all. Additionally, a person in possession of inside information may pass that information on to others to convince them not to trade without committing an offence. The proscribed conduct does not encompass either of these forms of activity, or non-activity. When undertaking its review of Australian insider trading laws, CAMAC considered whether it would be appropriate for an offence to occur in these circumstances but recommended that this aspect of insider trading law remain unchanged[123] as, since there is no other party to a trade, there is no party who is actually disadvantaged by that action or inaction.

## Contentious aspects of insider trading

It has been shown throughout this chapter that there are many contentious aspects to Australia's insider trading laws. In particular, (i) the legislation does not make it clear what is meant by the phrase 'possesses inside information' in s 1043A(1)(a) of the *Corporations Act* and judicial interpretation must be relied upon in order to determine the nature of the level of possession required; (ii) the tests for determining when, pursuant to s 1042D of the *Corporations Act*, a reasonable person would expect information to have a 'material' effect are unclear; and (iii) the tests for determining when a person 'ought reasonably to know' that certain information is inside information, in accordance with s 1043A(1)(b) of the *Corporations Act*, are clumsy and convoluted. These problems highlight the difficult nature of the current legislative framework and serve as examples of the inherent uncertainties which exist when attempting to understand the general application of Australia's insider trading laws.

---

122 *Corporations Act*, s 1043A (1) (emphasis added).
123 CAMAC, *Insider Trading Report*, above n 14, [3.5].

# 3 The application of insider trading laws to corporations

This chapter considers the theoretical basis for applying insider trading laws to corporations. This is done by considering the manner in which Australian insider trading laws apply to corporations and, in particular, whether a corporation is a 'person' caught by the prohibition of insider trading. A comparative review of the positions taken in other jurisdictions is undertaken and Australian cases which have focused on insider trading issues relevant to corporations are discussed. The historical and theoretical bases for applying insider trading laws to corporations are also considered, as well as whether it is appropriate for corporations to be subject to the prohibition of insider trading in Australia.

## A corporation as a 'person' caught by the prohibition of insider trading

While the elements of insider trading have been discussed in chapter 2, it is important to recall that under s 1043A of the *Corporations Act* it is an offence for a 'person' to engage in insider trading. The *Corporations Act* does not state whether a 'person' includes a corporation, as the term is not defined. However, there are several factors which make it clear that corporations *are* intended to be regarded as persons subject to the prohibition of insider trading – firstly, the operation of applicable principles of statutory interpretation; and secondly, the content of other relevant provisions within the *Corporations Act* which specifically refer to corporations.

General principles of statutory interpretation can assist in this context, as s 22(a) of the *Acts Interpretation Act 1901* (Cth), which applied when Part 7.10 of the *Corporations Act* was enacted, provided that:

> expressions used to denote persons generally (such as 'person', 'party', 'someone', 'anyone', 'no-one', 'one', 'another' and 'whoever'), include a body politic or corporate as well as an individual.[1]

---

1  Section 22(a) of the *Acts Interpretation Act 1901* (Cth) has since been repealed and replaced by s 2C(1), which is of similar effect. Of course, the overall context is a relevant consideration and a presumption that the term 'person' includes a body corporate can be rebutted if a

Despite a difficult legislative history for corporate legislation in Australia, the *Corporations Act* is quite clearly a Commonwealth statute, aided by the referral of powers to the Commonwealth by State Parliaments. Additionally, s 5C of the *Corporations Act* specifically states that the provisions of the *Acts Interpretation Act 1901* (Cth) apply to the *Corporations Act*. Thus, when the term 'person' is used in the *Corporations Act*, it will include a corporation (as a body corporate), unless a contrary intention is indicated.

Such a contrary intention is not indicated in the *Corporations Act* and it is clear from the nature and scope of other provisions of the *Corporations Act* that the prohibition of insider trading is intended to apply to corporations as well as natural persons, for the following three reasons:

> Firstly, there are specific exceptions to insider trading which are relevant only to corporations: for example, s 1043F of the *Corporations Act* provides an exception for bodies corporate which enter into Chinese Wall arrangements,[2] and s 1043I of the *Corporations Act* provides a specific exception for a corporation in relation to 'knowledge of its own intentions', due to an awareness of its own proposals relating to transactions or agreements concerning financial products issued by another person.
>
> Secondly, s 1042G of the *Corporations Act* specifically sets out circumstances in which a corporation will be considered to possess information that is possessed by an officer of the corporation.[3]
>
> Thirdly, the maximum penalties which may be imposed under the *Corporations Act* for insider trading differ between corporations and natural persons.[4] The maximum criminal penalty for a corporation is a fine of 45,000 penalty units (currently \$9,450,000),[5] three times the total value of the benefits obtained or loss avoided that are reasonably attributable to the offence, or 10 per cent of the corporation's annual turnover for the 12-month period in which the offence occurred, whichever is the greater; the maximum penalty for a natural person is ten years' imprisonment, or a fine of the greater of 4,500 penalty units (currently \$945,000) or three times the total value of the benefits obtained or loss avoided that are reasonably attributable to the offence, or both. Similarly, the maximum fine in civil penalty proceedings for insider trading is a fine of \$1,000,000 for a corporation and \$200,000 for a natural person.[6]

---

court finds that there is a contrary legislative intention: D C Pearce and R S Geddes, *Statutory Interpretation in Australia* (LexisNexis Butterworths, 8th ed, Sydney, 2014) 305.

2   The application of s 1043F of the *Corporations Act* is considered in detail in chapter 6.

3   The application of s 1042G of the *Corporations Act* is considered in detail in chapter 5.

4   Set out in item 310 of Schedule 3 of the *Corporations Act*.

5   As at the date of publication of this book, a penalty unit amounts to \$210.00: *Crimes Act 1914* (Cth), s 4AA.

6   *Corporations Act*, 1317G.

The existence of such provisions indicates that corporations are intended to be 'persons' subject to the prohibition of insider trading and that there is no 'contrary intention' in the *Corporations Act*, which might otherwise provide evidence that the broad definition of 'person' in the *Acts Interpretation Act* was not intended to apply. Thus, they offer support for the adoption of that broad definition in the context of insider trading. Therefore, under the current regulatory regime, the Australian prohibition of insider trading contained in the *Corporations Act* applies to both corporations and natural persons.

## International comparisons

It is useful to review the position adopted in other countries, as a comparison of Australian insider trading laws with those of other jurisdictions offers an opportunity to determine if there are common approaches taken in regulating this type of conduct, or if there are substantial differences in the system of regulation that would offer opportunities for appropriate amendment. While Australia's insider trading laws do not mirror those of any other jurisdiction in their application to corporations, it can be seen that there is no one uniform model amongst other jurisdictions in relation to the manner in which insider trading laws are applied to corporations or the availability or requirements of a Chinese Wall defence to insider trading by corporations. While deficiencies and problems may be identified in the application of insider trading laws to corporations in Australia, such deficiencies and problems are unlikely to be rectified by simply importing the legal position adopted in another jurisdiction. However, some aspects of the approach taken in other jurisdictions may afford suggestions for improvement in the Australian position. A significant difficulty arises when attempting to compare the application of insider trading laws to corporations in a variety of jurisdictions – there is a notable absence of applicable case law or corporate prosecutions on which to base any resulting analysis. The wording of the legislation can be compared and contrasted, but without judicial interpretation of the various provisions, it is difficult to make meaningful or informed comparisons.

Although, as noted earlier, almost all countries with securities exchanges prohibit insider trading,[7] there is no uniform application of such a prohibition to corporations. Of the jurisdictions reviewed in this book,[8] all prohibit insider

---

7   Franklin A Gevurtz, 'The Globalisation of Insider Trading Prohibitions' (2002) 15 *Transnational Lawyer* 63, 65–66; as discussed in chapter 1.

8   It is clearly beyond the scope of this book to examine the laws of every regulatory regime which prohibits insider trading – accordingly, a review of the laws of a select number of jurisdictions has been conducted – the European Union, Germany, Hong Kong, New Zealand, Singapore, the United Kingdom and the United States. These countries and jurisdictions have been chosen because they represent a variety of nations with securities markets, with varying characteristics and attributes, in an attempt to ensure a degree of diversity – they include common law jurisdictions (the United Kingdom, the United States, New Zealand, Hong Kong and Singapore) and civil law jurisdictions (Germany) – thus ensuring the laws do not all have the same common source; they include countries with well-developed

trading,[9] and all apply the prohibition to corporations, as well as to natural persons, as either a civil or criminal offence, or both. Indeed, the United Kingdom is the only jurisdiction to apply only civil liability for insider trading to corporations[10] – the criminal offence of 'insider dealing' under the *Criminal Justice Act 1993* (UK) applies only to 'individuals',[11] thus limiting the application of the criminal offence to natural persons only, with no direct criminal liability for a corporation for insider trading. However, the civil prohibition applies to corporations as well as natural persons.[12] It appears that the original rationale underlying the limitation on the application of criminal insider trading laws to natural persons in the United Kingdom was to specifically avoid the difficulties large corporations (such as merchant banks) would face if they were subject to insider trading laws, and not because it was thought generally undesirable to make corporations criminally

---

securities markets which have long prohibited insider trading (the United Kingdom, the United States, Hong Kong and Singapore) and those whose securities markets have only relatively recently criminalised or prohibited insider trading (Germany and New Zealand); and they include countries from a variety of continents and regions – Europe, the Americas, Asia and Australasia. A number of these jurisdictions were also analysed by CAMAC when it undertook a review of Australian insider trading laws, as set out in CAMAC, *Insider Trading Discussion Paper*, 2001, although the laws in several of the examined jurisdictions have changed significantly since that time.

9   In the European Union, *Regulation (EU) 596/2014 of the European Parliament and of the Council of 16 April 2014 on Market Abuse* (Market Abuse Regulation) and the *Directive 2014/57/EU of the European Parliament and of the Council of 16 April 2014 on Criminal Sanctions for Market Abuse*, OJ 2014 L 173.179 (Market Abuse Directive) set out a legal framework to be adopted by the Member States of the European Union as local legislation, prohibiting activities such as insider trading. As at the date of publication of this book, the 28 Member States of the European Union are Austria, Belgium, Bulgaria, Croatia, the Republic of Cyprus, the Czech Republic, Denmark, Estonia, Finland, France, Germany, Greece, Hungary, Ireland, Italy, Latvia, Lithuania, Luxembourg, Malta, the Netherlands, Poland, Portugal, Romania, Slovakia, Slovenia, Spain, Sweden and the United Kingdom. In Germany, insider trading is prohibited under s 14 of the *Wertpapierhandelsgesetz (Securities Trading Act) (WpHG)*. In Hong Kong, insider trading (commonly referred to in that jurisdiction as 'insider dealing') is regulated under Parts XIII and XIV of the *Securities and Futures Ordinance* (Hong Kong) cap 571. Section 241 of the *Financial Markets Conduct Act 2013* (NZ) prohibits insider trading. Division 3 of Part XII of the *Securities and Futures Act 2001* (Singapore) makes insider trading an offence in Singapore. In the United Kingdom, insider trading (commonly referred to in that jurisdiction as 'insider dealing') is prohibited as a criminal offence under Part V of the *Criminal Justice Act 1993* (UK) c 36 and as a civil offence under Part VIII of the *Financial Services and Markets Act 2000* (UK) c 8. In the United States, the anti-fraud provisions in SEC rule 10b-5, promulgated under s 10(b) of the *Securities Exchange Act of 1934*, 15 USC § 78a (1934), give rise to the insider trading prohibition.

10   Kern Alexander, 'UK Insider Dealing and Market Abuse Law: Strengthening Regulatory Law to Combat Market Misconduct', in Stephen M Bainbridge (ed), *Research Handbook on Insider Trading* (Edward Elgar, Cheltenham, 2013) 407, 412.

11   *Criminal Justice Act 1993* (UK) c 36, s 52.

12   Section 118B of the *Financial Services and Markets Act 2000* (UK) c 8 defines 'insiders' to include 'any person', which includes corporations: Schedule 1 of the *Interpretation Act 1978* (UK) c 30.

liable for insider trading.[13] However, this reasoning now seems somewhat incongruous given that corporations can still be subject to civil liability for insider trading under the *Financial Services and Markets Act 2000* (UK), which therefore still necessitates merchant banks implementing Chinese Walls and other such arrangements in order to avoid conflicts of interest and prevent the flow of information. All the other jurisdictions examined apply criminal liability for insider trading to corporations as well as natural persons.[14]

However, while all the jurisdictions examined apply insider trading laws to corporations as well as to natural persons in some form, there is no uniform manner in which those laws are applied. As is discussed in chapter 5, Australia has a set of statutory provisions in the *Corporations Act* which specifically sets out mechanisms for applying the elements of insider trading laws to corporations. However, most of the examined jurisdictions do not have such statutory provisions relating to corporations within the relevant legislation prohibiting insider trading and, as a result, the general principles of corporate criminal liability which are applicable in the relevant jurisdiction must be relied upon to determine the manner in which corporations may be found liable for insider trading.[15] The exception

---

13  Paul Davies, *Gower & Davies: Principles of Modern Company Law* (Sweet & Maxwell, London, 2012) 458.

14  In the European Union, the Market Abuse Directive provides in recital (18) that Member States should extend liability for the offences provided for in this directive to legal persons. In Germany, both natural persons and legal persons are subject to the prohibition of insider trading contained in the *Securities Trading Act (WpHG)*: The British Institute of International and Comparative Law, *Comparative Implementation of EU Directives (I) – Insider Dealing and Market Abuse* (2005) 41. In Hong Kong, the insider dealing provisions of the *Securities and Futures Ordinance* (Hong Kong) cap 571 apply to any 'person' who is 'connected with' a corporation under s 270, which includes both natural and legal persons, such as corporations: s 3 of the *Interpretation and General Clauses Ordinance* (Hong Kong) cap 1. Section 247(2) of the Ordinance also expressly states that a corporation can be a person connected with another corporation. Section 241 of the *Financial Markets Conduct Act 2013* (NZ) prohibits insider trading by any 'information insider', which is defined in s 234 of that act to be a 'person' in possession of inside information. The reference to a person includes both natural persons and legal persons, such as corporations: *Interpretation Act 1999* (NZ), s 29. Section 234(2) of the *Financial Markets Conduct Act 2013* (NZ) also provides that 'a listed issuer may be an information insider of itself'. Section 218 of the *Securities and Futures Act 2001* (Singapore) prohibits a 'person' from engaging in insider trading, which includes both natural and legal persons: *Interpretation Act 1965* (Singapore), s 2. In the United States, the insider trading prohibition applies to natural and legal persons, as evidenced by the applicable penalties under the *Insider Trading and Securities Fraud Enforcement Act of 1988* P.L. 100–704 – the maximum fine for insider trading by legal persons such as corporations is US$25,000,000, although a further penalty representing three times the profit made or loss avoided can also be imposed. Additionally, the first case brought against a corporation for insider trading was *Re Merrill Lynch, Pierce, Fenner and Smith*, 43 S.E.C. 933 (1968) in the United States. This case is discussed in detail in chapter 6.

15  Such as the European Union, Germany, the United Kingdom, the United States, New Zealand and Hong Kong.

is Singapore,[16] where the relevant statute adopts specific statutory rules to apply the elements of insider trading to corporations.[17] Additionally, even though corporations are subject to insider trading laws in most jurisdictions, a Chinese Wall defence for corporations[18] is not available in all jurisdictions – there is no separate Chinese Wall defence to insider trading in the European Union or Germany. A number of jurisdictions do have a Chinese Wall defence available for corporations in respect of liability for insider trading,[19] but as is seen in chapter 6, those defences are similar to the Chinese Wall defence found in s 1043F of the *Corporations Act*, but with a number of points of departure.

## The history and theory of the application of Australian insider trading laws to corporations

In Australia, it was originally unclear whether insider trading laws were intended to apply to corporations. The original prohibition of insider trading under the *State Securities Industry Acts* focused on a 'person-connection' rather than an 'information-connection', with primary liability for insider trading depending on a person being 'connected with a body corporate'. This approach resulted in a distinction between 'primary insiders' – those who possessed inside information and had a connection with the relevant corporation (such as directors, officers, substantial shareholders, and those who had some form of business

---

16  Section 226(1) of the *Securities and Futures Act 2001* (Singapore) specifically provides that:

  (a)  a corporation is taken to possess any information which an officer of the corporation possesses and which came into his possession in the course of the performance of duties as such an officer; and
  (b)  if an officer of a corporation knows or ought reasonably to know any matter or thing because he is an officer of the corporation, it is to be presumed, until the contrary is proved, that the corporation knows or ought reasonably to know that matter or thing.

  Section 236B of the *Securities and Futures Act 2001* (Singapore) also provides that:

  (1)  Where an offence of contravening any provision in this Part is proved to have been committed by an employee or an officer of a corporation (referred to in this section as the contravening person) –

  (a)  with the consent or connivance of the corporation; and
  (b)  for the benefit of the corporation,

  the corporation shall be guilty of that offence as if the corporation had committed the contravention, and shall be liable to be proceeded against and punished accordingly.

17  These provisions are returned to in chapter 5 when the application of insider trading laws to corporations in Australia is analysed in detail.
18  The Chinese Wall defence to insider trading is examined in detail in chapter 6.
19  United Kingdom: *Financial Services and Markets Act 2000* (UK) c 8, s 147, in conjunction with SYSC 10.2.3R of the Financial Conduct Authority Handbook; New Zealand: *Financial Markets Conduct Act 2013* (NZ), s 261; Hong Kong: *Securities and Futures Ordinance* (Hong Kong) cap 571, s 271(2); Singapore: *Securities and Futures Act 2001* (Singapore), s 226(2); the United States: rule 10b5–1c(2)(ii), promulgated pursuant to the *Securities Exchange Act of 1934*, 15 USC § 78a (1934), s 10(b).

or professional relationship with the corporation) – and 'secondary insiders' – generally tippees who knowingly received the inside information from a primary insider.

One of the very first Australian cases to consider the application of insider trading laws to corporations and the operation of the relevant provisions, at that time contained in s 128 of the *Securities Industry (NSW) Code*, was *Hooker Investments Pty Ltd v Baring Bros Halkerston & Partners Securities Ltd*.[20] This case concerned a proposed issue of shares in Email Ltd to a number of parties pursuant to an underwriting agreement. Hooker Investments, an existing shareholder of Email Ltd, sought an injunction to restrain the issue of shares to Baring Bros, one of the underwriters, on the basis that an employee of Baring Bros, a corporation, had come into possession of inside information about the financial and corporate affairs of Email Ltd. Accordingly, it was alleged that the receipt of the issue of shares in Email Ltd under the underwriting agreement would amount to insider trading by Baring Bros.

At that time, s 128(1) of the *Securities Industry (NSW) Code* provided that a person 'connected with a body corporate' must not deal in any of its securities 'if he is in possession of information that is not generally available and if it were likely materially to affect the price of those securities'.[21] Section 128(8) then set out the circumstances in which a person could be so connected. Young J of the Supreme Court of New South Wales determined that the circumstances set out in s 128(8) could relate only to natural persons, and that the provision was exhaustive rather than inclusive so, as a result, His Honour found that only a natural person could be regarded as being 'connected with a body corporate'. As a result, s 128 of the *Securities Industry (NSW) Code* could only apply to a natural person, so that a corporation could not have primary liability for insider trading.[22] A corporation could have liability as a secondary insider if it received information from a primary insider, but the relevant employee of Baring Bros did not fit within the definition of a primary insider, because his position could not 'reasonably be expected' to give him access to inside information (even if it actually did). Thus, there was no liability for insider trading as a result of the issue of shares to Baring Bros. The correctness of this aspect of the decision has since been questioned, despite the fact that the result and reasoning were approved on appeal by the Court of Appeal.[23] However, there is now a specific exception for underwriters in s 1043C of the *Corporations Act*, to allow for the purchase of shares by underwriters pursuant to underwriting agreements to occur without any liability arising for insider trading.

---

20 *Hooker Investments Pty Ltd v Baring Bros Halkerston & Partners Securities Ltd* (1986) 10 ACLR 462.
21 Ibid 465.
22 Ibid 466.
23 *Hooker Investments Pty Ltd v Baring Bros Halkerston & Partners Securities Ltd* (1986) 5 NSWLR 157 (Kirby P, Glass and McHugh JJA).

These issues also arose in the case of *Brockley Investments Ltd v Black*,[24] which concerned the operation of s 128 of the *Securities Industry (WA) Code*. Mr Black was a director of two corporations. Brockley Investments Ltd bought shares in one of those corporations (Western Reefs Ltd) from the other corporation (to be referred to as the 'selling corporation', as it was not referred to by name in the decision). Brockley Investments Ltd later alleged that Mr Black and the selling corporation possessed inside information which would preclude them both from dealing in the securities of Western Reefs Ltd. Basing its argument on the reasoning in *Hooker Investments Pty Ltd v Baring Bros Halkerston & Partners Securities Ltd*, the selling corporation asked for the claim against it to be struck out, on the basis that the insider trading prohibition applied only to natural persons and not to corporations. Master White did not agree with the reasoning of Young J in *Hooker Investments Pty Ltd v Baring Bros Halkerston & Partners Securities Ltd*, determining as a matter of statutory interpretation that it was not necessary for a corporation to be a person 'connected with a body corporate' in order for the prohibition of insider trading in s 128(3) of the *Securities Industry (WA) Code* to apply. Accordingly, Master White accepted that both natural and legal persons could have primary liability for insider trading, and the application to strike out the relevant claim was not successful.

The divergence between these two decisions results from differing interpretations of the loose drafting of the relevant provisions of the *Securities Industry Codes*. General provisions prohibited 'persons' from engaging in insider trading, with other later provisions applying the prohibition to 'bodies corporate' in certain specific circumstances, such as where an officer of the body corporate possessed inside information. The ultimate results of the two decisions can be reconciled on their facts, on the basis that, although a corporation could potentially be liable for insider trading, in *Hooker Investments Pty Ltd v Baring Bros Halkerston & Partners Securities Ltd* there could be no such liability because the relevant employee who possessed the information was not sufficiently senior for that information to be regarded as being in the corporation's possession. However, in *Brockley Investments Ltd v Black*, due to the fact that a director possessed the relevant information, such information could be attributed to the corporation. Regardless, it is no longer necessary to be concerned with the conflicting nature of these decisions, as it was specifically noted in the Explanatory Memorandum to the Corporations Legislation Amendment Bill 1991 (Cth) that the insertion of a definition of 'person' into the then applicable *Corporations Law* would include corporations and would therefore overcome the effect of the decision in *Hooker Investments v Baring Bros Halkerston & Partners Securities Ltd*.[25] The previous distinction between primary and secondary insiders was abolished

24　*Brockley Investments Ltd v Black* (1991) 9 ACLC 255.
25　Explanatory Memorandum to the Corporations Legislation Amendment Bill 1991 (Cth), [346]; Michael Ziegelaar, 'Insider Trading Law in Australia', in Gordon Walker, Brent Fisse and Ian Ramsay (eds), *Securities Regulation in Australia and New Zealand* (Lawbook, 2nd ed, Sydney, 1998) 554, 565.

at this time, to focus only on an 'information connection' rather than a 'person connection',[26] so that any person in possession of material information was then prohibited from insider trading. Thus, while these two decisions highlight the ambiguity that had previously existed as to the application of insider trading laws to corporations, that uncertainty has now been resolved.

The next case to consider the application of insider trading laws to corporations was *Ex Parte Sun Securities Ltd*.[27] This case concerned the application of the *Securities Industry (WA) Code*, which at that time provided, in s 128(6), that:

> a body corporate shall not deal in any securities at a time when any officer of that body corporate is precluded . . . from dealing in those securities.

Section 128(1) of the *Securities Industry (WA) Code* also provided that:

> A person who is, or any time in the preceding 6 months has been, connected with a body corporate shall not deal in any securities of that body corporate if by reason of his so being, or having been, connected with that body corporate he is in possession of information that is not generally available but, if it were, would be likely materially to affect the price of those securities.

Mr Smith, an officer of Sun Securities Ltd, was alleged to have been connected with another corporation, Australian Shipbuilding Industries Ltd, and to have been in possession of inside information concerning a proposed takeover of Australian Shipbuilding Industries. Mr Smith was also alleged to have negotiated and concluded the purchase of shares in Australian Shipbuilding Industries by Sun Securities while he possessed that inside information. As a result, action was brought against both Mr Smith and Sun Securities, with Sun Securities being the first corporation to be charged with insider trading.[28] Mr Smith and Sun Securities applied for an order nisi for writs of mandamus and prohibition and for further and better particulars of the offences contained in the charge, but these applications were dismissed at first instance and on appeal.[29]

When first hearing these applications, Kennedy J of the Supreme Court of Western Australia rejected a submission that for a corporation to commit the offence of insider trading 'it requires the element of fault or knowledge by the company to be proved'.[30] In this context, His Honour appears to have accepted clearly, without detailed analysis, that a corporation could be liable for insider trading under these provisions, but the proceedings against Sun Securities were

26 Explanatory Memorandum to the Corporations Legislation Amendment Bill 1991 (Cth), [37].
27 *Ex Parte Sun Securities Ltd* (1990) 1 ACSR 588.
28 Tomasic, *Casino Capitalism? Insider Trading in Australia* (Australian Institute of Criminology, Canberra, 1991) 17.
29 *Sun Securities v National Companies and Securities Commission* (1990) 2 ACSR 796.
30 *Ex Parte Sun Securities Ltd* (1990) 1 ACSR 588, 594.

ultimately discontinued after a jury acquitted Mr Smith of the insider trading charges at trial in February 1991.[31]

*Exicom Pty Ltd v Futuris Corporation Ltd*[32] was the next case to consider the application of insider trading laws to corporations, but the relevant statutory provision in this case was s 1002G of the *Corporations Law*. Exicom Pty Ltd wished to raise funds and sought the assistance of a number of potential investors, disclosing certain information to them as a result. The first investor later proposed to buy shares in Exicom on the open market. Exicom was able to obtain an interim order to restrain this purchase on the basis that the investor possessed inside information acquired as a result of the initial investment discussions with Exicom and the later purchase might amount to insider trading. Exicom and the second investor then entered into an agreement for the second investor to subscribe for shares in Exicom, thereby enabling Exicom to raise some necessary funds. The first investor applied for an order to prevent Exicom from issuing the shares to the second investor, on the basis that it would also amount to insider trading by Exicom, but the issue as to whether it would amount to insider trading by the second investor was not raised.

It was clearly accepted that the insider trading prohibition in s 1002G of the *Corporations Law* could apply equally to corporations as to natural persons, but the application from the first investor was dismissed on the basis that *a* corporation cannot be considered an 'insider' in respect of its *own* shares or in respect of information that relates to its *own* securities. The reasoning behind the decision was based on the notion that insider trading laws rely on the existence of a fiduciary duty and that, since a corporation cannot owe a fiduciary duty to itself, it cannot be regarded as an 'insider' in relation to its own information or in relation to its own shares.[33] As it is now well established that Australian insider trading laws are based not on a concept of fiduciary obligation but on a need to maintain and protect market integrity and efficiency, the basis of this decision has since been heavily criticised.[34]

Since that time, it appears to have been judicially accepted that insider trading laws apply equally to corporations as to natural persons. In the case of *Westgold Resources NL v St George Bank Ltd*,[35] it was alleged that a corporation which held a put option over certain shares could not lawfully exercise the option because it possessed inside information about the corporation over whose shares the option related, so that the exercise of the put option would amount to insider trading.

---

31  Roman Tomasic, 'Insider Trading Law Reform in Australia' (1991) 9 *Company and Securities Law Journal* 121, 122.

32  *Exicom Pty Ltd v Futuris Corporation Ltd* (1995) 13 ACLC 1758.

33  Ibid 1763 (Young J).

34  See, for example, Gregory Lyon and Jean J du Plessis, *The Law of Insider Trading in Australia* (Federation Press, Sydney, 2005) 16; Robert P Austin and Ian M Ramsay, *Ford's Principles of Corporations Law* (LexisNexis Butterworths, Sydney, 2018), 9.870.12; CAMAC, *Insider Trading Discussion Paper*, 2001, [2.110].

35  *Westgold Resources NL v St George Bank Ltd* [1988] WASC 352.

While it was clearly accepted in this case that the insider trading prohibition applied to that corporation, the application to restrain the exercise of the put option was refused due to the application of s 1015A of the *Corporations Law*, which exempted a bank or financial institution from the application of the insider trading prohibition where the relevant transaction amounted to an exercise of security or other activity conducted by a bank in the ordinary course of its banking business.[36]

Similarly, in *Ampolex Ltd v Perpetual Trustee Company (Canberra) Ltd (No 2)*,[37] the application of insider trading laws to corporations was clearly accepted without argument. This case involved a dispute, resulting from a drafting error, over the terms of convertible notes which Ampolex Ltd had issued. The convertible notes had been sold to a group of brokers and investors and they made an announcement to the ASX, stating what they believed to be the correct conversion ratio under the convertible notes. Ampolex Ltd claimed that those parties had engaged in insider trading because knowledge of the content of the forthcoming ASX announcement amounted to inside information. All the parties to the trade were aware of the relevant information and the group of brokers and investors applied for a summary dismissal of the action. However, the application was refused on the basis that a defence that the counterparty to a trade also possessed the relevant inside information (then contained in s 1002T(2)(b) of the *Corporations Act*, and now in s 1043M(2)(b) of the *Corporations Act*) could only be relied on in a criminal prosecution and not in civil proceedings.

In *Rivkin Financial Services Ltd v Sofcom Ltd*,[38] a set of civil proceedings brought by Rivkin Financial Services, a publicly listed corporation related to Mr Rene Rivkin,[39] against three corporations related to Mr Farooq Khan, the Court clearly accepted that corporations are subject to the prohibition of insider trading. Mr Khan had wished to significantly increase his holding in Rivkin Financial Services and, if possible, to gain control of the board, and as a result he bought a large parcel of shares through three corporations which he controlled. Rivkin Financial Services brought a civil action against Mr Khan and the three corporations which alleged, amongst other things, that as a result of those purchases the three corporations had engaged in insider trading. Rivkin Financial Services argued that the fact that Mr Khan wished to increase his shareholding

---

36 A similar, but not identical, exemption exists under the current *Corporations Regulations 2001* (Cth): Regulation 9.12.01(e) provides that s 1043A(1) of the *Corporations Act* does not have effect in relation to. . .

(e) a sale of financial products under:

(i)  a mortgage or charge of the financial products; or
(ii) a mortgage, charge, pledge or lien of documents of title to the financial products.

37 *Ampolex Ltd v Perpetual Trustee Company (Canberra) Ltd (No 2)* (1996) 14 ACLC 1514.
38 *Rivkin Financial Services Ltd v Sofcom Ltd* (2004) 51 ACSR 486.
39 Mr Rivkin was convicted of insider trading in an unrelated set of criminal proceedings in 2004: *R v Rivkin* (2004) 184 FLR 365.

and control its board was inside information and that the three corporations possessed that information through Mr Khan, who was the managing director of each corporation. Emmet J of the Federal Court did find that the information about Mr Khan's intentions was to be attributed to each of the three corporations,[40] but determined that there had in fact been no insider trading as the information was not material.[41] The application of insider trading laws to corporations was accepted without question in this case, but the manner in which the information was possessed by the three corporations was not analysed.

The facts of *ASIC v Citigroup*[42] were set out in some detail in chapter 2. In this set of civil penalty proceedings for insider trading brought against the Australian subsidiary of a global investment bank, it was clearly accepted that the insider trading prohibition applies to corporations. Even though there was an eventual finding that Citigroup had not actually engaged in insider trading – due to the fact that the relevant information was not considered to be material; the relevant employee did not actually possess inside information; the corporation was not taken to possess the alleged information since the employee was not an officer of the corporation; and the corporation was found to have an effective Chinese Wall in place – the applicability of insider trading laws to Citigroup, as a corporation, was never in question.

The case of *ASIC v Hochtief*[43] was a set of civil penalty proceedings brought by ASIC against Hochtief Aktiengesellschaft (Hochtief), the German-based construction corporation, in which Hochtief admitted liability for insider trading on a technical basis. Hochtief's Australian subsidiary (Hochtief Australia) was a substantial shareholder in Leighton Holdings Limited (Leighton), now known as Cimic Group Limited, and Hochtief wished it to increase that shareholding further. Hochtief, Hochtief Australia and Leighton had a common director, Mr Sassenfeld, who was also a member of Leighton's audit committee. Hochtief gave Hochtief Australia a trading direction to increase its shareholding in Leighton under the 'creeping exception',[44] and Hochtief Australia began to do so, but due to a low turnover of Leighton shares, it became apparent it would not be able to complete the full purchase required by the trading direction by the given deadline. In the meantime, Mr Sassenfeld and others on Leighton's board and audit committee were given papers confirming Leighton's profit for the relevant year. After this, Hochtief gave Hochtief Australia a trading variation, extending the completion date for

---

40 *Rivkin Financial Services Ltd v Sofcom Ltd* (2004) 51 ACSR 486, 517.
41 Ibid 516.
42 *ASIC v Citigroup* (2007) 160 FCR 35.
43 *ASIC v Hochtief* [2016] FCA 1489.
44 Section 611 (item 9) of the *Corporations Act* provides an exception to the takeover prohibition in s 606 for an acquisition of securities by a person if:

   (a) throughout the 6 months before the acquisition that person, or any other person, has had voting power in the company of at least 19%; and
   (b) as a result of the acquisition, none of the persons referred to in paragraph (a) would have voting power in the company more than 3 percentage points higher than they had 6 months before the acquisition.

the increase in the Leighton shareholding, and Hochtief Australia continued to purchase Leighton shares. A month later, Leighton made an announcement about its profit position, and the share price rose almost five per cent. ASIC brought civil penalty proceedings against Hochtief, alleging that it possessed inside information (being material information not generally available concerning Leighton's financial results) through Mr Sassenfeld, and that as a result of issuing the trading variation while it possessed that information, Hochtief had engaged in insider trading by procuring Hochtief Australia to trade in Leighton shares. Hochtief admitted liability for the breach and the parties settled on a statement of agreed facts.[45]

The change in position which can be observed in the review of the cases – from circumstances in which it was unclear whether Australian insider trading laws applied to corporations to those where it is now readily accepted they do – is attributable primarily to the adoption of a new regulatory regime and legislative modification. As discussed in chapter 2, Australian law has moved from a requirement that a 'primary insider' must be a 'person connected with a body corporate', to a system which no longer distinguishes between primary and secondary 'insiders' and applies the prohibition of insider trading more broadly to any 'person'. Even though there are in fact very few Australian insider trading cases which relate to corporations, those cases that do exist evidence the current clear acceptance that the insider trading regime applies to legal persons such as corporations, as well as to natural persons. However, most insider trading cases relate to natural persons – there have been no successful criminal proceedings or successful contested civil proceedings brought against a corporation for insider trading in Australia, with *ASIC v Hochtief*, in which liability was admitted by the corporation, the only example of a successful set of civil penalty proceedings. When considering the topic of this book – the criminal and civil liability of corporations for insider trading in Australia – the absence of such proceedings produces a number of challenges. The dearth of cases means that the opportunity to consider the judicial interpretation of the relevant provisions is extremely limited, and it is therefore not a topic addressed at length in the literature. However, that absence does not reduce the importance of the topic – indeed, the fact that there have been no successful contested proceedings brought against a corporation could potentially be remedied if the reforms proposed in this book were to be adopted, as they are aimed at better applying the insider trading laws to corporations and ensuring that there is certainty as to their operation.

## Why corporations should be liable for insider trading

Having shown that corporations are subject to the prohibition of insider trading in Australia, it is important to consider whether it is appropriate for corporations to continue to be caught by that prohibition. When CAMAC conducted its review of Australian insider trading laws in 2001 to 2003, it

---

45  See further, Juliette Overland, 'Recent Developments in Corporate Liability for Insider Trading: ASIC v Hochtief' (2017) 35 *Company and Securities Law Journal* 204.

considered whether it might be appropriate to limit the application of insider trading laws to natural persons. CAMAC noted that, if the application of insider trading laws was limited to natural persons, the legislative provisions could be simplified because there would be no need for the Chinese Wall defence for corporations.[46] However, CAMAC ultimately determined that there is no compelling reason why corporations should not be subject to the prohibition of insider trading, and that it was beneficial to retain the Chinese Wall defence for corporations. In particular, CAMAC considered that limiting the application of the insider trading prohibition to natural persons would undermine incentives for large organisations to control the internal flow of confidential information.[47]

While there are a number of different models of corporate criminal liability, as is discussed in chapter 4, those models are all clearly predicated on the basis that it is appropriate for corporations to have criminal liability, with the primary issue being the determination of the manner in which such liability is to be attributed. However, the difficulties associated with prosecuting and sentencing corporations have led to suggestions by some commentators that criminal liability should only be imposed on natural persons. This view is generally referred to as 'individualism', as it is argued that 'corporations don't commit offences, people do'.[48] Arguments in favour of individualism are commonly justified on the basis that corporations cannot be imprisoned, that significant fines cause hardship to the shareholders of the corporation rather than to those within the corporation who carry out the relevant criminal acts and omissions, and that the imposition of punishments upon corporations does little to actually deter criminal activity.[49] However, these views are generally countered by arguments in favour of 'collectivism' that, as corporate crimes are so often hard to detect, corporations are more likely to take internal action to prevent the relevant criminal conduct occurring, if the corporation itself is likely to have liability for any resulting crime.[50] As a result, the existence of corporate criminal liability can act as a deterrent to

---

46 CAMAC, *Insider Trading Discussion Paper*, above n 34, [1.54].

47 CAMAC, *Insider Trading Report*, 2003, [3.2].

48 Brent Fisse and John Braithwaite, 'The Allocation of Responsibility for Corporate Crime: Individualism, Collectivism and Accountability' (1988) 11 *Sydney Law Review* 469, 473.

49 John C Coffee, 'No Soul to Damn, No Body to Kick: An Unscandalized Inquiry into the Problem of Corporate Punishment' (1981) 79 *Michigan Law Review* 386, 387–389; Simon Chesterman, 'The Corporate Veil, Crime and Punishment' (1994) 19 *Melbourne University Law Review* 1064, 1072–1073.

50 Jonathan Clough and Carmel Mulhern, *The Prosecution of Corporations* (Oxford University Press, Melbourne, 2002) 7; John C Coffee, 'Corporate Crime and Punishment: A Non-Chicago View of the Economics of Criminal Sanctions' (1980) *American Criminal Law Review* 419, 421; Fisse and Braithwaite, above n 48, 489. Indeed, in 1929, Winn argued for direct criminal liability for corporations on the basis that they are more powerful than individuals and therefore more likely to cause harm, as well as the fact that the existence of corporate criminal liability is more likely to deter agents within the corporation from engaging in criminal conduct: C R N Winn, 'The Criminal Responsibility of Corporations' (1929) 3 *Cambridge Law Journal* 398, 412–413, 415.

those who would engage in criminal conduct within an organisation, with Fisse and Braithwaite stating that:

> Individualism persistently fails to capture the corporate significance of corporate operations over which the law seeks to exercise control. . . . The logic and practical imperatives of deterrence do not preclude corporate criminal responsibility, but, on the contrary, impel it.[51]

Some commentators take a 'middle ground' between individualism and collectivism, arguing that corporate criminal liability is only appropriate where no one individual can be identified as having criminal responsibility.[52] However, in Australia it is generally accepted that it is appropriate to impose criminal liability on corporations as well as natural persons.[53]

Corporations should remain subject to both criminal and civil liability for insider trading in Australia for a number of reasons. Firstly, the imposition of criminal liability for insider trading on corporations reinforces the notion that insider trading is regarded as a serious threat to market integrity and that all persons, natural and legal, should be subject to the prohibition of insider trading. Criminal sanctions are appropriate for any conduct which 'involves, or has the potential to cause, considerable harm to society or individuals, the environment or Australia's national interests, including securities interests'.[54] In this context, it is important to remember the reason for the prohibition of insider trading. As noted earlier, insider trading is prohibited in Australia on the basis of a 'market integrity' rationale – a rationale which aims to protect and ensure market integrity on two bases: that it is necessary for both market fairness and market efficiency. Accordingly, the question must be asked: is market integrity more likely to be protected and maintained if corporations are subject to the prohibition of insider trading, or would market integrity be better served by removing the application of insider trading laws to corporations? As insider trading has the potential to cause significant harm to Australia's securities markets, it is appropriate that all persons who may be regarded as engaging in such conduct be caught by the relevant prohibition and subject to criminal and civil liability. The impact of insider trading is not reduced or minimised merely because the conduct is engaged in by a corporation rather than a natural person.

---

51 Fisse and Braithwaite, above n 48, 510.
52 See, for example, Lim Win Ts'ai, 'Corporations and the Devil's Dictionary: The Problem of Individual Responsibility for Corporate Crimes' (1990) 12 *Sydney Law Review* 311, 313; Matthew Goode, 'Corporate Criminal Liability', in Neil Gunningham, Jennifer Norberry and Sandra McKillop (eds), *Environmental Crime* (Australian Institute of Criminology, Canberra, 1995) 6.
53 For example, the *Criminal Code* provides in s 12.1(2) that 'A body corporate may be found guilty of any offence, including one punishable by imprisonment.' See further, Juliette Overland, 'The Concept of Attribution in Corporate law: Making Corporations Liable for Criminal Conduct', in David Chaikin and Gordon Hook (eds), *Corporate and Trust Structures: Legal and Illegal Dimensions* (Australian Scholarly Publishing, Melbourne, 2018) 35.
54 Commonwealth Attorney-General's Department, Criminal Justice Division, *A Guide to Framing Commonwealth Offences, Infringement Notices and Enforcement Powers*, 2011, 12.

Secondly, the fact that a corporation has never been convicted of insider trading in Australia, and the only successful civil penalty proceedings for insider trading brought against a corporation involved an admission of liability, is not a compelling reason to simply cease to apply insider trading laws to corporations. Even if corporations were to have only civil instead of criminal liability for insider trading, the elements of insider trading must still be applied and proven, even if subject to a different standard of proof.[55] As noted earlier, there are a number of reasons why corporations may not have been the subject of successful contested proceedings for insider trading in Australia, including the complexity of Australian insider trading laws, particularly in relation to their application to corporations. If the difficulties in the application of insider trading laws to corporations can be identified and resolved, greater enforcement action for insider trading might be brought. In particular, any concerns that may relate to the operation or efficacy of Chinese Walls within corporations are better addressed by regulation aimed at improving such operation and efficacy, rather than by a determination that liability for insider trading should be removed or reduced. While the regulator may have a discretion to elect to pursue either criminal or civil proceedings against an alleged insider trader – whether that defendant is a natural person or a legal person – it would not be appropriate to remove insider trading liability for corporations, or to limit it to civil consequences only, as the significant impact of insider trading warrants the availability of both criminal and civil liability as a deterrent factor for all potential insider traders.

Finally, the fact that insider trading is extremely difficult to identify and detect reinforces the importance of continuing to apply criminal and civil liability for insider trading to corporations. The continuing existence of direct corporate liability for insider trading makes it more likely that corporations will take steps to proscribe such conduct and prevent it from occurring within the organisation. This will limit opportunities for individuals associated with the corporation to engage in insider trading, either on their own account or on behalf of the corporation.

Accordingly, for these reasons, the intended rationale to protect and maintain market integrity is best served by continuing to apply the prohibition of insider trading to corporations.

---

55 In civil proceedings for insider trading, the civil standard of proof, 'on the balance of probabilities', is applied, instead of the criminal standard, 'beyond a reasonable doubt'.

# 4 Corporate criminal and civil liability

As insider trading is a criminal offence, the manner in which a corporation can be liable for a criminal offence is the necessary focus of this chapter. In order to be able to properly analyse the application of the elements of insider trading to corporations – that is, to determine how a corporation can possess inside information; how a corporation can have the requisite knowledge that certain information is inside information; and how a corporation can engage in the relevant trading conduct – corporate criminal liability, and the nature of the physical and fault elements of criminal offences, need to be addressed and understood.

Determining the manner in which criminal liability should be imposed on corporations has long proved to be a complex and vexed legal issue. The common law has attempted to address the issue of corporate liability for crimes in two primary ways: through principles of vicarious liability and through direct liability, incorporating the identification doctrine. Additionally, specific statutory rules have been developed to provide for the application of the necessary elements of various criminal offences to corporations. While the *Corporations Act* contains particular provisions relating to corporate criminal liability for insider trading, and sets out rules for attributing the possession of information, knowledge and conduct of certain individuals to corporations, those provisions of the *Corporations Act* are not necessarily exclusive and may still allow the general law rules to operate, as is demonstrated in later chapters. Thus, this chapter considers the manner in which the law has developed rules to provide for corporate criminal liability under the general law, and then reviews the statutory rules which have been developed in order to apply principles of criminal liability to corporations. The specific provisions of the *Corporations Act* which relate to corporate criminal liability for insider trading are addressed in order to provide a clear context for the later topics, as is the civil penalty regime as it applies to insider trading.

## Models of corporate criminal liability

The common law has traditionally applied concepts of 'actus reus' (in essence, a guilty act) and 'mens rea' (a guilty mind) to most criminal offences. The 'actus reus' is the 'forbidden act' or unlawful conduct which gives rise to the offence,[1]

---

1   *R v Barker* (1983) 153 CLR 338, 370 (Dawson J).

and includes the relevant 'act or omission, the circumstances in which it takes place, and any consequences'.[2] The 'mens rea' is often considered to be 'an evil intention, or a knowledge of the wrongfulness of the act'.[3] The term also refers to a 'variety of states of mind, including intent, knowledge and recklessness'.[4] However, the *Criminal Code*, which provides for principles of criminal responsibility for Commonwealth offences, does not use the terms 'actus rea' or 'mens rea', but instead separates offences into 'physical elements' and 'fault elements'.[5]

The general law concepts of actus reus and mens rea were originally developed with individual offenders in mind,[6] and have often proved difficult to apply to corporations, due to the fact that a corporation can only act through its officers and agents and has no physical body or mind of its own.[7] Fisse has stated that:

> The attribution of criminal liability to corporations is an intractable subject; indeed, it is one of the blackest holes in criminal law.[8]

As a reflection of this difficulty, the first recorded cases of corporations being found liable for crimes involved offences of strict liability only.[9] Such cases concerned regulatory offences, like criminal nuisance, which required only that it be demonstrated that the relevant acts or omissions had occurred (the actus reus), without needing any proof of mens rea.[10]

The common law has now developed to recognise two primary models of corporate criminal liability: vicarious liability – where the corporation is liable for the criminal conduct of its employees or agents; and direct liability through the identification doctrine – where the corporation is actually regarded as having engaged in the criminal conduct itself due to the actions and intentions of its organs.[11] There are also two other significant theories of corporate criminal liability which have received statutory recognition, if not judicial endorsement, in Australia – the 'aggregation' doctrine – under which a corporation can be liable for the collective

---

2   David Brown, David Farrier, Luke McNamara, Alex Steel, Michael Grewcock, Julia Quilter and Melanie Schwartz, *Criminal Laws: Materials and Commentary on Criminal Law and Process in New South Wales* (Federation Press, 6th ed, Sydney, 2015) 144.

3   *Sherras v De Rutzen* (1895) 1 QB 918, 921, approved in *R v He Kaw Teh* (1985) 157 CLR 523, 528 (Gibbs CJ).

4   Brown et al, above n 2, 145.

5   *Criminal Code*, s 3.1(1).

6   Law Reform Commission of New South Wales, *Sentencing: Corporate Offenders*, Report No 10 (2003) [2.3].

7   Jonathan Clough and Carmel Mulhern, *The Prosecution of Corporations* (Oxford University Press, Melbourne, 2002) 71.

8   Brent Fisse, 'The Attribution of Criminal Liability to Corporations: A Statutory Model' (1992) 13 *Sydney Law Review* 277, 277.

9   For example, *R v Birmingham and Gloucester Railway Co* (1842) 114 ER 492; *R v The Great North of England Railway Co* (1846) 115 ER 1294.

10   Clough and Mulhern, above n 7, 72–73.

11   Law Reform Commission of New South Wales, above n 6, [2.5].

actions and intentions of more than one individual within the organisation;[12] and the 'organisational fault' model – which seeks to impose liability where there is perceived to be blameworthy conduct by the corporation itself, without needing to identify particular individuals whose actions and intentions must be attributed to the corporation.[13]

## Vicarious liability

Vicarious liability, a form of indirect liability, arises when one person is held responsible for the misconduct of another, due to the nature of the relationship between them. For example, employers are generally vicariously liable for the acts or omissions of their employees occurring within the scope of their employment.[14] Where the employer is a corporation, the corporation will bear the vicarious liability for the conduct of its employees, as would a natural person in the same position. Although vicarious liability is most commonly used in tort to impose liability for negligence, corporations can also be found vicariously liable for crimes in respect of the conduct of their officers or employees acting within the scope of their employment or authority.[15] Courts have generally not been willing to find corporations vicariously liable for crimes committed by their officers or employees where the crime is prohibited by statute, unless the statute indicates a clear legislative intent that there should be such liability.[16] In *Mousell Bros Ltd v London and North-Western Railway Co*,[17] Viscount Reading CJ stated that:

> Prima facie . . . a master is not to be made criminally responsible for the acts of his servant to which the master is not a party. But it may be the intention of the legislature, in order to guard against the happening of the forbidden thing, to impose a liability upon a principal even though he does not know of, and is not a party to, the forbidden act done by his servant. Many statutes are passed with this object. In those cases the legislature absolutely forbids the act and makes the principal liable without a mens rea.[18]

Where vicarious liability operates so that a corporation is considered to be guilty of a criminal offence, the corporation is not actually regarded as having engaged

---

12 Eric Colvin, 'Corporate Personality and Criminal Liability' (1995) 6 *Criminal Law Forum* 1, 18.
13 G R Sullivan, 'The Attribution of Culpability to Limited Companies' (1996) 55 *Cambridge Law Journal* 515, 524.
14 R P Balkin and J L R Davies, *Law of Torts* (LexisNexis Butterworths, 4th ed, Sydney, 2009) 719.
15 Meaghan Wilkinson, 'Corporate Criminal Liability – The Move Towards Recognising Genuine Corporate Fault' (2003) 9 *Canterbury Law Review* 142.
16 For example, *Mousell Bros Ltd v London and North-Western Railway Co* [1917] 2 KB 836, applied by the High Court of Australia in *R v Australasian Films Ltd* (1921) 29 CLR 195.
17 *Mousell Bros Ltd v London and North-Western Railway Co* [1917] 2 KB 836.
18 Ibid 844.

in the offence itself, but it has liability because of the relationship between the corporation and the person actually committing the offence.

The imposition of vicarious liability for criminal offences has been criticised because a corporation can be liable for the criminal acts of junior employees in circumstances in which the corporation derives no benefit from the relevant acts and, in very large organisations, there can be great difficulty in closely supervising every employee.[19] As a result, there are often 'due diligence' defences available under statutes which impose vicarious liability for criminal offences, which provide that there is no liability where a corporation has taken reasonable precautions to prevent the relevant act or omission occurring.[20] Additionally, criminal vicarious liability is usually only imposed for less serious offences, such as those which are regulatory in nature – for example, fair-trading, consumer protection and environmental offences – or where it would be impossible to enforce the offence without vicarious liability.[21] As a result, vicarious liability is not used, or proposed, as a model for corporate criminal liability for insider trading.

## Direct liability

The common law model of 'identification doctrine' – also known as 'organic theory' or the 'alter ego' doctrine[22] – operates to impose direct criminal liability on corporations, so that the actus reus and mens rea of certain officers or agents, such as the corporate organs, are taken to be those of the corporation.[23] This means that the corporation itself is regarded as having committed the crime, rather than merely being held responsible for crimes committed by others.

The identification doctrine relies on the concept of the 'directing mind and will' of a corporation, which originated from the judgment of Viscount Haldane LC[24] in the civil case of *Lennard's Carrying Co Ltd v Asiatic Petroleum Co Ltd*.[25] Under this doctrine, where there is a person who can be regarded as an organic

---

19  See, for example, James Gobert, 'Corporate Criminality: Four Models of Fault' (1994) 14 *Legal Studies* 393, 398.

20  Fisse, above n 8, 279. An example of such a 'due diligence' defence can be found in s 12.3(3) of the *Criminal Code* which provides that:

> Paragraph (2)(b) [which sets out the means by which authorisation or permission for relevant conduct might be established] does not apply if the body corporate proves that it exercised due diligence to prevent the conduct, or the authorisation or permission.

21  Clough and Mulhern, above n 7, 124.

22  Ross Grantham, 'Attributing Responsibility to Corporate Entities: A Doctrinal Approach' (2001) 19 *Company and Securities Law Journal* 168, 168; Sullivan, above n 13, 515. For ease of reference, the term 'identification doctrine' is used throughout this book.

23  Martin Wolff, 'On the Nature of Legal Persons' (1938) 54 *Law Quarterly Review* 494.

24  The Law Lords – Lord Dunedin, Lord Atkinson, Lord Parker of Waddington and Lord Parmoor – all concurred with Viscount Haldane LC's judgment.

25  *Lennard's Carrying Co Ltd v Asiatic Petroleum Co Ltd* [1915] AC 705.

part of the corporation, their actions and state of mind can be considered to be those of the corporation itself. Viscount Haldane LC stated that:

> A corporation is an abstraction. It has no mind of its own any more than a body of its own; its active and directing will must consequently be sought in the person of somebody who . . . may be called an agent, but who is really the directing mind and will of the corporation, the very ego and centre of the personality of the corporation. . . . That person may be under the direction of the shareholders in general meeting; that person may be the board of directors itself, or it may be, and in some corporations it is so, that that person has an authority co-ordinate with the board of directors given to him under the articles of association, and is appointed by the general meeting of the corporation, and can only be removed by the general meeting of the corporation.[26]

The concept of the directing mind and will of a corporation was further developed by Lord Denning in *H L Bolton (Engineering) Co Ltd v T J Graham & Sons Ltd*,[27] another civil case, where His Honour noted that:

> Some of the people in the company are mere servants and agents who . . . cannot be said to represent the mind or will. Others are directors and managers who represent the directing mind and will of the company and control what it does. The state of mind of these managers is the state of mind of the company. . . . Whether their intention is the company's intention depends on the nature of the matter under consideration, the relative position of the officer or agent and the other relevant facts and circumstances of the case.[28]

In *Tesco Supermarkets Ltd v Nattrass*,[29] the principle of the 'directing mind and will' of a corporation was then applied to criminal liability. This case involved criminal proceedings brought against Tesco Supermarkets under the *Trade Descriptions Act 1968* (UK) due to the advertisement of certain products at a price lower than the marked price on the products displayed in the supermarket. All the products marked at the lower advertised price had been sold and a shop assistant had replaced them on the shelf with products marked at the original higher price. The store manager, who, in accordance with the corporation's procedures, was responsible for supervising the shop assistant, was not aware that this had occurred. The *Trade Descriptions Act* contained a defence which could be relied on in such proceedings if it could be proved that:

(a) the commission of the offence was due to . . . the act or default of *another person*; and

---

26  Ibid 713–714.
27  *H L Bolton (Engineering) Co Ltd v T J Graham & Sons Ltd* [1957] 1 QB 159.
28  Ibid 172.
29  *Tesco Supermarkets Ltd v Nattrass* [1972] AC 153.

(b)  he [the corporation] took all reasonable precautions and exercised all due diligence to avoid the commission of such an offence. . . .[30]

Having been found guilty of the offence by the Magistrates Court, and after unsuccessfully appealing to the Divisional Court, Tesco Supermarkets appealed to the House of Lords on the basis that the offence was due to the act of the store manager, who was 'another person' within the meaning of s 24(1)(a), and that Tesco Supermarkets had taken all reasonable precautions and exercised all due diligence within the meaning of s 24(1)(b) of the *Trade Descriptions Act*, having set up proper systems for the running of the store. It was ultimately determined that Tesco Supermarkets was entitled to rely on the defence in s 24(1) of the *Trade Descriptions Act* on this basis.

Lord Reid approved the comments of Viscount Haldane LC[31] in *Lennard's Carrying Co Ltd v Asiatic Petroleum Co Ltd* and those of Lord Denning[32] in *H L Bolton (Engineering) Co Ltd v T J Graham & Sons Ltd*, noting that:

> A living person has a mind which can have knowledge or intention or be negligent and he has hands to carry out his intentions. A corporation has none of these: it must act through living persons, though not always one or the same person. Then the person who acts is not speaking or acting for the company. He is acting as the company and his mind which directs his acts is the mind of the company. There is no question of the company being vicari-ously liable. He is not acting as a servant, representative, agent or delegate. He is an embodiment of the company or, one could say, he hears and speaks through the persona of the company, within his appropriate sphere, and his mind is the mind of the company. If it is a guilty mind then that guilt is the guilt of the company. It must be a question of law whether, once the facts have been ascertained, a person in doing particular things is to be regarded as the company or merely as the company's servant or agent. In that case any liability of the company can only be a statutory or vicarious liability.[33]

Lord Reid then stated that:

> Normally the board of directors, the managing director and perhaps other superior officers of a company carry out the functions of management and speak and act as the company. Their subordinates do not. They carry out orders from above and it can make no difference that they are given some measure of discretion. But the board of directors may delegate some part of their functions of management giving to their delegate full discretion to act

---

30  *Trade Descriptions Act 1968* (UK), s 24(1) (emphasis added).
31  *Tesco Supermarkets Ltd v Nattrass* [1972] AC 153, 170.
32  Ibid.
33  Ibid.

independently of instructions from them. I see no difficulty in holding that they have thereby put such a delegate in their place so that within the scope of the delegation he can act as the company.[34]

The other Lords also approved the comments of Viscount Haldane LC in *Lennard's Carrying Co Ltd v Asiatic Petroleum Co Ltd* and Lord Denning in *H L Bolton (Engineering) Co Ltd v T J Graham & Sons Ltd*, and accepted the application of the principle of the 'directing mind and will' when considering the imposition of criminal liability on the relevant corporation, in this case Tesco Supermarkets.[35] The Lords also each separately determined that the store manager was not the directing mind and will of Tesco Supermarkets, so could properly be regarded as 'another person' for the purposes of the defence found in s 24(1)(b) of the *Trade Descriptions Act*.

The use of the identification doctrine to impose direct criminal liability on corporations – particularly in accordance with the statements of Lord Reid in *Tesco v Nattrass* – has been accepted and applied in a number of Australian cases[36] and approved by the High Court of Australia in the decision of *Hamilton v Whitehead*.[37] However, it must be acknowledged that there can be great difficulty in determining who actually is, or may be regarded as, the directing mind and will of a corporation. The directing mind and will of the corporation may be, as stated by Lord Reid in *Tesco v Nattrass*, the board of directors; the managing director; or a superior officer who 'carr[ies] out the functions of management and speak[s] and act[s] as the corporation'.[38] The concept does not apply to 'all servants of a company . . . who exercise some managerial discretion under the direction of superior officers'.[39] A person who is the directing mind and will of a corporation can only be a person or persons given 'full discretion to act independently of instruction' from the board.[40] Thus, this approach has been widely criticised

---

34  *Tesco Supermarkets Ltd v Nattrass* [1972] AC 153, 171. It was determined by Lord Reid that, as the store manager was not the directing mind and will of Tesco Supermarkets, he could be considered to be 'another person' for the purposes of the defence relied upon, and that Tesco Supermarkets had also engaged in an appropriate degree of due diligence – the board of Tesco Supermarkets had developed an operational system for the proper running of its stores, and had not delegated its managerial function to the store manager – so the store manager's acts were not the acts of the corporation: *Tesco Supermarkets Ltd v Nattrass* [1972] AC 153, 175.

35  See Lord Morris of Borth-Y-Gest at 180–181; Viscount Dilhorne at 187–188; Lord Pearson at 190; Lord Diplock at 199–200: *Tesco Supermarkets Ltd v Nattrass* [1972] AC 153.

36  See, for example, *Hanley v Automotive Food, Metals, Engineering, Printing and Kindred Industries Union* (2000) 100 FCR 530; *Collins v State Rail Authority (NSW)* (1986) 5 NSWLR 209; *Walplan Pty Ltd v Wallace* (1985) 8 FCR 27; *Trade Practices Commission v Tubemakers of Australia Ltd* (1983) 47 ALR 719; *G J Coles & Co Ltd v Goldsworthy* [1985] WAR 183; *Universal Telecasters (Qld) Ltd v Guthrie* (1978) 18 ALR 531.

37  *Hamilton v Whitehead* (1988) 166 CLR 121.

38  *Tesco Supermarkets Ltd v Nattrass* [1972] AC 153, 171.

39  Ibid.

40  *Tesco Supermarkets Ltd v Nattrass* [1972] AC 153, 171 (Lord Reid), 193 (Lord Pearson).

because it restricts liability to the conduct or fault of directors and high-level managers,[41] favouring larger corporations which will escape liability for acts of most employees,[42] and because criminal liability may be easily avoided by retaining an ultimate discretion within the board.[43]

In *Meridian Global Funds Management Asia Limited v Securities Commission*,[44] a case from New Zealand which went on appeal to the Privy Council, the identification doctrine was stated to be only one form of attribution available to determine direct corporate criminal liability. This case concerned an investment management corporation, Meridian, which had two senior employees who had used Meridian's funds to purchase shares in a listed corporation on Meridian's behalf. Due to the quantity of shares purchased, Meridian became a substantial shareholder of the listed corporation. The managing director and board of directors of Meridian were unaware of the share purchase, or that Meridian had become a substantial shareholder of the listed corporation, although the two senior employees had authority to make investments on behalf of Meridian. The relevant provisions of the *Securities Amendment Act 1988* (NZ) required a person who became a substantial shareholder of a listed corporation to notify the Securities Commission as soon as they knew, or ought to have known, that they had become a substantial shareholder.[45] One of the employees was the corporation's chief investment officer and his knowledge of the share purchase was attributed to Meridian, which meant Meridian ought to have known that it was a substantial shareholder of the listed corporation, placing it in breach of the notification obligation. This determination was made, not because the chief investment officer was considered to be Meridian's 'directing mind and will' but because it was considered by the Privy Council to be the natural construction of the statute.[46]

In reaching the decision in this case, the Privy Council emphasised that the decision of the House of Lords in *Tesco Supermarkets Ltd v Nattrass* 'was based not on general principle but on interpretation of particular statutory provisions',[47] in that case being those within the *Trade Descriptions Act 1968* (UK). Lord Hoffman[48] stated that, when determining whether a corporation is to be liable for a particular crime, the question to be answered is:

> whose act (or knowledge, or state of mind) was for this purpose intended to count as the act etc of the company? One finds the answer to this question by

---

41  Fisse, above n 8; Eilis Ferran, 'Corporate Attribution and the Directing Mind and Will' (2011) 127 *Law Quarterly Review* 239, 242.

42  Gobert, above n 19, 400; Colvin, above n 12, 15.

43  Jennifer Hill and Ronald Harmer, 'Criminal Liability of Corporations – Australia', in H De Doelder and K Tiedemann (eds), *Criminal Liability of Corporations* (Kluwer Law International, The Hague,1994) 71, 81–82.

44  *Meridian Global Funds Management Asia Limited v Securities Commission* [1995] AC 500.

45  *Securities Amendment Act 1988* (NZ), ss 20(3) and (4).

46  *Meridian Global Funds Management Asia Limited v Securities Commission* [1995] AC 500, 512.

47  Brown et al, above n 2, 253.

48  All other Lords agreed with Lord Hoffman in this decision.

applying the usual canons of interpretation, taking into account the language of the rule (if it is a statute) and its content and policy.[49]

Lord Hoffman then classified the rules of attribution into three separate groups: (i) *primary* rules of attribution – where the relevant acts were authorised by a resolution of the board of directors or unanimous agreement of shareholders; (ii) *general* rules of attribution – such as the rules of agency and vicarious liability, which operate in respect of natural persons as well as corporations; and (iii) *special* rules of attribution – to be determined by the courts for the purpose of applying particular rules. In such circumstances, the court must determine whose act or knowledge was intended by the legislature to be counted as the act or knowledge of the corporation, taking into account the policy of the relevant law.[50]

According to these classifications, the identification doctrine is regarded as one of the special rules of attribution, but not as the only way of determining direct corporate criminal liability. This means that it is not always necessary to determine who might be the directing mind and will of a corporation, as:

> it is a question of construction in each case as to whether the particular rule requires that the knowledge that an act has been done, or the state of mind with which it was done, should be attributed to the company.[51]

Following this decision would mean that employees who would not necessarily be regarded as the 'directing mind and will' of a corporation could still have their acts and intentions attributed to the corporation, depending upon the language, policy and intention of the relevant statute.[52]

While the decision in *Meridian Global Funds Management Asia Limited v Securities Commission* was criticised by many commentators for its lack of certainty and predictability, due to difficulties in determining whether a corporation is likely to have liability in any particular case,[53] it was welcomed by others for its flexibility and recognition of the 'realities of diffused organisational decision making'.[54] As noted in *ABC Developmental Learning Centres Pty Ltd v Wallace,*[55] a decision of Bell J of the Supreme Court of Victoria, the pronouncements of Lord Hoffman in *Meridian Global Funds Management Asia Limited v Securities Commission* have 'been frequently followed or cited with approval in various contexts':[56] for

---

49 *Meridian Global Funds Management Asia Limited v Securities Commission* [1995] AC 500, 507.
50 Ibid.
51 *Meridian Global Funds Management Asia Limited v Securities Commission* [1995] AC 500, 511.
52 Ross Grantham, 'Corporate Knowledge: Identification or Attribution' (1996) 59 *Modern Law Review* 732, 734.
53 See, for example, Clough and Mulhern, above n 7, 101.
54 See, for example, Grantham, above n 52.
55 *ABC Developmental Learning Centres Pty Ltd v Wallace* [2006] VSC 171 (3 May 2006).
56 Ibid 6.

example, by the Supreme Court of Western Australia,[57] the Federal Court,[58] the Supreme Court of South Australia,[59] the Supreme Court of New South Wales[60] and the Supreme Court of Victoria.[61] However, it was also noted in *ABC Developmental Learning Centres Pty Ltd v Wallace* that each of these instances involved cases which were regulatory in nature.[62] The statements made by Lord Hoffman in *Meridian Global Funds Management Asia Limited v Securities Commission* have not yet been adopted by the High Court of Australia, whose approval of the reasoning in *Tesco v Nattrass* in *Hamilton v Whitehead* remains the definitive pronouncement on direct corporate criminal liability in Australia. Additionally, despite the decision in *Meridian Global Funds Management Asia Limited v Securities Commission*, the identification doctrine seems to have remained the judicially preferred basis for corporate attribution in relation to serious crimes involving mens rea.[63]

As is discussed in detail in chapter 5, while the *Corporations Act* does provide specific statutory mechanisms for determining when a corporation is to be regarded as engaging in the relevant elements of insider trading, the *Corporations Act* does not exclude the general law or provide that the statutory mechanisms are to be exclusive. Thus, while these statutory mechanisms might be regarded as 'special rules of attribution' in accordance with the statements of Lord Hoffman in *Meridian Global Funds Management Asia Limited v Securities Commission*,[64] attribution through the identification doctrine, and as a result of the acts and intentions of the directing mind and will of a corporation, may also be available to attribute the elements of insider trading to corporations.

## Aggregation doctrine

Ordinarily, to find a corporation criminally liable for an offence, it is necessary to show that the person who engaged in the relevant actus reus also had the

---

57  *The City of Perth and Ors v DL (Representing the Members of People Living with Aids (WA) (Inc) and Ors* BC960167 [1996] EOC 92–796 (27 March 1996) (Ipp J).

58  *Australian Competition and Consumer Commission v J McPhee & Son (Australia) Pty Ltd* [1997] 469 FCA (19 May 1997) (Heerey J); *Australian Competition and Consumer Commission v Simsmetal Limited and Ors* [2000] FCA 818 (20 June 2000) (Heerey J); *Australian Competition and Consumer Commission v Australian Safeway Stores Pty Ltd and Another* (2003) 129 FCR 339 (Heerey, Sackville and Emmett JJ).

59  *Duke Group Limited (in liquidation) v Pilmer and Ors* (1999) 73 SASR 64 (Doyle CJ, Duggan and Bleby JJ); *Minister for Environment and Heritage v Greentree and Others* (2004) 138 FCR 198 (Sackville J).

60  *AAPT Ltd v Cable & Wireless Optus Ltd and Others* (1999) 32 ACSR 63 (Austin J).

61  *Director of Public Prosecutions Reference No 1 of 1996* [1998] 3 VR 352 (Callaway JA); *Emhill Pty Ltd v Bonsoc Pty Ltd* (2005) 55 ACSR 379 (Callaway JA).

62  *ABC Developmental Learning Centres Pty Ltd v Wallace* [2006] VSC 171 (3 May 2006) [12].

63  *Attorney-Generals' Reference (No 2 of 1999)* [2000] QB 796; Ferran, above n 41, 246.

64  *Meridian Global Funds Management Asia Limited v Securities Commission* [1995] AC 500, 507.

necessary mens rea.[65] However, the aggregation doctrine, also referred to as the doctrine of 'collective knowledge', enables the 'aggregation' of the conduct or knowledge of more than one individual within a corporation.[66] Even though no individual associated with the corporation would have criminal liability, the conduct or knowledge of two or more individuals who represent the corporation, or for whom the corporation is vicariously liable, can be aggregated so that the corporation has criminal liability.[67] Primarily developed in the United States,[68] this concept has been adopted in Australia in connection with civil liability, including liability for fraudulent misrepresentation,[69] but the High Court of Australia rejected the aggregation doctrine as a general principle for criminal liability in *R v Australasian Films Ltd*.[70] Despite this, the aggregation doctrine has been implemented in some Australian statutes – for example, s 12.4(2) of the *Criminal Code*.[71]

As is discussed in more detail in chapter 5, despite the fact that the provisions of the *Criminal Code* relating to corporate criminal liability do not apply to Chapter 7 of the *Corporations Act* and therefore do not apply to the insider trading provisions,[72] the current model of corporate liability for insider trading in Australia may enable the aggregation model to operate. The knowledge and actions of different individuals within a corporation can potentially be aggregated to attribute overall liability for insider trading to the corporation, regardless of whether any of those individuals would themselves have personal liability for insider trading. The new legislative provisions proposed in this book would remove the concept of aggregation from the current statutory provisions so that a corporation is only liable for insider trading where a person who possesses inside information, which the corporation is taken to possess, also knows or ought reasonably to know that the information is inside information and either engages in or authorises the relevant conduct or gives advice about the relevant conduct. This is consistent with the rationale for the prohibition of insider trading in Australia – the protection of market integrity – and corporate criminal liability will only arise where an informational advantage might actually be obtained.

---

65  Clough and Mulhern, above n 7, 106.
66  Colvin, above n 12, 18–19.
67  Sullivan, above n 13, 527.
68  See, for example, *United States v Bank of England*, 821 F2d 844 (1987).
69  See, for example, *Krakowski v Eurolynx Properties Ltd* (1995) 182 CLR 563.
70  *R v Australasian Films Ltd* (1921) 29 CLR 195.
71  Section 12.4(2) of the *Criminal Code* provides that:

If:

(a)  negligence is a fault element in relation to a physical element of an offence; and
(b)  no individual employee, agent or officer of the body corporate has that fault element,
that fault element may exist on the part of the body corporate if the body corporate is negligent when viewed as a whole (that is, by *aggregating* the conduct of any numbers of its employees, agents or officers) (emphasis added).

72  *Corporations Act*, s 769A.

## Organisational fault

The organisational fault model of liability operates on the basis that while there may be circumstances where there is no particular individual whose conduct is actually criminal, the 'organisational conduct' of the corporation itself is blameworthy and the corporation should be held criminally liable.[73] This model also responds to the criticism of the 'directing mind and will' form of direct liability, that merely because one managerial representative of a corporation may be at fault, it does not necessarily mean that the corporation as a whole should be regarded as being at fault.[74] 'Organisational fault' can arise under statute where the actus reus of the offence is committed by a person for whom the corporation is vicariously liable and the overall conduct of the corporation fulfils the mens rea through a corporate policy of non-compliance or a failure to take reasonable precautions or exercise due diligence.[75] It has been suggested that the organisational fault model is most suitable for serious offences where it is necessary to consider corporate blameworthiness.[76] The *Criminal Code* provides an example of this model of liability in s 12.3(2).[77] Organisational fault is not currently applied in relation to corporate liability for insider trading, and it is not proposed to be applied as part of the new reforms set out in this book as, once again, the new reforms are focused on ensuring that market integrity is protected and corporations will only have liability where an informational advantage might actually be obtained.

## Statutory principles of corporate criminal liability

In addition to the mechanisms available under the general law, statutory regimes may also provide particular rules for determining corporate criminal liability. By way of example, Part 2.5 of the *Criminal Code* sets out general principles of criminal responsibility for Commonwealth offences. As noted earlier, instead of using the common law terminology of 'actus reus' and 'mens rea', s 3.1(1) of the *Criminal Code* provides that offences consist generally of 'physical elements' and 'fault elements'. The *Criminal Code* describes a variety of matters which may amount to a fault element – intention, knowledge, recklessness or negligence.[78] A physical

---

73  Sullivan, above n 13, 524.
74  Brent Fisse and John Braithwaite, 'The Allocation of Responsibility for Corporate Crime: Individualism, Collectivism and Accountability' (1988) 11 *Sydney Law Review* 468, 504.
75  Fisse, above n 8, 279; James Gobert, 'Corporate Criminality: New Crimes for the Times' (1994) *Criminal Law Review* 722, 723.
76  Clough and Mulhern, above n 7, 124.
77  Section 12.3(2) of the *Criminal Code* sets out means by which a fault element can be attributed to a corporation, by:

(c)  proving that a corporate culture existed within the body corporate that directed, encouraged, tolerated or led to non-compliance with the relevant provision; or
(d)  proving that the body corporate failed to create and maintain a corporate culture that required compliance with the relevant provision.

78  *Criminal Code*, s 5.1.

element may be conduct, a result of conduct or a circumstance in which conduct, or a result of conduct, occurs.[79]

Section 3.2 of the *Criminal Code* then states that:

> In order for a person to be found guilty of committing an offence the follow-ing must be proved:
>
> (a) the existence of such physical elements as are, under the law creating the offence, relevant to establishing guilt;
> (b) in respect of each such physical element for which a fault element is required, one of the fault elements for the physical element.

It is clear that an offence may have more than one physical element.[80] The major-ity of the High Court of Australia noted in *The Queen v LK*[81] that the *Crimi-nal Code* applies fault elements to particular physical elements of an offence and makes no provision for the specification of a fault element that does not directly relate to a specified physical element.[82]

Despite the use of different terminology, in *The Queen v LK*, French J approved the statement that the drafting of the *Criminal Code* adopted 'the usual analytical division of criminal offences into the actus reus and the mens rea or physical ele-ments and fault elements'.[83] Part 2.5 of the *Criminal Code* also sets out general principles pursuant to which corporate criminal responsibility can be established and s 12.1(2) provides that a corporation can be found guilty of any offence. This part of the *Criminal Code* also provides specific rules for determining when a physical element[84] and a fault element[85] are to be attributed to a corporation.

---

79 *Criminal Code,* s 4.1(1).
80 *Ansari v The Queen* [2010] HCA 18, [50] (French CJ).
81 *The Queen v LK* [2010] HCA 17 (Gummow, Hayne, Crennan, Kiefel and Bell JJ).
82 Ibid 132.
83 Criminal Law Officers Committee of the Standing Committee of Attorneys-General, *Model Criminal Code, Chapter 2: General Principles of Criminal Responsibility*, Final Report (1992) 9; as approved in *The Queen v LK* [2010] HCA 17, [42] (French J).
84 Section 12.2 of the *Criminal Code* provides as follows:

> If a physical element of an offence is committed by an employee, agent or officer of a body corporate acting within the actual or apparent scope of his or her employment, or within his or her actual or apparent authority, the physical element must also be attributed to the body corporate.

85 Section 12.3(1) of the *Criminal Code* provides that a fault element must be attributed to a corporation that expressly, tacitly or impliedly authorises or permits an offence. Pursuant to s 12.3(2) such an authorisation or permission may be established by:

> (a) proving that the body corporate's board of directors intentionally, knowingly or reck-lessly carried out the relevant conduct, or expressly, tacitly or impliedly authorised or permitted the commission of the offence; or
> (b) proving that a high managerial agent of the body corporate intentionally, knowingly or recklessly engaged in the relevant conduct, or expressly, tacitly or impliedly authorised or permitted the commission of the offence; or

However, the provisions in the *Criminal Code* are just one example of a set of statutory rules providing for corporate criminal liability and they apply only to Commonwealth offences.[86] Additionally, certain statutes restrict the application of the rules contained within the *Criminal Code*. In particular, the *Corporations Act* provides that the operation of Part 2.5 of the *Criminal Code* does not apply to any offences created under Chapter 7 of the *Corporations Act*,[87] and a separate regime for corporate criminal liability for those offences is created in s 769B of the *Corporations Act*. The insider trading prohibition, contained in Part 7.10 of Chapter 7 of the *Corporations Act*, is therefore an offence excluded from the operation of Part 2.5 of the *Criminal Code*, and the principles of corporate criminal liability contained in that part are not applied to insider trading.

In relation to the conduct of a corporation, which is usually relevant to the physical element of a criminal offence, s 769B(1) of the *Corporations Act* provides that conduct engaged in on behalf of a body corporate:

(a)  by a director, employee or agent of the body, within the scope of the person's actual or apparent authority; or

(b)  by any other person at the direction or with the consent or agreement (whether express or implied) of a director, employee or agent of the body, where the giving of the direction, consent or agreement is within the scope of the actual or apparent authority of the director, employee or agent;

is taken for the purposes of a provision of this Chapter, or a proceeding under this Chapter, to have been engaged in also by the body corporate.

The conduct caught by s 769B(1) of the *Corporations Act* goes further than that which would be caught by s 12.2 of the *Criminal Code*, as s 769B(1) of the *Corporations Act* includes conduct engaged in by a person at the direction or with consent or agreement of a director, employee or agent, even if it is *not* within the scope of the first person's authority.

In relation to criminal offences where it is necessary to establish the state of mind of a body corporate, which will usually be relevant to fault elements, s 769B(3) of the *Corporations Act* provides that:

If, in a proceeding under this Chapter in respect of conduct engaged in by a body corporate, it is necessary to establish the state of mind of the body, it is sufficient to show that a director, employee or agent of the body [corporate],

---

(c)  proving that a corporate culture existed within the body corporate that directed, encouraged, tolerated or led to non-compliance with the relevant provision; or

(d)  proving that the body corporate failed to create and maintain a corporate culture that required compliance with the relevant provision.

86  *Criminal Code*, s 2.1.
87  *Corporations Act*, s 769A.

being a director, employee or agent by whom the conduct was engaged in within the scope of the person's actual or apparent authority, had that state of mind.

In Division 3 of Part 7.10 of the *Corporations Act*, which contains the insider trading prohibition, there is an additional means of establishing a corporation's possession of information and knowledge, which may be relevant for both the physical and fault elements of insider trading. For example, s 1042G(1) of the *Corporations Act* states that, for the purposes of Division 3 of Part 7.10:

(a)  a body corporate is taken to possess any information which an officer of the body corporate possesses and which came into his or her possession in the course of the performance of duties as such an officer; and
(b)  if an officer of a body corporate knows any matter or thing because he or she is an officer of the body corporate, it is to be presumed that the body corporate knows the matter or thing.

Section 1042G(2) also specifically states that 'this section does not limit the application of section 769B in relation to this Division'.[88] As the insider trading laws are intended to maintain and protect 'market integrity', it is most appropriate to utilise a particular set of provisions focused on achieving that rationale, rather than relying on the general statutory provisions applicable to the majority of Commonwealth criminal offences, which do not necessarily have similar aims or appropriate application to insider trading.[89]

## Civil liability for insider trading

A civil penalty regime for various forms of corporate misconduct was introduced in February 1993,[90] in order to:

- define a number of provisions of the *Corporations Law* as 'civil penalty provisions';
- enable the court to make a 'civil penalty order' in relation to a contravention of a civil penalty provision;
- retain criminal sanctions in relation to a contravention of a civil penalty provision. . .; [and]

88  These provisions are examined in detail in chapter 5.
89  See further, Juliette Overland, 'The Concept of Attribution in Corporate Law: Making Corporations Liable for Criminal Conduct', in David Chaikin and Gordon Hook (eds), *Corporate and Trust Structures: Legal and Illegal Dimensions* (Australian Scholarly Publishing, Melbourne, 2018) 35.
90  The regime was introduced into the then *Corporations Act 1989* (Cth) by the *Corporate Law Reform Act 1992* (Cth), and later amended by the *Corporate Law Economic Reform Program Act 1999* (Cth).

- enable the court to order a person who contravenes a civil penalty provision to compensate the company.[91]

The civil penalty regime was intended to give ASIC a greater range of enforcement options, consistent with the concept of an 'enforcement pyramid' developed by Ayres and Braithwaite[92] in accordance with their theory of 'responsive regulation'.[93] It was later extended to market misconduct offences,[94] which had the effect that insider trading could be the subject of civil penalty proceedings as well as criminal prosecutions.[95] Despite this, to date there have been only three sets of civil penalty proceedings brought for insider trading:

1   *ASIC v Petsas & Miot*;[96]
2   *ASIC v Citigroup*;[97] and
3   *ASIC v Hochtief*.[98]

In light of this, it is worth noting ASIC's own comment that it will 'generally pursue criminal action for insider trading given the seriousness of the misconduct'.[99]

For a corporation, the maximum possible penalties available for a contravention of the insider trading prohibition in civil penalty proceedings are:

a   a civil penalty of up to $1,000,000;[100] and
b   a compensation order to a person who suffered damage as a result of the contravention.[101]

The persons who are most likely to suffer damage as a result of insider trading contraventions are the trading counterparties, even though they may be unaware of it at the time, due to the anonymous nature of most trading in financial products.[102]

---

91   Explanatory Memorandum to the Corporate Law Reform Bill 1992, [18].
92   Ian Ayres and John Brathwaite, *Responsive Regulation: Transcending the Deregulation Debate* (New York: Oxford University Press, Oxford, 1992).
93   Michelle Welsh, 'Civil Penalties and Responsive Regulation: The Gap Between Theory and Practice' (2009) 33 *Melbourne University Law Review* 908, 912.
94   As a result of the *Financial Services Reform Act 2001* (Cth) amendments to the *Corporations Act*.
95   The notes accompanying s 1043A of the *Corporations Act* now state that a failure to comply with the section is an offence (note 1), and also a civil penalty provision (note 2).
96   *ASIC v Petsas and Miot* [2005] FCA 88.
97   *ASIC v Citigroup Global Markets Australia Pty Ltd* [2007] FCA 963.
98   *ASIC v Hochtief* [2016] FCA 1489.
99   ASIC, *Report 387, Penalties for Corporate Wrongdoing*, 2014, 25.
100  *Corporations Act*, s 1317G(1A). The maximum civil penalty for a natural person is $200,000.
101  *Corporations Act*, s 1317HA(1).
102  A natural person may also be disqualified from managing a corporation under s 206C of the *Corporations Act*, but this does naturally not apply to corporations.

The cases of *ASIC v Citigroup* and *ASIC v Hochtief*, which are discussed in detail elsewhere in this book, are the only examples of insider trading proceedings brought against corporations in Australia and both are sets of civil penalty proceedings. Citigroup successfully defended the civil penalty proceedings brought against it in 2007, and Hochtief admitted liability in civil penalty proceedings in 2016, with the appropriate civil penalty determined to be a fine of $400,000.

ASIC appears to primarily focus on bringing enforcement action for insider trading against individuals, and to prefer criminal prosecutions where available – this is most likely due to the comparatively low civil penalties and greater presumed deterrent effect of criminal prosecutions. As a result, it appears that civil penalty proceedings for insider trading against corporations are most likely to be utilised where a corporation admits liability, as was the case in *ASIC v Hochtief*.[103]

## A model of corporate liability for insider trading in Australia

It can be seen that there are a variety of models that are available for determining corporate liability under both the general law and statute, with complex and intricate variations. Currently, corporate liability for insider trading in Australia operates through a combination of models because the statute does not exclude the operation of the general law, and also incorporates concepts of direct liability under the *Corporations Act*. The manner in which these different models currently operate are explored in detail in the next chapter.

In this book, it is proposed that a new model of direct liability be adopted as the exclusive means for determining the liability of corporations for insider trading in Australia – it would operate as a set of 'special rules of attribution' for determining whose acts and knowledge are to be regarded as the acts and knowledge of the relevant corporation.[104]

It causes significant confusion and uncertainty as to the operation of the law for multiple models of liability to operate concurrently in relation to the liability of corporations for insider trading. As discussed in detail in chapter 1, insider trading is prohibited in Australia in accordance with a market integrity rationale, intended to ensure market fairness and promote market efficiency. Underlying this rationale is the desire to prevent certain participants from gaining an unfair advantage over others, and limiting their opportunities to trade on the basis of information which is not available to all participants. The model of liability to be imposed should reflect this rationale. Accordingly, a model of direct liability, in which a corporation will have liability for insider trading where it is regarded

---

103 See further, Juliette Overland, 'Making the Most of a Lost Opportunity: Do Civil Proceedings for Insider Trading Need to be Reformed?' (2018) 33 *Australian Journal of Corporate Law* 364.

104 Using the language of Lord Hoffman in *Meridian Global Funds Management Asia Limited v Securities Commission* [1995] AC 500, 507.

as having engaged in the prohibited conduct itself, is the only model which is truly consistent with this aim. A corporation will only be obtaining an unfair advantage over other participants in securities markets where it can be regarded as engaging in insider trading itself. Further, a corporation does not obtain an unfair advantage over other market participants, if officers, employees or agents who may possess inside information are not aware that other officers, employees or agents may be trading or procuring trading in financial products to which that information might relate. As a result, the model of direct liability proposed in this book has the following characteristics – a corporation would only be taken to have engaged in insider trading if the person who engaged in or authorised the relevant trading conduct on the corporation's behalf, within the actual or apparent scope of their authority, also possessed the relevant information and had the requisite knowledge that it was inside information. Under the operation of the new provisions, there would be no vicarious liability and no liability by aggregation. The new provisions, which would set out when a corporation is taken to possess inside information, to have the requisite knowledge that the information is inside information and when it is taken to have engaged in the relevant trading conduct, would provide for the direct liability of the corporation.

# 5 Attributing the elements of insider trading to corporations

Having considered the principles of corporate criminal and civil liability in chapter 4, this chapter focuses on the manner in which the elements of insider trading are attributed to corporations. There are several issues which must be addressed: when an alleged insider trader is a corporation, how does that corporation possess information? How does a corporation have knowledge that certain information is inside information? How does a corporation engage in the relevant trading conduct? How do the relevant provisions of the *Corporations Act* operate, and are general law principles of the identification doctrine and agency rules also to be considered? Accordingly, this chapter is comprised of three major parts: attributing the possession element to corporations; attributing the knowledge element to corporations; and attributing the trading element to corporations. The legal complexities associated with each of these issues is examined, to attempt to reach a definitive answer in relation to the liability of corporations for insider trading, and to highlight legislative difficulties and inconsistencies that could be overcome with reform. An analysis of these issues reveals significant uncertainty in the attribution of the elements of insider trading to corporations, which can only be resolved by significant legislative amendment.[1]

## The relevant elements of insider trading

In order to determine the manner in which insider trading is to be attributed to corporations, the following elements must be examined – the possession of inside information; the knowledge that certain information is inside information; and the relevant trading conduct.

As noted earlier in chapter 2, s 1043A of the *Corporations Act* sets out the offence of insider trading, which can be summarised as having the following elements: (i) a person possesses certain information; (ii) the information is not generally available; (iii) if the information were generally available, it would be

---

1  Much of the material addressed in this chapter is also discussed in detail in Juliette Overland, 'Reforming Australian Insider Trading Laws: A New Model of Corporate Criminal Liability – Part 1' (2017) 32 *Australian Journal of Corporate Law* 314.

material information; (iv) the person knows (or ought reasonably to know) that the information is not generally available, and, that if the information were generally available, it would be material information; and (v) while in possession of the information, the person trades in relevant financial products or procures another person to do so, or engages in tipping.

Elements (ii) and (iii) will not be applied any differently when the alleged insider trader is a corporation rather than a natural person, as it will be a question of determining, based on the relevant tests in ss 1042C and 1042D of the *Corporations Act*, whether the relevant information is generally available, and, if it were, whether that information would be material. However, it is not immediately clear how a corporation can be shown to satisfy elements (i), (iv) and (v) – that is, it needs to be determined how a corporation can be considered to possess information (the 'possession element'); how a corporation can be considered to know (or be considered to ought reasonably to know) that information is not generally available and, if it were, that the information would be material (the 'knowledge element'); and how a corporation can be considered to trade, or procure trading, in financial products or engage in tipping (the 'trading element').

Section 1043A of the *Corporations Act* states that:

(3)  For the purposes of the application of the *Criminal Code* in relation to an offence based on subsection (1) . . .

   (a)  (1)(a) is a physical element, the fault element for which is as specified in paragraph (1)(b).[2]

As the element set out in paragraph (1)(a) of s 1043A is that 'a person (the insider) possesses inside information' and the element set out in paragraph (1)(b) is that 'the insider knows, or ought reasonably to know, that the matters specified in paragraphs (a) and (b) of the definition of inside information in section 1042A are satisfied in relation to the information',[3] this means that the physical element of insider trading is the possession element, and the fault element is the knowledge

---

2   As discussed in chapter 4, s 3.1(1) of the *Criminal Code* provides that offences generally consist of 'physical elements' and 'fault elements'. Although s 769A of the *Corporations Act* provides that Part 2.5 of the *Criminal Code* does not apply to offences created under Chapter 7 of the *Corporations Act*, Part 2.5 of the *Criminal Code* (which comprises ss 12.1 to 12.6) is concerned only with 'Corporate Criminal Responsibility'. Thus, s 3.1 of the *Criminal Code* is still generally applicable to insider trading. When the current insider trading regime was inserted into the *Corporations Act*, it was noted that the insider trading provisions 'are *Criminal Code* compliant': Explanatory Memorandum, Financial Services Reform Bill 2001 (Cth), [15.23].

3   As set out earlier in chapter 2, s 1042A of the *Corporations Act* provides that 'inside information' means information in relation to which the following paragraphs are satisfied:

   (a)  the information is not generally available; and
   (b)  if the information were generally available, a reasonable person would expect it to have a material effect on the price or value of particular Division 3 financial products.

element. The conduct described in s 1043A(1)(c) of the *Corporations Act* relates to trading in relevant financial products – whether by applying for them, acquiring or disposing of them, or entering into an agreement to do any of those things.[4] Section 1043A(1)(d) concerns the procuring of another person to do any of those things, and s 1043A(2) concerns the communication of inside information to another person likely to do any of those things or procure another person to do so. While this is the conduct which a person who possesses inside information, and who knows or ought reasonably to know that it is inside information, must not engage in, such conduct is not stated to be a 'physical element' of insider trading. In this chapter, it is determined how these three elements of insider trading can be applied to corporations. As is demonstrated below, there are a number of statutory mechanisms and general law principles which can be used to determine when a corporation has possession of information, when a corporation has certain knowledge, and when a corporation has engaged in particular conduct. However, as is also demonstrated, the manner of their application is not at all certain.

## Attributing the possession element to corporations

The meanings of the terms 'information' and 'possession' were discussed in detail in chapter 2, and it was noted there that the pronouncements of Spigelman CJ in *R v Hannes*[5] make it clear that, in the context of insider trading, the possession of information requires actual 'awareness' of the relevant information, not mere physical possession or access to the information. Therefore, when applying this element to corporations, the question to be answered is – how does a corporation come to have actual 'awareness' of information?

Within Division 3 of Part 7.10 of the *Corporations Act* there is a provision under which a corporation is taken to possess information that is possessed by one of its officers in certain circumstances. Section 1042G(1)(a) of the *Corporations Act* provides that:

> a body corporate is taken to possess any information which an officer of the body corporate possesses and which came into his or her possession in the course of the performance of duties as such an officer.

In *ASIC v Citigroup*,[6] this provision was the only mechanism considered by the Court when determining whether Citigroup possessed certain information relating to the proposed takeover of Patrick by Toll. In that case, Jacobson J

---

4   As set out earlier in chapter 2, section 1043A(1) of the *Corporations Act* expressly states that an insider must not (whether as principal or agent):

   (c)  apply for, acquire, or dispose of, relevant Division 3 financial products, or enter into an agreement to apply for, acquire, or dispose of, relevant Division 3 financial products.

5   *R v Hannes* (2000) 158 FLR 359.
6   *ASIC v Citigroup* (2007) 160 FCR 35. This case was discussed in detail in chapter 2 and is the subject of further detailed discussion in chapter 6.

determined that even if the proprietary trader, Mr Manchee, had possessed the relevant information, that information was not taken to have been possessed by Citigroup under s 1042G(1)(a) because he was not an 'officer' of the corporation within the meaning of s 9 of the *Corporations Act*.[7] Similarly, in *ASIC v Hochtief*,[8] s 1042G(1)(a) of the *Corporations Act* was the only mechanism considered when determining whether Hochtief possessed inside information possessed by one of its directors.[9] As there are other potential mechanisms which could also be used to determine whether a corporation possesses certain information, before the application of s 1042G(1)(a) is examined, it is important to consider whether it is actually intended to be the exclusive mechanism for this purpose.

There are three reasons why s 1042G(1)(a) of the *Corporations Act* should *not* be regarded as the exclusive means for determining when a corporation possesses inside information: (i) the language of s 1042G(1)(a) itself indicates an absence of exclusivity; (ii) cases which have interpreted other statutes which use the same or very similar language to s 1042G(1)(a) have found that there is an absence of exclusivity; and (iii) in order to make sense of other provisions of the *Corporations Act*, it is necessary to infer a lack of exclusivity in s 1042G(1)(a).

When reaching these conclusions in relation to the interpretation of s 1042G(1) (a) of the *Corporations Act* (and other sections of this statute), careful examination and interpretation of the language used is necessary in order to discern the true meaning and underlying intention and, in this context, principles of statutory interpretation are clearly relevant.

While clearly all words must be given their 'plain and ordinary meaning',[10] when interpreting words and phrases used in the *Corporations Act* which have not been judicially considered in that context, principles of statutory interpretation allow reference to be had to cases which interpret their meaning when used in other statutes.[11] Additionally, an interpretation which allows all words used within the statute to have 'some meaning and effect' is to be preferred over an interpretation which would result in certain words being considered meaningless or redundant.[12]

---

7 This was despite the fact that the proprietary trader had a daily limit of $10,000,000: *ASIC v Citigroup* (2007) 160 FCR 35, 99; Keith Kendall and Gordon Walker, 'Insider Trading in Australia', in Stephen M Bainbridge (ed), *Research Handbook on Insider Trading* (Edward Elgar, Cheltenham, 2013) 365, 378–379.

8 *ASIC v Hochtief* [2016] FCA 1489.

9 Ibid 62.

10 See, for example, *Cody v J H Nelson Pty Ltd* (1947) 74 CLR 629, 647 (Dixon J); *Herbert Adams Pty Ltd v Federal Commission for Taxation* (1932) 47 CLR 222, 228 (Dixon J); D C Pearce and R S Geddes, *Statutory Interpretation in Australia* (LexisNexis Butterworths, 8th ed, Sydney, 2014) 61.

11 See, for example, *Gett v Tabet* (2009) 254 ALR 504, [289]; *Marshall v Director-General, Department of Transport* (2001) 205 CLR 603, [62] (McHugh J); Pearce and Geddes, above n 10, 10.

12 *Commonwealth v Baume* (1905) 2 CLR 405, 404 (Griffith CJ); *Beckwith v R* (1976) 135 CLR 569, 574 (Gibbs J); Pearce and Geddes, above n 10, 62.

Section 1042G(1)(a) of the *Corporations Act* is not expressed in language which indicates a legislative intention that it be regarded as an exclusive mechanism. Looking again at the precise language of s 1042G(1) – it states that:

For the purposes of this Division:

(a) a body corporate *is taken to* possess any information which an officer of the body corporate possesses and which came into his or her possession in the course of the performance of duties as such an officer.[13]

The opening phrase – 'For the purposes of this Division, a body corporate is taken to possess . . . ' – does not require or imply exclusivity. Indeed, it is expressly stated in s 1042G(2) that 'this section does not limit the application of section 769B in relation to this Division'. Since s 769B of the *Corporations Act* contains the rules of corporate criminal responsibility which are applicable to Chapter 7 of the Act in place of Chapter 2.5 of the *Criminal Code*, this means that the relevant rules from s 769B will also be applicable, further indicating that s 1042G of the *Corporations Act* is not intended to be exclusive.

In *Rowe v Transport Workers Union of Australia*,[14] Cooper J of the Federal Court considered whether the general law identification doctrine was applicable to determining whether an industrial association had engaged in certain conduct, or if only the specific statutory rules set out in s 298B of the *Workplace Relations Act 1996* (Cth) were relevant. Section 298B(2) of the *Workplace Relations Act* provided that certain 'action done by one of the [prescribed bodies or persons] *is taken to* have been done by an industrial association'.[15] To that extent, it is similar to s 1042G(1)(a) of the *Corporations Act* providing that a body corporate *is taken to* possess information possessed by an officer in certain circumstances. Cooper J found that the phrase 'is taken to' implies an additional alternative statutory mechanism, rather than an exclusive one, which:

as a matter of construction, [is] not intended to exclude the operation of the directing mind principle. . . . Indeed, the operation of the principle and the two sections may overlap.[16]

In order to make sense of later provisions of the *Corporations Act*, it is also necessary to assume that other mechanisms (such as other statutory provisions and the general law rules) can also operate to attribute the possession of information to a corporation. Importantly, s 1043F of the *Corporations Act*, which sets out the

---

13 Emphasis added.
14 *Rowe v Transport Workers Union of Australia* (1998) 160 ALR 66.
15 Emphasis added.
16 *Rowe v Transport Workers Union of Australia* (1998) 160 ALR 66, 81, approved in *Hadgkiss v Sunland Constructions Pty Ltd* [2007] FCA 346 (14 March 2007) (Keifel J) and in *Hanley v Automotive, Food, Metals, Engineering, Printing and Kindred Industries Union* [2000] FCA 1188 (24 August 2000) (Ryan, Moore and Goldberg JJ).

Chinese Wall defence for corporations, refers to 'information in the possession of an officer *or an employee*'. If s 1042G(1) is to be the only means by which the possession of information can be attributed to a corporation, requiring that it be possessed by an officer of the corporation, the words 'or an employee' in s 1043F of the *Corporations Act* would be meaningless, as information possessed by a mere employee would be irrelevant. Further, in the Explanatory Memorandum, Corporate Law Economic Reform Program (Audit Reform and Corporate Disclosure) Bill 2003 (Cth), which repealed a redundant definition of 'officer' in s 82A of the *Corporations Act*, there is a statement that 'in cases where particular provisions of the *Corporations Act* dealing with personnel are intended to extend to employees, this will be expressly stated'.[17] If the Chinese Wall defence is intended to apply when *employees* possess information, s 1042G(1)(a) of the *Corporations Act* must not be an exclusive mechanism because it does not provide for a corporation to possess information known only to an employee who is not an officer. While some might regard this as only a drafting error in need of minor correction,[18] such an interpretation still creates significant uncertainty as to the intended operation of these provisions.

The need to rely on general law principles of attribution in connection with the possession of information by corporations is recognised by Qu,[19] but he does so based on a view that s 1042G(1)(a) of the *Corporations Act* contains a rebuttable presumption that the information possessed by an officer is also possessed by the corporation, and that general law principles of attribution can be used to rebut that presumption.[20] While, for the reasons discussed earlier, the language of s 1042G(1) of the *Corporations Act*, in stating that 'a body corporate is taken to possess any information which an officer of the body corporate possesses', is not intended to be exhaustive, it does not necessarily follow that this creates a rebuttable presumption in this instance. If this statutory rule could be rebutted by demonstrating that the general law rules would not attribute possession of the relevant information to the corporation, it means that the statutory rule would only apply to attribute the possession of information to a corporation when the general law rules also have that effect. If the statutory rule had that effect but the general law rules did not, and the general law rules could then be used to rebut the statutory rule, it would have the overall effect that only the operation of the general law would be relevant, thereby making the statutory provision redundant. This cannot have been the legislative intention behind this provision. The better view must be that both the general law rules and the statutory rules can be relied on as alternative means of attributing the possession of information to a corporation.

17  Explanatory Memorandum, Corporate Law Economic Reform Program (Audit Reform and Corporate Disclosure) Bill 2003 (Cth), [5.574].
18  See, for example, Kevin A Lewis, 'A Decade On: Reforming the Financial Services Law Reforms' (Paper presented at Sixth Annual Supreme Court Corporate Law Conference, Sydney, 23 August 2011).
19  Charles Zhen Qu, 'How Statutory Civil Liability is Attributed to a Company: An Australian Perspective Focusing on Civil Liability for Insider Trading by Companies' (2006) 32 *Monash Law Review* 177.
20  Ibid 191.

Thus, it can be seen that, without exclusivity in s 1042G(1)(a) of the *Corporations Act*, other mechanisms can apply to attribute the possession of information to a corporation, even though the provisions of the *Criminal Code* are excluded.[21] This is despite the fact that in *ASIC v Citigroup* and in *ASIC v Hochtief* only the operation of s 1042G(1)(a) of the *Corporations Act* was considered in this context. One can infer from the judgment in *ASIC v Citigroup* that arguments relating to alternative means of attributing the possession of information to a corporation such as Citigroup were not presented to the Court, particularly since it appears that ASIC assumed that the proprietary trader in question would be regarded as an officer of Citigroup and that s 1042G(1)(a) would therefore apply.[22]

In *Rivkin Financial Services Ltd v Sofcom Ltd*,[23] Emmet J found that, while the alleged inside information was not actually material and therefore that no insider trading had taken place, the three corporations controlled by Mr Khan did possess the information about Mr Khan's intentions to attempt to increase his shareholding and gain control of the board. However, His Honour did not give reasons for that determination and did not analyse any provisions of the *Corporations Act* or consider the general law in this context. As a result, this decision does not assist in determining how corporations might possess inside information and which mechanisms are to be used for that purpose.

Other mechanisms which could potentially be used to determine when a corporation possesses certain information are, firstly, other provisions in the *Corporations Act*, such as s 1042G(1)(b) and s 769B(3), and secondly, general law agency rules and the identification doctrine.

Section 1042G(1)(b) of the *Corporations Act* provides that:

> if an officer of a body corporate knows any matter or thing because he or she is an officer of the body corporate, it is to be presumed that the body corporate knows that matter or thing.

Is 'information' a matter or thing? Even if information is not a 'thing', it clearly includes matter, as the definition of 'information' in s 1042A of the *Corporations Act* states that information includes:

(a) *matters* of supposition and other *matters* that are insufficiently definite to warrant being made known to the public; and
(b) *matters* relating to the intentions, or likely intentions, of a person.[24]

---

21 *Corporations Act*, s 769A.
22 *ASIC v Citigroup* (2007) 160 FCR 35, 99–101. Black notes that 'ASIC did not seek to establish attribution under the *Corporations Act 2001* (Cth), s 769B, or the general law in that case': Ashley Black, 'Insider Trading and Market Misconduct' (2011) 29 *Company and Securities Law Journal* 313, 320.
23 *Rivkin Financial Services Ltd v Sofcom Ltd* (2004) 51 ACSR 486. The facts of this case were set out in chapter 2.
24 Emphasis added.

Additionally, s 1042C(1)(a) of the *Corporations Act* provides that information is generally available if, amongst other things, it consists of readily observable *matter*. Thus, it appears that information can include a 'matter' and therefore s 1042G(1)(b) may be used to determine when a corporation possesses certain information.

Some commentators, such as Lyon and du Plessis[25] and Black,[26] apply s 1042G(1)(b) of the *Corporations Act* only to the knowledge element of insider trading – whether there was knowledge that the relevant information was not generally available and likely to be material. Others, such as Austin and Ramsay[27] and Hambrook,[28] consider that it is applicable to both the possession element and the knowledge element of insider trading. The title of s 1042G gives little assistance – the section is titled 'Information in Possession of Officer of Body Corporate'. Reliance on this heading[29] would support the proposition that s 1042G(1)(b) actually relates to an alleged insider's *possession* of inside information, rather than the knowledge that he or she may have about the *qualities* of that information. However, later paragraphs of s 1042G(1) of the *Corporations Act* provide that:

(c)  if an officer of a body corporate, in that capacity, is reckless as to a circumstance or results, it is to be presumed that the body corporate is reckless as to that circumstance or result; and

(d)  for the purposes of paragraph 1043M(2)(b), if an officer of a body corporate ought reasonably to know any matter or thing because he or she is an officer of the body corporate, it is to be presumed that the body corporate ought reasonably to know that matter or thing.

Neither of these additional subsections appear to relate exclusively to the possession of information, or knowledge as to the qualities of that information, so

---

25  Gregory Lyon and Jean J du Plessis, *The Law of Insider Trading in Australia* (Federation Press, Sydney, 2005) 57.

26  Ashley Black, 'The Reform of Insider Trading Law in Australia' (1992) 15 *University of New South Wales Law Journal* 214, 225.

27  Robert P Austin and Ian M Ramsay, *Ford's Principles of Corporations Law* (LexisNexis Butterworths, Sydney, 2018) 9.870.2.

28  J P Hambrook, 'Market Misconduct and Offences', in *Australian Corporations Law Principles and Practice* (LexisNexis Butterworths, Sydney, 2018) 7.13.0145.

29  Section 13(1) of the *Acts Interpretation Act 1901* (Cth) provides that:

All material from and including the first section of an Act to the end of:

(a)  if there are no Schedules to the Act – the last section of the Act; or,

(b)  if there are one or more Schedules to the Act – the last Schedule to the Act; is part of the Act.

In the Explanatory Memorandum to the Acts Interpretation Amendment Bill 2011 (Cth), which inserted this provision into the *Acts Interpretation Act 1901* (Cth) when enacted, it was noted that the 'new section 13 is intended to capture all headings . . . within the Act'. However, it was also noted that, while headings are to be regarded as part of an Act, the weight to be given to headings 'will ordinarily be less than the words of the section itself': Explanatory Memorandum to the Acts Interpretation Amendment Bill 2011 (Cth), [93].

it seems that the heading of s 1042G is not helpful in this respect and that s 1042G(1) of the *Corporations Act* contains provisions which are capable of relating to both elements of insider trading. Therefore, s 1042G(1)(b) appears to be applicable to both the possession and knowledge elements of insider trading, and therefore to determining when a corporation may have possession of certain information. However, the differing approaches on the availability of this subsection to attribute the possession of information to a corporation illustrate the difficulties of interpretation and uncertainty created by these provisions and highlight the need for legislative reform.

Section 769B(3) of the *Corporations Act* provides that:

> If, in a proceeding under this Chapter in respect of conduct engaged in by a body corporate, it is necessary to establish the *state of mind* of the body, it is sufficient to show that a director, employee or agent of the body, being a director, employee or agent by whom the conduct was engaged in within the scope of the person's actual or apparent authority, had that state of mind.[30]

If the 'state of mind' of the body corporate can include the possession of information, this provision may also be a potential means of determining when a corporation has such possession. Section 769B(10)(c) states that:

> A reference to the state of mind of a person includes a reference to the *knowledge*, intention, opinion, belief or purpose of the person and the person's reason for the person's intention, opinion, belief or purpose.[31]

Since the possession of information does require 'awareness' and therefore knowledge of the contents of the information,[32] it is arguable that this provision is relevant to the possession element of insider trading – the possession of inside information. The state of mind of a corporation can conceivably also relate to awareness of the qualities of that information – such as whether it is generally available or material – which would equate to the knowledge element. Thus, it appears that s 769B(3) of the *Corporations Act* can relate to both the possession element and the knowledge element of insider trading and can be considered in both contexts to determine whether a corporation is to be regarded as having engaged in insider trading.

Therefore, having established that s 1042G(1)(a) of the *Corporations Act* is not the exclusive mechanism for determining when a corporation may possess inside information, and having determined that there are a number of possible mechanisms which may be used to determine when a corporation possesses

---

30 Emphasis added.
31 Emphasis added.
32 In accordance with the pronouncements of Spigelman CJ in *R v Hannes* (2000) 158 FLR 359, 398.

information – ss 1042G(1)(a), 1042G(1)(b) and 769B(3) of the *Corporations Act*, as well as general law rules – each can now be analysed in order to determine how that possession occurs.

### Statutory mechanisms

Returning again to s 1042G(1)(a) of the *Corporations Act*, the precise language of the section states that:

> a body corporate is taken to possess any information which an officer of the body corporate possesses and which came into his or her possession in the course of the performance of duties as such an officer.

Thus, in order for information to be possessed by a corporation in accordance with s 1042G(1)(a) of the *Corporations Act*, there are two requirements which must be satisfied: (i) the information must be possessed by an *officer* of the corporation; and (ii) the information possessed by the officer must have come into his or her possession *in the course of performing his or her duties*.

In *ASIC v Citigroup*,[33] determining whether the relevant proprietary trader who allegedly possessed inside information was an officer of Citigroup was treated as a 'threshold question' as to whether that information could be attributed to the corporation,[34] as evidenced by the following statement of Jacobson J of the Federal Court:

> Even if Mr Manchee was in possession of inside information, his knowledge is not attributable to Citigroup *unless* he was an officer of that body corporate.[35]

The requirement under s 1042G(1)(a) of the *Corporations Act* that information will only be taken to be possessed by a corporation where it is acquired by an officer, will generally require that the person must be a director, company secretary or senior executive, as the term 'officer' is defined in s 9 of the *Corporations Act* to mean:

(a)  a director or secretary of the corporation; or
(b)  a person:
 (i)  who makes, or participates in making, decisions that affect the whole, or a substantial part, of the business of the corporation; or
 (ii)  who has the capacity to significantly affect the corporation's financial standing; or

---

33  *ASIC v Citigroup* (2007) 160 FCR 35.
34  Ibid 99.
35  Ibid.

(iii) in accordance with whose instructions or wishes the directors of the corporation are accustomed to act (excluding advice given by the person in the proper performance of functions attaching to the person's professional capacity or their business relationship with the directors or the corporation); or

(c) a receiver, or receiver and manager, of the property of the corporation; or
(d) an administrator of the corporation; or
(e) an administrator of a deed of company arrangement executed by the corporation; or
(f) a liquidator of the corporation; or
(g) a trustee or other person administering a compromise or arrangement made between the corporation and someone else.

It is for this reason that, in *ASIC v Citigroup*, the information allegedly possessed by the proprietary trader was not regarded as being possessed by Citigroup itself, as the proprietary trader did not fall within this definition of an 'officer'. He was clearly not a director or company secretary of Citigroup, or any form of trustee or insolvency controller within the meaning of paragraphs (c) to (g) of the definition in s 9, and he was also not a 'shadow director' of Citigroup, being 'a person in accordance with those instructions or wishes the directors of the corporation are accustomed to act' as required by paragraph (b)(iii).[36] This meant that the decision as to whether he was an officer of Citigroup was an issue which turned on:

whether he was a person:

- who made, or participated in making, decisions that affected the whole, or a substantial part, of the business of Citigroup; or
- who had the capacity to affect significantly the financial standing of Citigroup.[37]

These parts of the definitions of 'officer', found in paragraphs (b)(i) and (b)(ii), are concerned with 'identifying persons who are involved in the management of the corporation'.[38] Mr Manchee, the proprietary trader, did not have 'any involvement in policy making or decisions that affected the whole or a substantial part of the business of Citigroup'.[39] He was one of five proprietary traders employed by Citigroup and he did not have any employees reporting to him or have any other responsibilities aside from proprietary trading. The fact that he had a daily trading limit of $10,000,000 did not 'make him a person who had the capacity to affect Citigroup's financial standing', as

36 Ibid.
37 Ibid.
38 Ibid.
39 Ibid.

this was not a significant sum 'in the context of Citigroup's very substantial business'.[40]

Thus, only a person who fulfils at least one of the elements of the s 9 definition of 'officer' will be a person whose possession of information will be attributed to a corporation pursuant to s 1042G(1)(a) of the *Corporations Act*. By contrast, s 1042H(1)(a) of the *Corporations Act* provides that each member of a partnership is regarded as possessing any information which another member of the partnership came to possess in their capacity as a member, and any information which an *employee* of the partnership possesses and which came into his or her possession in the course of the performance of their duties. So a partner in a partnership will be taken to possess information that is acquired by a member of the partnership or any employee but, under s 1042G(1)(a) of the *Corporations Act*, a corporation is only taken to possess information acquired by or known to an officer.

As noted earlier, s 1042G(1)(a) of the *Corporations Act* provides that, for a corporation to be considered to possess information, the relevant officer who possesses the information must have acquired it *in the course of the performance of their duties*. Although the phrase 'in the course of performance of duties' is not defined in the *Corporations Act*, or in any other available Australian legislation, it is a concept which is relevant to the duties of directors, particularly in cases concerning conflicts of interest where it is necessary to consider whether certain information or opportunities came to directors in their capacity as a director or in a personal capacity.

In *Peso Silver Mines v Cropper*,[41] a director who acquired an interest in a mining claim, which had been previously offered to and rejected by the corporation of which he was a director, was found not to be liable to account to the corporation for any of the profits he made because he had been approached 'not in his capacity as a director' but 'as an individual member of the public'.[42] In *Regal Hastings v Gulliver*,[43] directors who took up shares in an investment, so that the corporation of which they were directors could also participate, were found to be liable to account to the corporation for the relevant profits because the opportunity to take up the investment only came to them because they were directors of the corporation.[44] In *Boardman v Phipps*,[45] a trustee of a trust and the solicitor for the trust were both found to be in breach of duty and liable to account to the trust for profits they made when they purchased certain shares in a corporation in which the trust had a substantial holding, because information about the shares came to them only because of their position as trustee and solicitor, and because they would never have acquired the information if they were not acting for the trust.[46] The common feature in each of these cases is that information or an opportunity

---

40  Ibid 101.
41  *Peso Silver Mines v Cropper* [1966] SCR 673.
42  Ibid 682.
43  *Regal Hastings v Gulliver* [1967] 2 AC 134.
44  Ibid 158.
45  *Boardman v Phipps* [1967] 2 AC 46.
46  Ibid 118.

that would not have been acquired or available 'but for' the person's connection with the corporation is generally regarded as being information or an opportunity which has been acquired in the course of the performance of a person's duties.

Therefore, returning to the possession of inside information, the requirement in s 1042G(1)(a) of the *Corporations Act* that information be acquired by an officer 'in the course of performance of duties' clearly requires a nexus between the duties that the particular officer ordinarily performs, or is authorised to perform, for the corporation and the manner in which the information comes into that officer's possession.

This requirement gives rise to an important issue: what is the position if information may be considered to have been acquired in two or more different capacities, only one of which relates to the performance of the officer's duties? For example: what is the status of information which could have been acquired in either a private or a professional capacity? What is the status of information which could have arisen in one of two different professional capacities, one of which is unrelated to the performance of the officer's duties?

Information which is acquired in a private capacity is necessarily excluded from the operation of s 1042G(1)(a) of the *Corporations Act*, because it falls outside the performance of the officer's duties. For example, if an officer of a corporation is informed of some inside information by a close personal friend at a social event, the director is unlikely to have received the information 'in the course of performing his or her duties', and therefore the corporation will not be regarded as possessing the information pursuant to s 1042G(1)(a) of the *Corporations Act*. By contrast, if the officer was informed of the inside information by a client of the corporation at a formal business meeting, the officer would be more likely to be regarded as acquiring the information 'in the course of performing his or her duties' and so the information would also be considered to be possessed by the corporation pursuant to this provision.

However, the distinction between information acquired in a private capacity and information acquired in a professional capacity may not always be easily drawn. What would be the result if an officer acquired information in a context which had both private and professional aspects? How are such issues to be determined? The difficulties associated with this question can be demonstrated by the following example: an officer may, over time, become very friendly with a client of the corporation, so that they sometimes socialise together. Both the officer and the client may regularly, as part of their professional activities, attend industry functions for networking and marketing purposes. If the officer and client were to run into each other at such a function and then, when the function ended, move on to a bar for a post-function drink where they discussed both professional and social topics, would information passed on to the officer by the client be information acquired in the course of the officer's performance of his or her duties? The attendance at the industry function suggests a professional capacity, but the post-function drinks are more likely to be described as a mere social occasion, giving the event a more private capacity. Is this really a satisfactory test, particularly in light of the reason for the prohibition of insider trading in Australia? Since insider trading is prohibited in order to attempt to protect and maintain market integrity, ensuring a fair and efficient market, the application of the prohibition to corporations should be focused on ensuring that the corporation does not obtain an unfair informational advantage, rather than on the manner in which the information comes into the possession of various officers or employees.

What then of information acquired in another professional capacity? It is not uncommon for officers of corporations to have other professional roles and responsibilities outside their 'primary' corporate role. For example, a director may be on the board of more than one corporation. Where such a director acquires inside information, how is it to be determined in which capacity he or she was acting when they acquired it? Austin and Ramsay[47] consider that, if one corporation controls enough shares in a second corporation to be able to appoint an officer of the first corporation as a director of the second, any information acquired by that officer while serving as a director of the second corporation will be possessed by the first corporation as well, because the information will be acquired by the officer in the course of performing his or her duties for the first corporation. However, in circumstances where a person is a director of two unrelated corporations, with no relationship or link between the two roles, there is generally no possession of information by one corporation if the director acquires the information while performing duties for the second corporation.[48] Austin and Ramsay[49] suggest that the common law agency rules may be relevant here, so that, if a person is a director of two corporations and acquired information in the course of performing their duties for the second corporation, the first corporation would only be considered to possess the information if the director was under a duty to acquire it for, or disclose it to, the first corporation and could do so without breaching any duties to the second corporation from which it was acquired.[50] Alternatively, if the director was regarded as being the 'directing mind and will' of both corporations at general law, each corporation could be regarded as possessing the information under the identification doctrine,[51] as is discussed below. However, once again, insider trading laws should be directed to ensuring a corporation does not obtain an unfair informational advantage, rather than focusing on the capacity in which an officer was acting when he or she came to possess inside information.

Section 1042G(1)(b) of the *Corporations Act* may also be used as a mechanism for determining that certain information is possessed by a corporation. As set out earlier, s 1042G(1)(b) states that:

> if an officer of a body corporate knows any matter or thing because he or she is an officer of the body corporate, it is to be presumed that the body corporate knows that matter or thing.

---

47  Austin and Ramsay, above n 27, [16.220].
48  *Re David Payne & Co Ltd* [1904] 2 Ch 608.
49  Austin and Ramsay, above n 27, [16.220].
50  *Harkness v Commonwealth Bank of Australia Ltd* (1993) 32 NSWLR 543; *El Ajou v Dollar Land Holdings Plc* [1994] 2 All ER 685, 698.
51  *Endresz v Whitehouse* (1997) 24 ACSR 208, 228.

Thus, in order for information to be possessed by a corporation in accordance with s 1042G(1)(b) of the *Corporations Act* there are two requirements which must be satisfied: (i) the information must be known by an officer of the corporation; and (ii) the officer must know the information because he or she is an officer of the corporation.

The requirement that the person who knows the information must be an officer of the corporation is the same as for s 1042G(1)(a) and the definition of the term 'officer' in s 9 of the *Corporations Act* will be equally applicable.

A requirement that a person knows information *because* he or she is an officer of a corporation is similar but not identical to the requirement in s 1042G(1)(a) of the *Corporations Act* that the officer *acquired information in the course of performance of their duties*. The phrase 'because he or she is an officer' is not defined in the *Corporations Act* or in any other available Australian legislation. However, it clearly requires a link between the position the person occupies within the corporation and the circumstances which lead to the person 'knowing' the information. Consequently, it will necessarily lead to the same or a similar result as under s 1042G(1)(a) of the *Corporations Act*, where information acquired in a private capacity will not be attributed to the corporation. Thus, despite the variation in language used, there is likely to be little discernible difference between the operation of these two potential mechanisms of determining when a corporation will possess inside information.

Turning now to s 769B(3) of the *Corporations Act*, another potential means of determining when a corporation possesses inside information, it has been noted earlier that this statutory provision states that:

> If, in a proceeding under this Chapter in respect of conduct engaged in by a body corporate, it is necessary to establish the state of mind of the body, it is sufficient to show that a director, employee or agent of the body, being a director, employee or agent by whom the conduct was engaged in within the scope of the person's actual or apparent authority, had that state of mind.

There are two requirements which must be satisfied to show that a corporation had a certain state of mind in these circumstances, an awareness of information in order to amount to possession – under s 769B(3) of the *Corporations Act*: (i) a director, employee or agent of the corporation must be aware of the relevant information; and (ii) the same director, employee or agent of the corporation must have engaged in certain conduct, within the scope of the person's actual or apparent authority.

Section 769B(3) of the *Corporations Act* is widely drafted so that any director,[52] employee or agent can possess the relevant information. Unlike ss 1042G(1)(a)

---

52 The term 'director' is extensively defined in s 9 of the *Corporations Act*, which states that:

'director' of a company or other body means:
(a) a person who:
(i) is appointed to the position of a director; or

and 1042G(1)(b) discussed earlier, it is not limited to an officer of the corporation, but also applies to employees who possess relevant information. An employment relationship is typically one in which an employee enters into a contract of service with an employer, in contrast to a contract for services entered into between a principal and an independent contractor. While the totality of the relationship needs to be examined, the key criteria which are usually addressed to determine if there is an employment relationship are: the degree of control exercised, the mode of remuneration, whether there is an obligation to provide and maintain equipment, the obligation to work, the hours of work and provision of holidays, the deduction of income tax and the delegation of work.[53]

Section 769B(3) of the *Corporations Act* also extends further to agents of a corporation. An agent of a corporation may also be a director, officer or employee of the corporation, but that is not necessarily the case. Agency is a relationship under which an agent agrees to act or, in the case of apparent authority, appears to act, on behalf of a principal, and under their control and direction, in relation to a particular matter, usually with the agent having the ability to effect a legal relationship between the principal and third parties.[54] General law rules of agency will apply to determine whether a particular person is considered to be a corporation's agent (whether by express actual authority, implied actual authority or apparent authority). Independent contractors, who are not regarded as employees, will generally be considered to be agents of a corporation.

While it might be possible for a variety of agents who are engaged by corporations to come into the possession of inside information, the most likely agent to be representing a corporation while coming into possession of inside information is a securities broker, or another type of securities intermediary. Security broking services may be provided by specialist securities brokers, or investment banks which offer their clients a wide range of financial intermediary services.[55]

Accordingly, it can be seen that s 769B(3) of the *Corporations Act*, in applying to directors, employees and agents of a corporation, extends significantly beyond the scope of ss 1042G(1)(a) and 1042G(1)(b). However, while under

---

      (ii)  is appointed to the position of an alternate director and is acting in that capacity; regardless of the name that is given to their position; and

  (b)  unless the contrary intention appears, a person who is not validly appointed as a director if:

      (i)  they act in the position of a director; or

      (ii)  the directors of the company or body are accustomed to act in accordance with the person's instructions or wishes.

53  *Hollis v Vabu* (2001) HCA 44; *Stevens v Brodribb Sawmilling Co Pty Ltd* (1986) HCA 1.

54  *International Harvester Co of Australia Pty Ltd v Carrigan's Hazledene Pastoral Co* (1958) 100 CLR 644, 652; *Peterson v Maloney* (1951) 84 CLR 91, 94.

55  Such services may include issuing, buying and selling of securities, and the giving of related financial advice, securities underwriting and financial advisory services in connection with takeovers, mergers and acquisitions, divestitures, restructurings, joint ventures and privatisations, as well as a range of trading, investment research, financing asset management and foreign exchange dealings: Andrew Tuch, 'Investment Banks as Fiduciaries: Implications for Conflicts of Interest' (2005) 2 *Melbourne University Law Review* 478, 486.

this provision any director, employee or agent may have the relevant state of mind, being the awareness of certain information amounting to possession, it is only considered to be the state of mind of the corporation if the same person engaged in certain conduct in the scope of their actual or apparent authority. The relevant conduct for insider trading can be described as the trading, or procuring of trading, in relevant financial products. As noted earlier, this is specifically set out in s 1043A(1) of the *Corporations Act*, which has the title 'Prohibited Conduct by Person in Possession of Inside Information', where it is stated that an insider:

must not (whether as principal or agent):

(c) apply for, acquire, or dispose of, relevant Division 3 financial products, or enter into an agreement to apply for, acquire, or dispose of, relevant Division 3 financial products; or

(d) procure another person to apply for, acquire, or dispose of, relevant Division 3 financial products, or enter into an agreement to apply for, acquire, or dispose of, relevant Division 3 financial products.

An additional form of prohibited conduct is set out in s 1043A(2) of the *Corporations Act*, where it is stated that an insider must not:

directly or indirectly, communicate the information, or cause the information to be communicated, to another person if the insider knows, or ought reasonably to know, that the other person would or would be likely to:

(c) apply for, acquire, or dispose of, relevant Division 3 financial products, or enter into an agreement to apply for, acquire, or dispose of, relevant Division 3 financial products; or

(d) procure another person to apply for, acquire, or dispose of, relevant Division 3 financial products, or enter into an agreement to apply for, acquire, or dispose of, relevant Division 3 financial products.

This means that, for s 769B(3) of the *Corporations Act* to apply, the person in possession of the relevant inside information must also be the same person who traded, or procured the trading, in the relevant financial products, or engaged in tipping.

It must also have been within the person's actual or apparent authority to do so. When assessing whether an act is done within the scope of authority – actual or apparent – general law principles of agency will be relevant. It will be necessary to establish that the person either had: (i) express actual authority;[56] (ii) implied actual authority;[57] or (iii) apparent authority,[58] to engage in that conduct as part

---

56 As described in *Freeman & Lockyer v Buckhurst Park Properties (Mangal) Ltd* [1964] 2 QB 480, 502.
57 As described in *Hely-Hutchinson v Brayhead Ltd* [1968] 1 QB 549, 583.
58 As described in *Crabtree-Vickers v Australian Direct Mail* (1975) 33 CLR 72.

of their ordinary duties, or as part of the broader role for which they are retained by the corporation. Such a person is likely to include, for example, an employee specifically authorised to buy and sell shares on a corporation's behalf, such as the proprietary trader whose activities were the subject of *ASIC v Citigroup*,[59] and employees who advise clients of the corporation on share trading and facilitate their resulting trading, such as securities brokers. As the relevant conduct includes the procuring of trading, it will also include a senior manager or executive who directs a more junior employee to engage in the actual trading that occurs.

Thus, the ability to trade in financial products, or procure such trading, must be conduct in which the relevant person engages, with some form of authority. The fact that the actual trading in question was not expressly authorised or permitted will not prevent the conduct from being considered to be within the scope of that general authority.[60]

Where the person who engaged in the relevant trading conduct also possesses the relevant inside information, s 769B(3) of the *Corporations Act* will therefore operate so that the corporation will also be considered to possess the information. This section must be contrasted with ss 1042G(1)(a) and 1042G(1)(b) of the *Corporations Act*, which do not contain any requirement that the relevant officer who possesses inside information also engage in the relevant trading conduct.

### General law agency rules

As the *Corporations Act* does not provide an exclusive mechanism for determining when information is possessed by a corporation, as was demonstrated earlier in this chapter, general law mechanisms are still available as an additional means of determining when a corporation possesses inside information.

At general law, a corporation may be regarded as possessing information that is known to an authorised agent (who need not be the directing mind and will of a corporation) if the following conditions are satisfied: (i) the information is acquired by the agent in his or her capacity as a representative of the corporation;[61] (ii) the agent has authority to receive information on the corporation's behalf and a duty to disclose the information to the corporation;[62] and (iii) the agent is not under a duty to another person to refrain from communicating the information to the corporation.[63] If an agent of a corporation satisfying these criteria possesses certain inside information, the corporation could also be considered to possess that information pursuant to the general law agency rules.

As noted earlier in the discussion concerning s 769B(3) of the *Corporations Act*, an agent of a corporation may also be a director, officer or employee of the

---

59  *ASIC v Citigroup Global Markets Australia Pty Ltd* (2007) 160 FCR 35.
60  See, for example, *Meridian Global Funds Management Asia Limited v Securities Commission* [1995] AC 500.
61  *Societe Generale de Paris v Tramways Union Co Ltd* (1884) 14 QBD 424.
62  *Beach Petroleum NL and Claremont Petroleum NL v Johnson* (1993) 115 ALR 411, 568–569.
63  *Re Marseilles Extension Railway Company* (1971) LR 7 Ch App 161.

corporation, but that is not necessarily the case, and general law rules of agency will apply to determine whether a particular person is considered to be a corporation's agent (again, whether by express actual authority, implied actual authority or ostensible authority). However, merely because an agent of the corporation knows certain relevant information, the corporation will not be found to possess it, if the agent did not acquire the information in their capacity as a representative of the corporation. This raises similar issues to those which arise in connection with ss 1042G(1)(a) and 1042G(1)(b) of the *Corporations Act*, where a corporation will only be regarded as possessing inside information if an officer of the corporation came into possession of the information in the course of performance of their duties, or because he or she was an officer of the corporation. Information acquired by an agent in another professional capacity, or privately, will not be information which the principal corporation is considered to possess.

Although the agent must have a duty to disclose the information to the corporation, in order for knowledge to be regarded as the information of the corporation, a failure to actually make such a disclosure will not prevent the corporation from being considered to possess the information.[64] Thus, if the agent has acquired the information while representing the corporation, but does not pass the information on to the corporation as required, the corporation will still be regarded as possessing the information under general law agency rules.

If the information acquired by an agent is information which is confidential to another person, and it would breach the agent's duty to that other person to disclose the information to the corporation, the agent is bound not to disclose the information and the corporation will not be regarded as possessing the information known to the agent.[65] This will be the case even if the agent would otherwise have been obliged to disclose the information to the corporation.

### Identification doctrine

As noted earlier, various cases have found that the words 'is taken to' in legislation similar to s 1042G(1)(a) of the *Corporations Act* indicate a lack of exclusivity and allow 'the operation of the directing mind principle'[66] in addition to statutory mechanisms.

The general law identification doctrine provides that certain people act not just as agents of a corporation but as the corporation itself, so that their acts and intentions are taken to be those of the corporation, as discussed in chapter 4. Such persons, referred to as the directing mind and will of a corporation, may

---

64  Deborah A DeMott, 'When Is a Principal Charged with an Agent's Knowledge?' (2003) *Duke Journal of Comparative and International Law* 291, 313.

65  *Kelly v Cooper* [1993] AC 205, 214.

66  *Rowe v Transport Workers Union of Australia* (1998) 160 ALR 66, 81. Approved in *Hadgkiss v Sunland Constructions Pty Ltd* [2007] FCA 346 (14 March 2007) (Keifel J) and in *Hanley v Automotive, Food, Metals, Engineering, Printing and Kindred Industries Union* [2000] FCA 1188 (24 August 2000) (Ryan, Moore and Goldberg JJ).

possess information which is then regarded as being possessed by the corporation itself. Such persons include: (i) a person under the direction of the shareholders in general meeting; (ii) the board of directors; and (iii) a person who has the authority of the board of directors, given under the corporation's constitution and appointed by the shareholders.[67]

As the board of directors is responsible for the overall management of a corporation, information which is known collectively to the board will automatically be imputed to the corporation.[68] Similarly, if the board of directors has delegated their day-to-day management powers to a managing director or chief executive officer, the corporation will be regarded as possessing information which is possessed by that managing director or chief executive officer.[69] However, if the information is possessed by one director only, who is not a managing director, that will not be sufficient for the information to be considered to be possessed by the corporation, as such a director will not ordinarily be regarded as the directing mind and will of the corporation, unless the board has delegated particular authority to that director.

The ultimate test of whether a person is the directing mind and will of a corporation is whether the person manages and controls the actions of the corporation in relation to the relevant activity.[70] For example, while a corporation may have a managing director who ordinarily would be regarded as the directing mind and will of the corporation in relation to most of its activities, if a particular employee has been given authority to act for the corporation in relation to a certain transaction or certain types of transactions (for example, to undertake securities trading on the corporation's behalf) and the person has been vested with 'authority, control, discretion and a significant degree of responsibility'[71] in relation to the relevant transactions, that employee can be regarded as the corporation's directing mind and will in relation to the securities trading but not in relation to other activities. This makes it possible for more than one person to be regarded as a corporation's directing mind and will in relation to a variety of different activities of the corporation.[72] However, as there is no separation of the relevant actus reus and mens rea between different people within a corporation when the identification doctrine is relied upon, in order for a corporation to be regarded as engaging in the offence under this doctrine, the person who is the directing mind and will of the corporation will need to engage in, or satisfy, all the relevant elements, so that the person's acts and intentions are regarded as those of the corporation. Accordingly, when applying the principles of the identification doctrine to the liability of corporations for insider trading, it will therefore be necessary to demonstrate that the person who is regarded as being the directing mind and will of

---

67   *Lennard's Carrying Co Ltd v Asiatic Petroleum Co Ltd* [1915] AC 705, 713–714.
68   *Houghton and Co v Nothard, Lowe and Wills Ltd* [1928] AC 1, 18–19.
69   *Re Rossfield Group Operations Pty Ltd* [1981] Qd R 372, 377.
70   *El Ajou v Dollar Land Holdings Ltd Plc* [1994] 2 All ER 685.
71   *Bell Group Ltd (in Liq) v Westpac Banking Corporation (No 9)* (2008) 70 ACSR 1, [539].
72   *Brambles Holdings v Carey* (1976) 2 ACLR 126.

the relevant corporation possessed the relevant information, had the necessary knowledge that it was inside information and engaged in the relevant trading conduct.

### Collective knowledge

At general law it is possible, in certain circumstances, to find that a corporation has collective knowledge, comprised of separate pieces of information known by more than one person within the corporation.[73] Not every piece of information held by separate employees can be aggregated,[74] and a distinction is made between the aggregation of mere knowledge of facts and the aggregation of a particular state of mind – while the first type of aggregation is often possible, the second is rare.[75]

In *Re Chisum Services*,[76] it was acknowledged by Wootten J of the Supreme Court of New South Wales that the aggregation of knowledge of facts within a corporation was possible, but only if one of the people who possessed some of the information was under a duty to communicate it to the other person (for example, if the first person reported to the second person) or if both people in possession of separate pieces of information reported to the same superior and had a duty to communicate it to him or her.[77]

As was stated by Owen J of the Supreme Court of Western Australia in *The Bell Group Ltd (in Liq) v Westpac Banking Corporation (No 9)*:[78]

> Whether a court is prepared to infer that a company had particular knowledge or had a particular state of mind, based on collective knowledge of its officers and agents, depends on the circumstances of the case. It may depend on the type of information and the effect that such a piece of information may have (or should have had) on the particular employee. It will also depend on the particular employees' positions, their duties and responsibilities, and their proximity to the relevant transaction.[79]

Thus, at general law it may be possible for separate pieces of information possessed by more than one person to be aggregated, so that the corporation is deemed to possess *all* the information. However, there are no known cases concerning insider trading in which the concept of collective knowledge has been applied. The concept of collective knowledge is not expressly addressed

---

73  *The Bell Group Ltd (in Liq) v Westpac Banking Corporation (No 9)* (2008) 70 ACSR 1, 539; *Krakowski v Eurolynx Properties* (1995) 130 ALR 1, 16.
74  *The Bell Group Ltd (in Liq) v Westpac Banking Corporation (No 9)* (2008) 70 ACSR 1, 539.
75  Ibid 540.
76  *Re Chisum Services* (1982) 7 ACLR 641.
77  Ibid 650.
78  *The Bell Group Ltd (in Liq) v Westpac Banking Corporation (No 9)* (2008) 70 ACSR 1.
79  Ibid 542.

by the *Corporations Act* in relation to insider trading, as s 1042G(1)(a) refers only to a body corporate being taken to possess information which 'an officer' possesses and s 1042G(1)(b) provides only that if 'an officer' of a body corporate knows any matter or thing, it is presumed that the body corporate knows it. Section 769B(3) of the *Corporations Act* links the state of mind of 'a director, employee or agent' with conduct that person engages in within the scope of his or her authority. However, it is possible, in the absence of express language to the contrary, to determine that if separate pieces of information were known to two different officers of a corporation, the corporation could be regarded as possessing all of that information which together amounts to inside information.

### Relationship with continuous disclosure obligations

It is useful to consider the continuous disclosure obligations which exist under the ASX Listing Rules and require listed public corporations to immediately notify the ASX:

> once an entity is or becomes aware of any information concerning it that a reasonable person would expect to have a material impact on the price or value of the entity's securities.[80]

In Chapter 19 of the ASX Listing Rules, the term 'aware' is given the following meaning:

> An entity becomes aware of information if, and as soon as, an officer of the entity . . . has, or ought reasonably to have, come into possession of the information in the course of the performance of their duties as an officer of that entity.[81]

The continuous disclosure obligations contained in the ASX Listing Rules are considered to be 'critical to the integrity and efficiency of the ASX market'.[82] The ASX states that the definition of 'aware' is based on s 1042G of the *Corporations*

---

80  ASX, Listing Rules, LR 3.1.
81  Prior to May 2013, when this definition was amended, an entity was considered to be 'aware' of information when a director or executive officer of the entity had, or ought reasonably to have, come into possession of the information in the course of the performance of their duties as director or executive officer of that entity.
82  ASX, Listing Rules, *Guidance Note 8, Continuous Disclosure: Listing Rules 3.1–3.1B*, 2018, 4. As noted by the ASX, the view has also received judicial endorsement, as evidenced by the statement of the New South Wales Court of Appeal (comprised of Spigelman CJ, Beazley JA and Giles JA) in *James Hardie Industries NV v ASIC* [2010] NSWCA 332, [355], where it was noted that the policy objective of the continuous disclosure obligations is to 'enhance the integrity and efficiency of Australian capital markets by ensuring that the market is fully informed'.

*Act.*[83] There is, however, an important distinction as, under the ASX Listing Rules, a corporation is regarded as being aware of information not only where the relevant person has come into possession of the information in the course of performance of their duties but also where they *ought reasonably to have come into possession of the information.* This distinction has resulted in the continuous disclosure obligations being interpreted as having both subjective and objective elements, so that where a director or an executive officer of a corporation has access to information, even without actual knowledge of the contents, they are deemed to have it in their possession.[84] Thus, despite the similarity underlying the rationale for continuous disclosure rules and insider trading laws – both existing to protect and maintain market integrity – the difference in significant aspects of the statutory requirements means that, in this context, the continuous disclosure obligations are of little assistance in interpreting the insider trading laws.

The ASX offers an explanation for including information that an officer 'ought reasonably to have come into possession of' as information of which a corporation is 'aware', by stating that it is intended to prevent corporations from seeking to avoid their obligations and liability 'by not bringing market sensitive information to the attention of its officers in a timely manner'.[85] However, for insider trading laws, such a position clearly falls outside the judicial interpretation of the meaning of 'possession' of inside information. It is certainly not desirable that two sets of rules dealing with similar issues and with the same underlying rationale should differ significantly in this respect.[86]

### Different mechanisms for determining when a corporation possesses information

Having determined that there are a number of mechanisms which are available to determine when a corporation possesses information – the statutory provisions found in ss 1042G(1)(a), 1042G(1)(b) and 769B(3) of the *Corporations Act* and the general law principles of the identification doctrine and agency rules – the differences between these methods can now be analysed.

Sections 1042G(1)(a) and 1042G(1)(b) of the *Corporations Act* require the person who possesses the information to be an officer of the corporation;

---

83 ASX, Listing Rules, *Guidance Note 8, Continuous Disclosure: Listing Rules 3.1–3.1B*, 2018, 12.

84 *ASIC v Fortescue Metals Group Ltd* [2011] FCAFC 19 (18 February 2011), [185]. Although the ultimate decision of the Full Court of the Federal Court was overturned on appeal, the High Court of Australia did not address the issue of objective and subjective considerations in relation to the possession of information: *Forrest v ASIC; Fortescue Metals Group Ltd v ASIC* [2012] HCA 39 (2 October 2012).

85 ASX, Listing Rules, *Guidance Note 8, Continuous Disclosure: Listing Rules 3.1–3.1B*, 2018, 10.

86 While it is beyond the scope of this book to consider potential amendments to the continuous disclosure obligations under the *Listing Rules* as well as the insider trading laws under the *Corporations Act*, it is hoped that any future reforms made to both the *Corporations Act* and the *ASX Listing Rules* may lead to greater consistency between these two interrelated sets of rules.

s 769B(3) of the *Corporations Act* has potential application to directors, employees and agents; and the general law requires the person to be the directing mind and will of the corporation, or an agent of the corporation with authority to receive the information and a duty to disclose it. While the person who is regarded as the directing mind and will of a corporation will generally be a 'superior officer'[87] and is likely to fall within the definition of 'officer' contained in s 9 of the *Corporations Act*, this will not necessarily be the case. Indeed, not all officers of a corporation would be regarded as the corporation's directing mind and will.

Whether a particular agent with authority to receive the information and a duty to disclose it would be an officer or the directing mind and will of the corporation will obviously depend on the circumstances, but as an agent may be a person external to the corporation (such as a securities broker) it is certainly possible that such an agent would be neither an officer of the corporation nor the corporation's directing mind and will. Such an agent may also be an employee who is neither an officer of the corporation or the directing mind and will. Sections 1042G(1)(a) and 1042G(1)(b) of the *Corporations Act* require either that the information known by the relevant officer came into his or her possession 'in the course of the performance of duties' as an officer or was known by them 'because he or she is an officer of the corporation'. Both require a clear nexus with the person's role or duties as an officer of the corporation and therefore exclude information acquired in a private capacity. Section 769B(3) of the *Corporations Act* requires no such nexus with the person's role or duties when coming into possession of the information, but does require that the person also engaged in the relevant conduct – in this case, the trading or procuring or trading in relevant financial products, or tipping. Under the general law, information obtained by an agent of the corporation with authority to receive the information and a duty to disclose it must also be obtained in the course of performing the agent's duties for the corporation. However, there is no such requirement for possession by a person who is the directing mind and will of a corporation, as the information will still be possessed by the corporation if it is possessed by the person who is its directing mind and will, regardless of how it is obtained. It also seems that the doctrine of collective knowledge has potential operation, so that a corporation may be regarded as being in possession of several different pieces of information, each possessed by a different person within the corporation.

As noted in chapter 3, most of the examined jurisdictions do not have statutory provisions within the relevant legislation prohibiting insider trading which set out the particular manner in which the elements of the insider trading laws are to be applied to corporations – this includes the European Union, Germany, the United Kingdom, the United States, New Zealand and Hong Kong. As a result, the general principles of corporate criminal liability which are applicable in the relevant jurisdiction must be relied upon to determine the manner in which corporations may be found liable for insider trading. The exception is Singapore, which has a set of specific statutory rules to apply the elements of insider trading

---

87  *Tesco Supermarkets Ltd v Nattrass* [1972] AC 153, 171.

to corporations. Section 226(1) of the *Securities and Futures Act 2001* (Singapore) specifically provides that:

(a)  a corporation is taken to possess any information which an officer of the corporation possesses and which came into his possession in the course of the performance of duties as such an officer; and
(b)  if an officer of a corporation knows or ought reasonably to know any matter or thing because he is an officer of the corporation, it is to be presumed, until the contrary is proved, that the corporation knows or ought reasonably to know that matter or thing.

Section 236B(1) of the *Securities and Futures Act 2001* (Singapore) also provides that:

> Where an offence of contravening any provision in this Part is proved to have been committed by an employee or an officer of a corporation (referred to in this section as the contravening person) –
>
> (a)  with the consent or connivance of the corporation; and
> (b)  for the benefit of the corporation,
>
> the corporation shall be guilty of that offence as if the corporation had committed the contravention, and shall be liable to be proceeded against and punished accordingly.

It is not recommended that Australian insider trading laws adopt the model utilised in jurisdictions such as the European Union, Germany, the United Kingdom, the United States, New Zealand and Hong Kong, where there are no statutory provisions within the relevant legislation prohibiting insider trading providing for the manner in which the elements of insider trading are to be applied to corporations. Such a position would create additional uncertainty and in Australia would require reliance only on the common law agency rules or identification doctrine, or necessitate the use of the existing principles of corporate criminal responsibility contained in the *Criminal Code* but currently excluded from operation in respect of insider trading. Instead, the drafting of improved statutory provisions to better provide for the attribution of the elements of insider trading to corporations is the basis of the reforms proposed.

The Singaporean provisions are similar to those in Australia, having developed particular statutory rules for determining when a corporation possesses information, has knowledge and engages in an offence. Indeed, s 226(1)(a) of the *Securities and Futures Act 2001* (Singapore) is almost identical to s 1042G(1)(a) of the *Corporations Act*, but this is not surprising since the Singaporean insider trading laws were modelled on the Australian provisions.[88] As a result, the Singaporean

---

88  Hse-Yu Chiu, 'Australian Influence on the Insider Trading Laws in Singapore' (2002) *Singapore Journal of Legal Studies* 574.

position, as a set of insider laws derived from Australia's own, does not provide an alternative base on which to model potential reforms to the Australian legislation.

The concurrent operation of both the general law and statute in this area, with overlapping but differing sets of rules, leads to significant difficulty and uncertainty in determining when a corporation possesses inside information, has knowledge that certain information is inside information and engages in the relevant trading conduct. It is not desirable that such uncertainty exists, particularly as the general law rules have also been demonstrated to apply, but with their application untested judicially in this context. Legislative reform is vital in order to provide clarity and certainty in relation to the liability of corporations for insider trading.

It can be seen, from the earlier analysis, that the different mechanisms which may be used to attribute the possession of information to corporations are capable of giving quite varied results. As has been noted, in *ASIC v Citigroup* and *ASIC v Hochtief*, the Courts considered the operation of just one of these mechanisms, s 1042G(1)(a) of the *Corporations Act*, and did not address any other statutory mechanisms or the operation of the general law. By contrast, Qu[89] regards the general law as relevant to rebut statutory presumptions which might otherwise apply elements of the offence to a corporation. A careful review of the element of possession leads to the necessary conclusion that both the statutory provisions and general law rules operate concurrently to provide a variety of mechanisms which can be used to establish that a corporation possesses inside information. The *Corporations Act* is silent on the application of the general law, but the operation of the general law is not excluded. This is in contrast to other sections of the *Corporations Act* which expressly refer to the general law – for example, s 133 of the *Corporations Act* excludes the operation of the general law in relation to pre-registration contracts[90] and s 236(3) of the *Corporations Act* abolishes the general law derivative action,[91] whereas s 185 of the *Corporations Act* expressly provides that the statutory directors' duties and obligations contained in ss 180 to 184 operate in addition to those which exist under the general law.[92]

---

89  Qu, above n 19, 191.

90  Sections 131 and 132 of Part 2B.3 of the *Corporations Act* set out the statutory rules relating to preregistration contracts and s 133 provides:

> This Part replaces any rights or liabilities anyone would otherwise have on the preregistration contract.

91  Section 236(1) and (2) of the *Corporations Act* provide for the statutory derivative action and s 236(3) provides:

> The right of a person at general law to bring, or intervene in, proceedings on behalf of a company is abolished.

92  Section 185 of the *Corporations Act* provides:

> Sections 180 to 184:
>
> (a)  have effect in addition to, and not in derogation of, any rule of law relating to the duty or liability of a person because of their office or employment in relation to a corporation; and

Cases interpreting other pieces of legislation which use the same or very similar language to these provisions make it clear that the general law is not intended to be excluded and, in order to make sense of other provisions of the *Corporations Act*, it is necessary to infer that the general law is also intended to apply. Even when considering the statutory tests alone, there is confusion as to which of those tests relates to the possession of information and which relates to the requisite knowledge. For example, as noted earlier, there is a divergence of opinion as to whether s 1042G(1)(b) of the *Corporations Act* applies only when attempting to determine whether a corporation had the requisite knowledge, or whether it is applicable to both the possession of information *and* the requisite knowledge. This uncertainty needs to be resolved.

In addition to the uncertainty which exists in determining whether both statutory and general law mechanisms are available to determine when a corporation possesses information, each of various available mechanisms applies a different set of tests – some require that, for a corporation to be considered to possess information that a natural person possesses, the natural person must be an officer of that corporation,[93] whereas others will operate in respect of any employee or agent who is able to act on the corporation's behalf.[94] Some require that there be a link or nexus with the person's role within the corporation.[95] Some require that the possession of information must be linked to the relevant conduct,[96] while others do not.[97] When the general law mechanisms are also considered, the confusion compounds, as the principles of the identification doctrine will apply so that a corporation possesses information which is possessed by its 'directing mind and will', with no necessary connection with their role or other elements of the offence. The proposed reforms set out in detail in chapter 8 are intended to remedy these many problems.

## Attributing the knowledge element to corporations

As noted earlier, the 'knowledge element' of insider trading is that a person knows, or ought reasonably to know, that the relevant information possessed is not generally available, and that if it were, a reasonable person would expect it to be material. That is, the person knows, or ought reasonably to know, that the relevant information is 'inside information'.[98] Therefore, the next issues to

---

    (b)  do not prevent the commencement of civil proceedings for a breach of a duty or in respect of a liability referred to in paragraph (a).

93  *Corporations Act*, ss 1042G(1)(a) and 1042G(1)(b).
94  *Corporations Act*, s 769B(3).
95  *Corporations Act*, ss 1042G(1)(a), 1042G(1)(b) and 769B(3).
96  *Corporations Act*, s 769B(3).
97  *Corporations Act*, ss 1042G(1)(a) and 1042G(1)(b).
98  As set out earlier, the knowledge element of insider trading, contained in s 1043A(1)(b) of the *Corporations Act*, is that:

    the insider knows, or ought reasonably to know, that the matters specified in paragraphs (a) and (b) of the definition of inside information in section 1042A are satisfied in relation to the information.

be addressed in this chapter are how a corporation comes to have the requisite knowledge of these matters and when it is that a corporation 'ought reasonably to know' something.

As there has never been a criminal prosecution brought against a corporation for insider trading in Australia, and no successful contested civil penalty proceedings, the application of the knowledge element of insider trading to a corporation has never been considered judicially.[99] However, this important issue concerning the liability of corporations for insider trading is unnecessarily unwieldy and complex, with a number of statutory mechanisms which can be used to determine that a corporation has certain knowledge, in addition to the general law principles of the identification doctrine.

### Statutory mechanisms

There are two provisions in the *Corporations Act* which could potentially be used to determine when a corporation has certain knowledge, and which therefore may be applicable to the knowledge element of insider trading: (i) s 104G(1)(b) of the *Corporations Act*; and (ii) s 769B(3) of the *Corporations Act*.

Section 1042G(1)(b) of the *Corporations Act* has already been examined earlier in the context of the possession element.[100] In order to establish that a corporation had certain knowledge under the operation of this section, it must be established that: (i) an officer of the corporation had the relevant knowledge; and (ii) the officer had the knowledge because he or she was an officer of the corporation. The application of this section in relation to the knowledge element does differ from its application to the possession element, as it is more difficult to determine how a person is likely to have knowledge of the qualities of certain information *because* he or she is an officer of a corporation.

Section 1042G(1)(b) of the *Corporations Act* requires an officer of the corporation to have the relevant knowledge. Thus, the definition of 'officer' set out

---

The matters specified in paragraphs (a) and (b) of the definition of 'inside information' in s 1042A of the *Corporations Act* are:

(a)  the information is not generally available; and

(b)  if the information were generally available, a reasonable person would expect it to have a material effect on the price or value of particular Division 3 financial products.

99  It was not necessary for this issue to be addressed in *ASIC v Citigroup* (2007) 160 FCR 35 due to the determinations made by the Court in relation to the other elements of insider trading.

100  Section 1042G(1)(b) of the *Corporations Act* provides that 'if an officer of a body corporate knows any matter or thing because he or she is an officer of the body corporate, it is to be presumed that the body corporate knows that matter or thing'. It was noted earlier that some commentators view s 1042G(1)(b) of the *Corporations Act* as relevant only to the knowledge element of insider trading, whereas others consider that it is also applicable to both the possession element and the knowledge element. On either interpretation, s 1042G(1)(b) of the *Corporations Act* is relevant to the knowledge element.

in s 9 of the *Corporations Act*[101] must be satisfied, so the person will generally need to be a director, secretary or senior executive of the corporation. Then, the relevant officer must have the knowledge because he or she was an officer of the corporation. As noted earlier, the phrase 'because he or she is an officer' is not defined in the *Corporations Act* or in any other Australian legislation, but in cases concerning directors' duties and fiduciary obligations, the courts make it clear that there must be a causal link between the position the person occupies within the corporation and the reason they have acquired that particular knowledge,[102] thereby excluding knowledge acquired or resulting from a private role or as a member of the general public.

While this may be a concept which is fairly easy to apply to the possession element of insider trading – to determine whether a person came into the *possession* of information because of their position within a corporation – it is much more difficult to apply to the knowledge element. This element obviously requires a person to have knowledge of certain qualities of the information – whether it is generally available and likely to be material – so how can it be said that a person has that sort of knowledge *because* he or she is an officer of a particular corporation? If the person acquires the relevant information in connection with their role as an officer – for example, while working on a particular transaction – and it is made clear to them by the person imparting the information that it is confidential and would be likely to affect the price of certain financial products, it could potentially be said that the officer had such knowledge *because* of their position. However, if they came into possession of the information in connection with their role as an officer, but were not expressly told that it was confidential and would be likely to affect the price of certain financial products, it is difficult to conclude that the person would have that knowledge *because* he or she was an officer of the corporation.

It may be the case that certain people are more likely to be aware of these qualities of information – when it is generally available and when it is likely to be material – because they have a certain occupation. For example, a proprietary trader or securities broker is more likely to be knowledgeable about such matters than many other employees or executives within an organisation. However, merely because a person has a certain occupation which enables him or her to better assess the qualities of certain information than others, and also happens to be an officer of a corporation, does not necessarily lead to the conclusion that he or she had that knowledge *because* they are an officer. Thus, the application of this provision to the knowledge element of insider trading is unclear and contains significant ambiguity.

As noted earlier, s 769B(3) of the *Corporations Act* provides that:

> If, in a proceeding under this Chapter in respect of conduct engaged in by a body corporate, it is necessary to establish the state of mind of the body, it

---

101  This definition was set out in full and discussed earlier.
102  See, for example, *Peso Silver Mines v Cropper* [1966] SCR 673; *Regal Hastings v Gulliver* [1967] 2 AC 134; and *Boardman v Phipps* [1967] 2 AC 46, as discussed earlier.

is sufficient to show that a director, employee or agent of the body, being a director, employee or agent by whom the conduct was engaged in within the scope of the person's actual or apparent authority, had that state of mind.[103]

Section 769B(3) of the *Corporations Act* is clearly also relevant to the knowledge element of insider trading, due to the inclusion of 'knowledge' as the definition of 'state of mind' in s 769B(10)(c).

In order to establish that a corporation had certain knowledge under s 769B(3) of the *Corporations Act*, there are two requirements which must be satisfied: (i) a director, employee or agent of the corporation must have the relevant knowledge; and (ii) the same director, employee or agent of the corporation must have engaged in the relevant conduct, within the scope of the person's actual or apparent authority.

As noted earlier in relation to the 'possession element', to which this section can also be applied, while any director, employee or agent may have the relevant knowledge, it is only considered to be the knowledge of the corporation if the same person engaged in the relevant conduct which, for insider trading, is not the physical element – the possession of the inside information – but the trading, or procuring of trading, in financial products, or tipping – the 'trading element'. Accordingly, for s 769B(3) of the *Corporations Act* to apply so that the corporation is regarded as having the relevant knowledge, the person with the knowledge that the information is inside information must also be a person who engaged in the relevant trading conduct.

It must also have been within the person's actual or apparent authority to trade or procure trading in the relevant financial products, or engage in tipping. As discussed earlier, this means that the general law principles of agency must be relied upon to establish such authority as part of their ordinary duties, or as part of the broader role for which they are retained by the corporation. However, the fact that the actual trading conduct in question was not specially authorised or permitted will not prevent the conduct from being considered to be within the scope of that general authority.[104]

Where the person who engaged in the relevant conduct knows that the relevant information is not generally available and would be likely to be material, s 769B(3) of the *Corporations Act* will therefore operate so that the corporation is considered to have such knowledge. This section can be contrasted with s 1042G(1)(b) of the *Corporations Act*, which does not require any link between the knowledge element and the trading element of insider trading.

---

103 As previously set out, s 769B(10)(c) of the *Corporations Act* provides that:

> A reference to the state of mind of a person includes a reference to the *knowledge*, intention, opinion, belief or purpose of the person and the person's reason for the person's intention, opinion, belief or purpose
>
> (emphasis added).

104 See, for example, *Meridian Global Funds Management Asia Limited v Securities Commission* [1995] AC 500.

## General law principles

As well as utilising the statutory mechanisms in ss 1042G(1)(b) and 769B(3) of the *Corporations Act*, general law principles may also be relevant to determine when a corporation has the requisite knowledge.

As noted earlier, s 1042G(2) of the *Corporations Act* states that 'this section does not limit the application of section 769B in relation to this Division', indicating that ss 1042G and 769B of the *Corporations Act* can both be applied and that s 1042G(1)(a) is not the exclusive means of determining when a corporation possesses inside information. For the same reasons, as it is part of the same section, s 1042G(1)(b) of the *Corporations Act* is clearly not intended to be the exclusive means of determining when a corporation has the knowledge that certain information is inside information.

Likewise, s 769B(3) of the *Corporations Act* does not appear to require exclusivity, or the exclusion of the general law rules, as it uses the phrase 'it is sufficient to show', which does not indicate an intention that it be exclusive, or that the general law should be excluded. There are a number of cases in which the courts have determined that such language when used in other statutes extends liability beyond the general law rules, but does not exclude them.[105] For example, in the case of *Universal Telecasters (Qld) Ltd v Guthrie*,[106] the liability of a television station for broadcasting an advertisement that allegedly contained 'false or misleading statements concerning the existence of or amounts of price reductions' in breach of s 53(e) of the former *Trade Practices Act 1974* (Cth). The corporation's sales manager looked after all dealings and communications concerning the advertisement, including viewer complaints. In order to be able to rely on a defence in s 85(3) of the former *Trade Practices Act*, the television station needed to establish that it 'did not know and had no reason to suspect that its publication would amount to a contravention'. Section 84(1) of the former *Trade Practices Act* provided that 'where . . . it is necessary to establish the intention of the corporation, *it is sufficient to show* that a servant or agent had the particular intention'.[107] The Full Court of the Federal Court found that the language in this section did not exclude the general law and the identification doctrine was still relevant to determine whether or not the knowledge of the sales manager should be attributed to the corporation. Although the sales manager had received complaints about the advertisement and should have had reason to suspect the contravention, the Court determined by majority[108] that this did not amount to intention within the scope of s 84(1), and that the sales manager was not the

---

105  *Universal Telecasters (Qld) Ltd v Guthrie* (1978) 32 FLR 360; *Walplan Pty Ltd v Wallace* (1985) 8 FCR 27; *Sydbank Soenderjylland A/S v Bannerton Holdings Pty Ltd* (1996) ATPR 41–525; *Ballard v Sperry Rand Aust Ltd* (1975) 8 ALR 696; see also, Jonathan Clough and Carmel Mulhern, *The Prosecution of Corporations* (Oxford University Press, Melbourne, 2002) 127.
106  *Universal Telecasters (Qld) Ltd v Guthrie* (1978) 32 FLR 360.
107  Emphasis added.
108  Bowen CJ and Franki J (Nimmo J dissenting).

directing mind and will of the television station and therefore that his knowledge was not that of the corporation itself.

Thus, in addition to the statutory mechanisms, it appears that general law rules can also be used to determine when a corporation has the necessary knowledge to satisfy the knowledge element of insider trading.

### Identification doctrine

As discussed earlier, there are certain persons who may be considered to be the 'directing mind and will' of a corporation under the identification doctrine, so that their acts and intentions are taken to be those of the corporation itself. Depending on the circumstances, such persons may include the board of directors, a managing director or a superior officer of the corporation, so long as they have 'full discretion to act independently of instruction' from the board.[109] If a person who is considered to be the directing mind and will of a corporation has the necessary knowledge that certain information is inside information, the corporation will therefore be regarded as having that knowledge. There is no need to demonstrate that the person, or persons, regarded as the corporation's directing mind and will acquired the relevant knowledge *because* they are the directing mind and will of the corporation, or in the course of performing their duties. However, the need to demonstrate that the person who is the directing mind and will of the corporation has engaged in, or satisfies, all the relevant elements means that it will be necessary to show that the person who is the directing mind and will of the relevant corporation possessed the relevant information, had the necessary knowledge that it was inside information and engaged in the relevant trading conduct.

Such a person may be anyone who manages and controls the actions of the corporation in relation to the relevant activity[110] which, when considering insider trading, may be a person who has been given authority to undertake securities trading on the corporation's behalf, regardless of whether they are a director or officer of the corporation, so long as the person is entitled to undertake such activities without direction or instruction. In the case of *ASIC v Citigroup*,[111] it is unlikely that Mr Manchee, the proprietary trader who had engaged in the relevant trading in Patrick shares, could be regarded as the directing mind and will of Citigroup in relation to proprietary trading, because it was clear that he was one of five proprietary traders who reported to Mr Darwell, the Head of Equities and Derivatives at Citigroup, and he was clearly subject to Mr Darwell's direction and instruction.[112]

---

109  *Tesco Supermarkets Ltd v Nattrass* [1972] AC 153, 171 (Lord Reid).
110  *El Ajou v Dollar Land Holdings Ltd Plc* [1994] 2 All ER 685.
111  *ASIC v Citigroup Global Markets Australia Pty Ltd* (2007) 160 FCR 35.
112  Ibid 98–101.

## Agency principles

As discussed earlier, at general law a corporation can be considered to possess information which is possessed by an agent, who need not be the directing mind and will of the corporation, if certain conditions are satisfied. However, such rules appear to more obviously relate to the actual possession or awareness of information rather than knowledge or a state of mind. Cases on this topic concern the imputation of knowledge about certain facts or circumstances that a corporation was deemed (or not deemed) to know, due to the possession of that information by an agent, not knowledge amounting to an intention or 'mens rea'.[113] Additionally, the relevant criteria are very difficult to apply to knowledge amounting to a corporation's state of mind. For example, a requirement that the agent have authority to receive information on behalf of the corporation and a duty to disclose it, is applicable to knowledge of certain matters or facts, but not a subjective state of mind. How can a person be authorised to have a certain state of mind or knowledge? It is not possible to say that an agent can be authorised to know that certain information is not generally available or is likely to be material. However, it could be possible that an agent who is authorised to receive information on behalf of a corporation and who has a duty to disclose it, might then have the knowledge that the information is inside information. While this issue does not appear to have been considered judicially, the potential application of agency rules to the knowledge element of insider trading is clearly problematic and uncertain.

## Different mechanisms for establishing the knowledge of corporations

Both the statutory mechanisms under ss 1042G(1)(b) and 769B(3) of the *Corporations Act*, which can be used to determine when a corporation has certain knowledge, expressly require that a nexus with the person's role or authority be demonstrated, either because the relevant director, employee or agent with the knowledge engaged in the relevant conduct in the scope of their actual or apparent authority,[114] or because the relevant officer had the knowledge *because* he or she was an officer of the corporation.[115] This is not explicitly required under the general law principles of the identification doctrine, as it does not matter how the directing mind and will came to have the relevant knowledge, only that such

---

113  See, for example, *Societe Generale de Paris v Tramways Union Co Ltd* (1884) 14 QBD 424; *Beach Petroleum NL and Claremont Petroleum NL v Johnson* (1993) 115 ALR 411; *Re Marseilles Extension Railway Company* (1971) LR 7 Ch App 161; *International Harvester Co of Australia Pty Lt v Carrigan's Hazledene Pastoral Co* (1958) 100 CLR 644; *Peterson v Maloney* (1951) 84 CLR 91; *Kelly v Cooper* [1993] AC 205.

114  *Corporations Act*, s 769B(3).

115  *Corporations Act*, s 1042G(1)(b).

knowledge should be regarded as the knowledge of the corporation. The general law rules of agency are difficult to apply to knowledge of information, rather than possession, and would create significant uncertainty if relied upon in this context.

Section 769B(3) of the *Corporations Act* enables the knowledge of a corporation to be established by showing that a director, employee or agent of the corporation had the relevant knowledge *and* engaged in the 'relevant conduct' *within the scope of their actual or apparent authority*. However, s 1042G(1)(b) of the *Corporations Act* does not require the person with the requisite knowledge to have also engaged in the relevant conduct. The general law identification doctrine does not expressly contain any such requirement in relation to conduct, although it will generally be necessary to show that the person who is the directing mind and will of a corporation had the requisite intention and engaged in certain conduct, which should therefore be regarded as the acts and intentions of the corporation.

The general law ordinarily requires that the person who is considered to be the directing mind and will of the corporation carries out a 'function of management' with authority before their state of mind can be attributed to the corporation. Section 1042G(1)(b) requires that the person with the relevant knowledge be an officer of the corporation, but s 769B(3) of the *Corporations Act* has no such requirement – encompassing any director, employee or agent – and does not require the person to have any particular role or degree of authority, so long as the relevant conduct they engage in falls within their own area of authority, regardless of how limited that authority may be. They need not have the ability to act independently or without instruction as is required under the general law to demonstrate that a person is the corporation's directing mind and will.

Thus, there is great divergence between the different statutory and general law mechanisms as to the status of the person who may have the relevant knowledge, whether there are any particular requirements as to how they came to have such knowledge and whether there must also be any link to the relevant conduct for the offence.

This divergence leads to significant uncertainty as to how the knowledge element of insider trading is actually to be applied to corporations, where there are three potential mechanisms – s 1042G(1)(b) of the *Corporations Act*, s 769B(3) of the *Corporations Act* and the general law identification doctrine – available to attribute that knowledge element to a corporation, each with different requirements. Commercial and legal certainty would obviously benefit from a more clearly articulated application of the law in this respect. The reforms proposed in this book are intended to overcome this uncertainty by excluding the general law provisions and creating one statutory mechanism for attributing knowledge to a corporation. The new statutory provisions would provide that a body corporate is taken to know, or to ought reasonably to know, that information is inside information if an officer, employee or agent of the body corporate knows, or ought reasonably to know, this. These provisions would not require that the officer, employee or agent have such knowledge as a result of their position or role within the corporation, but would require that the person who has such knowledge be the same person who engaged in or authorised the relevant trading conduct.

### Demonstrating that a corporation 'ought reasonably' to have certain knowledge

As well as determining when a corporation is regarded as 'knowing' that certain information is inside information, it also needs to be determined when a corporation will be in a position where it 'ought reasonably to know' that certain information is inside information, as the knowledge element set out in s 1043A(1)(b) of the *Corporations Act* requires that it be demonstrated that:

> the insider knows, *or ought reasonably to know*, that the matters specified in paragraphs (a) and (b) of the definition of inside information in section 1042A are satisfied in relation to the information.[116]

Thus, it needs to be determined when a corporation 'ought reasonably' to know that certain information is not generally available and is likely to be material.

Section 1042G(1)(d) of the *Corporations Act* states that:

> for the purpose of paragraph 1043M(2)(b), if an officer of a body corporate ought reasonably to know any matter or thing because he or she is an officer of the body corporate, it is to be presumed that the body corporate ought reasonably to know that matter or thing.

Section 1043M(2) provides a defence to insider trading if the other party to the trade also knew, or ought reasonably to have known, of the inside information before trading.[117] Thus, while s 1042G(1)(d) might appear to assist in determining when a corporation 'ought reasonably to know' something, the fact that it is expressly limited to s 1043M(2)(b) of the *Corporations Act* means that it does not apply to the knowledge element of insider trading.

By contrast, s 1002E of the previous legislative regime, the repealed *Corporations Law*, provided that:

> (b) if an officer of a body corporate knows or ought reasonably to know any matter or thing because he or she is an officer of a body corporate, it is to be presumed that the body corporate knows or ought reasonably to know that matter or thing.

Unlike the current s 1043A(1)(b) of the *Corporations Act*, s 1002E(b) of the *Corporations Law* was not limited in application to a provision such as the current s 1043M.

---

116 Emphasis added.
117 Section 1043M(2) of the *Corporations Act* provides that:

> In a prosecution brought against a person for an offence based on subsection 1043A(1) because the person entered into, or procured another person to enter into, a transaction or agreement at a time when certain information was in the first-mentioned person's possession:
>
> (b) it is a defence if the other party to the transaction or agreement knew, or ought reasonably to have known, of the information before entering into the transaction or agreement.

Thus, while the current regulatory regime provides in s 1042G(1)(b) of the *Corporations Act* that if an officer knows a matter or thing because he or she is an officer of a body corporate, the body corporate is presumed to know that matter or thing, there is no equivalent provision in relation to matters or things that the officer, and therefore the body corporate, *ought reasonably* to know. The Explanatory Memorandum to the Financial Services Reform Bill 2001, which inserted the current insider trading regulatory regime into the *Corporations Act* when enacted, does not reveal any reason why an equivalent provision was not incorporated into the *Corporations Act*.

However, even if such a provision did exist, in the same way that it is difficult to apply s 1042G(1)(b) to show that a person knew that certain information was inside information 'because' they were an officer of a corporation, as discussed earlier, it would also be difficult to demonstrate that a person *ought reasonably* to know that information was inside information because he or she was an officer.

There are no other provisions in the *Corporations Act* which would apply to assist in determining when a corporation 'ought reasonably to know' something. Thus, there appears to be a gap in the legislation in relation to the application of this aspect of the knowledge element to corporations. As discussed in chapter 2, the courts have determined that, when considering whether a person 'ought reasonably to know' that certain information was not generally available and was likely to be material, the question is subjective to the particular defendant, having regard to all of the relevant circumstances.[118] This means that one considers whether the particular defendant in question ought to have had such knowledge, so in the case of a corporation it would require an assessment as to whether that particular corporation 'ought reasonably' to have known that the information was inside information. Knowledge of directors, officers, agents or employees might be relevant to this assessment, but without any guidance from the statute or the courts as to when a corporation should be regarded as being in a position where it 'ought reasonably' to have that knowledge, significant uncertainty exists. As this matter has never been considered judicially, the uncertainty is further exacerbated.

## International comparisons

Singapore is the only jurisdiction amongst those examined which has a specific provision providing for the attribution of knowledge to a corporation. As noted earlier, s 226(1)(b) of the *Securities and Futures Act 2001* (Singapore) specifically provides that:

> if an officer of a corporation knows or ought reasonably to know any matter or thing because he is an officer of the corporation, it is to be presumed, until the contrary is proved, that the corporation knows or ought reasonably to know that matter or thing.

---

118 *R v Rivkin* (2004) 184 FLR 365, 384.

This provision combines the concepts contained in ss 1042G(1)(b) and 1042G(1)(d) of the *Corporations Act*.[119] However, as has been noted, under the *Corporations Act* it is only presumed that a corporation 'ought reasonably to know' a matter or thing that an officer of the body corporate ought reasonably to know because he or she is an officer of the body corporate for the purposes of s 1043M(2)(b), when a defence to insider trading is available if the other party to the trade also knew, or ought reasonably to have known, of the inside information before trading. The Singaporean provision does not limit the circumstances in which a corporation 'ought reasonably to know a matter or thing', so the provision is of wider application in connection with knowledge that a corporation has, or ought reasonably to have, which could include knowledge that certain information is inside information. In that respect, s 226(1)(b) of the *Securities and Futures Act 2001* (Singapore) is very similar to s 1002E of the repealed *Corporations Law*.

In the reforms set out in this book, it is proposed that a new provision be included in the *Corporations Act*, so that a body corporate would be taken to know, or to ought reasonably to know, that information is inside information if an officer, employee or agent of the body corporate has, or ought reasonably to have, that knowledge. However, the provision would not import a requirement that the officer, employee or agent have such knowledge (or that the officer, employee or agent ought reasonably to have such knowledge) *because* he or she is such an officer, employee or agent of the corporation. As previously identified, it is extremely difficult to show that a person knew, or ought reasonably to have known, that certain information was inside information 'because' of a position he or she held within a corporation.

As has been noted, the application of the knowledge element of insider trading to a corporation has not been considered judicially. However, an examination of the *Corporations Act* indicates that both statutory provisions and general law rules can be used to determine when a corporation knows that certain information is inside information. The differences and discrepancies between the various rules create significant uncertainty. Each of the rules attribute to the corporation the state of mind of a person within or connected to the corporation in some way – whether an officer, director, employee, agent or other person. The status of such a person and the nature of the connection required vary from rule to rule. Some rules require a nexus between the person's state of mind and their position within the corporation, and others do not. Some rules require that the

---

119 As noted earlier, s 1042G(1)(b) of the *Corporations Act* provides that:

> if an officer of a body corporate knows any matter or thing because he or she is an officer of the body corporate, it is to be presumed that the body corporate knows that matter or thing.

Section 1042G(1)(d) of the *Corporations Act* provides that:

> for the purposes of paragraph 1043M(2)(b), if an officer of a body corporate ought reasonably to know any matter or thing because he or she is an officer of the body corporate, it is to be presumed that the body corporate ought reasonably to know that matter or thing.

person who had the relevant state of mind also engaged in the relevant conduct, while others have no such requirement. This creates further uncertainty when it becomes clear that both the general law and statutory rules are applicable when determining when a corporation actually engages in the relevant conduct and these rules contain variations similar to those found when attempting to determine the corporation's state of mind. Additionally, it is particularly unclear how it can be determined when a corporation 'ought reasonably to know' that information is inside information. All of these ambiguities lead to the clear conclusion that it is increasingly difficult to be certain when the knowledge element will be made out when applying the insider trading laws to corporations, and that reform is needed in this area.

## Attributing the trading element to corporations

As noted earlier, the final element of insider trading, as set out in s 1043A(1) of the *Corporations Act*, is that:

> the insider must not (whether as principal or agent):
>
> (c)  apply for, acquire, or dispose of, relevant Division 3 financial products, or enter into an agreement to apply for, acquire, or dispose of, relevant Division 3 financial products; or
>
> (d)  procure another person to apply for, acquire, or dispose of, relevant Division 3 financial products, or enter into an agreement to apply for, acquire, or dispose of, relevant Division 3 financial products.

Further prohibited conduct is set out in s 1043A(2), pursuant to which an insider must not:

> directly or indirectly, communicate the information, or cause the information to be communicated, to another person if the insider knows, or ought reasonably to know, that the other person would or would be likely to:
>
> (c)  apply for, acquire, or dispose of, relevant Division 3 financial products, or enter into an agreement to apply for, acquire, or dispose of, relevant Division 3 financial products; or
>
> (d)  procure another person to apply for, acquire, or dispose of, relevant Division 3 financial products, or enter into an agreement to apply for, acquire, or dispose of, relevant Division 3 financial products.

The conduct described in s 1043A(1)(c) relates, in essence, to trading in relevant financial products – whether by applying for them, acquiring or disposing of them, or entering into an agreement to do any of those things. Section 1043A(1) (d) concerns the procuring of another person to do any of those things and s 1043A(2) relates to tipping. While this is the conduct which a person who possesses inside information, and who knows or ought reasonably to know that the information is inside information, must not engage in, it is not the 'physical element' of insider trading.[120]

The issue to be determined in relation to the trading element in this chapter is how a corporation can be regarded as engaging in the relevant conduct of trading, or the procuring of trading, in relevant financial products, or tipping. As is demonstrated, the existing statutory mechanisms and general law principles of the identification doctrine can both be used to determine when a corporation has engaged in this form of conduct.

### Statutory mechanisms

Unlike the 'possession element' and the 'knowledge element' of insider trading, Division 3 of Part 7.10 of the *Corporations Act* (Market Misconduct and Other Prohibited Conduct Relating to Financial Products and Financial Services) does not contain a specific provision relating to corporations and the 'trading element' of the offence. Accordingly, there is only one provision in the *Corporations Act* which could be used to determine when a corporation engages in certain conduct, and which may therefore be applicable to the trading element of insider trading – s 769B(1) of the *Corporations Act*.

Section 769B(1) of the *Corporations Act* provides that:

> Subject to subsections (7) and (8),[121] conduct engaged in on behalf of a body corporate:
>
> (a)  by a director, employee or agent of the body, within the scope of the person's actual or apparent authority; or
> (b)  by any other person at the direction or with the consent or agreement (whether express or implied) of a director, employee or agent of the body, where the giving of the direction, consent or agreement is within the scope of the actual or apparent authority of the director, employee or agent;
>
> is taken for the purposes of this Chapter[122] or a proceeding under this Chapter, to have been engaged in also by the body corporate.

---

120  As has been noted earlier, s 1043A(3)(a) of the *Corporations Act* states that 'for the purposes of the application of the *Criminal Code*' in relation to insider trading under s 1043A(1), 'paragraph (1)(a) is a physical element'. Section 1043A(1)(a) relates not to the trading or procuring of trading in financial products, but to the possession of information.

121  Sections 769B(7) and 769B(8) of the *Corporations Act* are not relevant in this context, as they exclude the operation of the section in connection with the provision of financial services and financial products in certain circumstances.

122  Being Chapter 7 of the *Corporations Act*, in which the insider trading prohibition is contained.

Accordingly, in order for conduct to be attributed to a corporation in accordance with s 769B(1) of the *Corporations Act*, there are two possible mechanisms available, either of which may be satisfied.

Under the first: (i) the conduct must be undertaken on behalf of the corporation; (ii) the conduct must be engaged in by a director, employee or agent of the corporation; and (iii) the conduct must be within the scope of the person's actual or apparent authority.

Under the second: (i) the conduct must be undertaken on behalf of the corporation; (ii) the conduct may be engaged in by any person; (iii) the conduct must be done at the direction, or with the consent or agreement, of a director, employee or agent of the corporation; and (iv) it must be within the scope of the actual or apparent authority of the director, employee or agent to give the relevant direction, consent or agreement.

The phrase 'conduct engaged in on behalf of a body corporate' has not yet been considered in this book, as it is not used in any of the statutory provisions analysed in relation to the possession element and knowledge element of insider trading. However, cases in other contexts have determined that a person is taken to engage in conduct 'on behalf of' a corporation if the person intends to do an act 'as a representative of' or 'for' the corporation, or in the course of the corporation's business, affairs or activities.[123] The phrase 'on behalf of' does not have a strict legal meaning but it requires 'some involvement' with the 'activities of the corporation' and will clearly encompass acts done by an employee in the course of his or her employment, as well as activities of a broader nature.[124] It has a similar meaning to the phrase 'in the course of [a] body corporate's affairs or activities'.[125]

This means that, in relation to insider trading, the relevant conduct must be engaged in on the corporation's behalf, and not by a person intending to trade on their own account. By way of example, the proprietary trader in *ASIC v Citigroup*[126] was clearly acting 'on behalf' of Citigroup when engaged in proprietary trading – buying and selling securities in the corporation's name, as part of the activities permitted by the terms of his employment, from which the corporation was intended to benefit.[127] However, an employee of a corporation, buying shares in his or her own name, intending to keep any personal profits resulting from the trading, will not be acting on behalf of that corporation.

123 *Lisciandro v Official Trustee in Bankruptcy* (1996) 69 FCR 180; *NMFM Property Pty Ltd v Citibank (No 10)* (2000) 186 ALR 442; *Downey v Carlson Hotels Asia Pacific Pty Ltd* [2005] QCA 199.

124 *Walplan Pty Ltd v Wallace* (1985) 8 FCR 27, 37 (Lockhart J).

125 Ibid.

126 *ASIC v Citigroup Global Markets Australia Pty Ltd* (2007) 160 FCR 35.

127 As discussed earlier, the insider trading claims made against Citigroup were not successful for a number of reasons, including the fact that the trader was not considered to have actually possessed any inside information and, because he was not an officer of Citigroup, Jacobson J determined that any information he might have possessed was not to be taken to be possessed by Citigroup anyway.

Section 769B(1) of the *Corporations Act* is widely drafted so that any director, employee or agent can engage in the relevant conduct. The term 'director' and the meanings of the terms 'employee' and 'agent' have already been discussed in detail earlier. With such a broad category of persons specified, and subject to satisfying the other necessary limbs of the mechanisms in s 769B(1), any trading, procuring of trading or tipping engaged in by any director, employee or agent of the corporation will be regarded as having been engaged in by the corporation.

When considering whether certain conduct is within the scope of a person's actual or apparent authority, it is worth noting that s 349 of the former *Workplace Relations Act 1996* (Cth) used language very similar to s 769B(1) of the *Corporations Act*, providing that:

Any conduct engaged in on behalf of a body corporate by:

(a)  an officer, a director, employee or agent of the body corporate within the scope of his or her actual or apparent authority; or

(b)  any other person at the direction or with the consent or agreement (whether express or implied) of an officer, director, employee or agent of the body corporate, where the giving of the direction, consent or agreement is within the scope of the actual or apparent authority of the officer, director, employee or agent;

shall be taken, for the purposes of this Act, to have been engaged in also by the body corporate.

The meaning of the phrase 'within the scope of his or her actual or apparent authority' was considered in this context by the Full Court of the Federal Court in *Hanley v Automotive, Food, Metals, Engineering, Printing & Kindred Industries Union*.[128] In that case, the Court stated, in a joint judgment, that:

there must at least be circumstances which would justify a belief on the part of a person dealing with the 'officer, director, employee or agent' that that 'officer, director, employee or agent' is acting with authority.[129]

The fact that certain conduct may have been unlawful will not place that conduct outside the scope of a person's authority – otherwise a corporation would be able to avoid liability for all unlawful conduct engaged in by its officers, employees or agents.[130]

---

128  *Hanley v Automotive, Food, Metals, Engineering, Printing & Kindred Industries Union* (2000) 100 FCR 530.

129  Ibid 544 (Ryan, Moore and Goldberg JJ).

130  *Trade Practices Commission v Tubemakers of Australia Ltd* (1983) 47 ALR 719, 742 (Toohey J); *Hanley v Automotive, Food, Metals, Engineering, Printing & Kindred Industries Union* (2000) 100 FCR 530, [83] (Ryan, Moore and Goldberg JJ); *Australasian*

Concepts of actual and apparent authority are well defined in the general law in relation to agency, and have been discussed earlier in relation into the possession element and knowledge element. Here, it will be necessary to demonstrate that the person either had sufficient authority to trade or procure trading in the relevant financial products or engage in tipping as part of their ordinary duties, or as part of the broader role for which they are retained by the corporation. Such a person is likely to include, for example, an employee specifically authorised to buy and sell shares on a corporation's behalf, such as the proprietary trader whose activities were the subject of *ASIC v Citigroup*,[131] and employees who advise clients of the corporation on share trading and facilitate such trading, such as securities brokers.

Thus, the ability to trade in financial products, or procure such trading, or give advice in relation to those activities, must be conduct in which the relevant person engages, with some form of authority. The fact that the actual trading in question was not specially authorised or permitted will not prevent the conduct from being considered to be within the scope of that general authority.[132]

If the relevant trading conduct is not undertaken by a director, employee or agent of the corporation (which is already a wide category of roles), it may still be regarded as having been undertaken by the corporation if it is done on the corporation's behalf at the direction, or with the consent or agreement, of a director, employee or agent of the corporation. This very broad language enables the conduct to be undertaken by *any person* on the corporation's behalf, if the necessary direction, consent or agreement can be demonstrated. It also means that it does not need to be demonstrated that it was within the scope of the usual role or responsibilities of the person who engaged in the conduct to carry out such activities, if they received a direction, consent or agreement to do so on the relevant occasion from a director, employee or agent of the corporation.

It must also be within the scope of the actual or apparent authority of the director, employee or agent to give such a direction, consent or agreement to another person to engage in the conduct on behalf of the corporation. Once again, the general law principles of agency will be used to determine whether such actual or apparent authority existed. This would encompass a situation where a senior executive of a corporation directs a more junior employee to undertake trading on behalf of the corporation, even if the more junior employee was not ordinarily authorised to carry out such an activity, so long as the senior executive has the necessary authority to do so.

Is s 769B(1) of the *Corporations Act* intended to be an exclusive mechanism for determining when a corporation engages in relevant conduct? Cases interpreting

---

*Brokerage Ltd v Australia and New Zealand Banking Corporation Ltd* (1934) 52 CLR 430, 451.

131  *ASIC v Citigroup Global Markets Australia Pty Ltd* (2007) 160 FCR 35.

132  See, for example, *Meridian Global Funds Management Asia Limited v Securities Commission* [1995] AC 500.

similar statutory provisions in other pieces of legislation have found that they extend the operation of the general law, rather than exclude it.[133] In *Hanley v Automotive, Food, Metals, Engineering, Printing & Kindred Industries Union*,[134] when considering the operation of s 349 of the former *Workplace Relations Act 1996* (Cth) which, as noted earlier, used very similar language to s 769B(1) of the *Corporations Act*, Ryan, Moore and Goldberg JJ of the Federal Court stated that the section:

> does not exclude the operation of common law vicarious liability or direct liability under the principles in *Tesco Ltd v Nattrass*. . . . Rather, it provides an alternative statutory mechanism for imposing direct liability on a body corporate.[135]

Accordingly, it can be argued that, in the absence of any express language to the contrary, the relevant general law principles are not excluded and s 769B(1) is not intended to be an exclusive statutory mechanism for determining when a corporation engages in particular conduct. As a result, both s 769B(1) of the *Corporations Act* and the general law rules of the identification doctrine are potentially relevant to determining when a corporation trades or procures trading in securities, or engages in tipping.

### Identification doctrine

As discussed earlier, at general law a corporation may be found to have engaged in certain criminal conduct if it is undertaken by a person who is considered to be the corporation's directing mind and will. The nature of the directing mind and will of a corporation may include the following people: (i) a person under the direction of the shareholders in general meeting; (ii) the board of directors; or (iii) a person who has the authority of the board of directors, given under the corporation's constitution and appointed by the shareholders.[136]

If such persons trade, or procure trading, in relevant financial products, or engage in tipping, the corporation may be regarded as having engaged in that conduct. This will clearly include the situation where the board of directors, or a managing director or chief executive, authorises particular trading activity. As

---

133 See, for example, *Trade Practices Commission v Queensland Aggregates Pty Ltd* (1982) 44 ALR 391, 404 (Morling J); *Trade Practices Commission v Tubemakers of Australia Ltd* (1983) 47 ALR 719, 739 (Toohey J); *Hanley v Automotive, Food, Metals, Engineering, Printing & Kindred Industries Union* (2000) 100 FCR 530, 544 (Ryan, Moore and Goldberg JJ).

134 *Hanley v Automotive, Food, Metals, Engineering, Printing & Kindred Industries Union* (2000) 100 FCR 530.

135 Ibid 544.

136 *Lennard's Carrying Co Ltd v Asiatic Petroleum Co Ltd* [1915] AC 705, 713–714, as discussed in chapter 4.

discussed earlier, the ultimate test of whether a person is the directing mind and will of a corporation is whether the person manages and controls the actions of the corporation in relation to the relevant activity.[137] So, even though a corporation may have a managing director who ordinarily would be regarded as the directing mind and will of the corporation in relation to most of its activities, if a particular employee has been given authority to act for the corporation in securities trading on the corporation's behalf, so long as that employee has been vested with 'authority, control, discretion and a significant degree of responsibility'[138] in relation to the relevant transactions, that employee can be regarded as the corporation's directing mind and will in relation to the securities trading but not other activities.

### Different mechanisms for establishing the conduct of corporations

When determining whether a corporation has engaged in certain conduct, the statutory mechanisms in s 769B(1) of the *Corporations Act* offer a variety of alternatives – they include conduct undertaken by a director, employee or agent on the corporation's behalf, so long as the conduct is within the scope of the person's actual or apparent authority, as well as conduct undertaken by any person on the corporation's behalf if undertaken at the direction of, or with the agreement or consent of, a director, employee or agent given within the scope of their actual or apparent authority. The general law will permit conduct engaged in by the directing mind and will of the corporation to be attributed to the corporation if the person engages in the relevant conduct. There is no requirement at general law that the particular conduct be within the scope of the authority of the person who is regarded as the corporation's directing mind and will. However, for an employee to be regarded as the directing mind and will of a corporation, as noted earlier, that employee must have been vested with 'authority, control, discretion and a significant degree of responsibility'[139] in relation to the relevant transactions. For an employee to be regarded as being in such a position, it would be highly likely that the general agency principles relating to actual and apparent authority would be satisfied anyway.

Thus, as with the various tests for determining the possession of information for the physical element and the knowledge of the corporation for the fault element of insider trading, there is a wide variance between the role of the relevant person and any link between their role, and their authority, before the corporation is considered to have engaged in the relevant conduct. The wide variation in the role of the relevant person whose conduct is relevant, the presence or absence of a requirement for a nexus with that role, creates significant uncertainty in determining when a corporation will be regarded as having engaged in certain

---

137 *El Ajou v Dollar Land Holdings Ltd Plc* [1994] 2 All ER 685.
138 *The Bell Group Ltd (in Liq) v Westpac Banking Corporation (No 9)* (2008) 70 ACSR 1, [539].
139 Ibid.

conduct. This uncertainty – which exists for regulators who seek to enforce the law as well as corporations who are required to comply with it – should be remedied by legislative reform in order that there can be an appropriate level of clarity and certainty in connection with the attribution of this element of insider trading to corporations.

Like the knowledge element of insider trading, the application of the trading element to a corporation has not been considered judicially. However, this chapter has revealed that both statutory provisions and general law rules can be used to determine when a corporation has engaged in the prohibited conduct, creating significant uncertainty due to the differing elements of those mechanisms – s 769B(1) of the *Corporations Act* and the general law rules of the identification doctrine do not contain the same elements or tests.

## Preliminary conclusions and recommended reforms

The reforms recommended in this book would remedy the many difficulties and problems with the attribution of the elements of insider trading to corporations as identified in this chapter. It is proposed that the operation of the general law be expressly excluded from the statutory regime applying insider trading laws to corporations, and that a new set of provisions be adopted to provide for a model of direct liability as the exclusive means for determining when a corporation possesses inside information, has knowledge that the information is inside information and trades or procures trading in relevant financial products, or engages in tipping.

The proposed amendments to the *Corporations Act* are set out in full in chapter 8. The reforms specifically provide that the only means by which a body corporate would be liable for the insider trading prohibitions in s 1043A are those set out in what would be a new s 1042G of the *Corporations Act*, to be entitled 'Liability of Bodies Corporate'. This would exclude the operation of the general law, so that the identification doctrine and the rules of agency would not operate in relation to the application of the elements of insider trading to a corporation in this context. The operation of s 769B of the *Corporations Act* would also be specifically excluded, and Part 2.5 of the *Criminal Code* would continue to be excluded, so that there are not multiple statutory mechanisms which may apply, using different tests, to determine when a corporation satisfies the various elements of insider trading.

The new s 1042G would specifically state that a body corporate will be taken to possess information if an officer, employee or agent of the body corporate possesses the information, and would not limit the application of the law to information possessed only by officers of a corporation. The new section would not require that the officer, employee or agent came to possess the information in the course of their duties or because they are an officer, employee or agent of the corporation. However, other provisions would apply so that a corporation would only be regarded as having engaged in insider trading if the person who possessed the information also had the requisite knowledge that it was inside information and engaged in, or authorised, the prohibited conduct of trading or procuring of trading in relevant financial products or tipping, within the actual or apparent scope of their authority. Thus, aggregation would not be possible and a link with the prohibited conduct would be required before a corporation would be considered to have engaged in insider trading.

The new s 1042G of the *Corporations Act* would also specifically state that a body corporate would be taken to know, or to ought reasonably to know, that information is inside information if it was known, or ought reasonably to have been known, by an officer, employee or agent of the body corporate. In a similar manner to the proposed new position in relation to the possession of information, the new section would not require that the officer, employee or agent have such knowledge as a result of their position or role within the corporation. The new s 1042G would provide that a body corporate would be taken to engage in the relevant trading conduct if an officer, employee or agent of the body corporate engages in the conduct on behalf of the body corporate within the scope of their actual or apparent authority, or any person engages in the conduct on behalf of the body corporate with the authorisation of an officer, employee or agent of the body corporate. The section would further provide that conduct is taken to be authorised by a person if the conduct is undertaken at that person's direction, or with the person's consent or agreement (whether express or implied), where the giving of the direction, consent or agreement is within the scope of the actual or apparent authority of that person.

The model proposed is one of direct liability, so that a corporation would itself be regarded as having engaged in insider trading, rather than having vicarious liability for conduct engaged in by others. Such a model is appropriate, as it is only where a corporation actually engages in insider trading that market integrity is threatened. Accordingly, even though the new provisions would provide that a corporation would be taken to possess information that is possessed by an officer, employee or agent, the new requirement that a corporation would only be liable for insider trading if the same person also had the requisite knowledge that the information is inside information, and engaged in or authorised the relevant conduct within the scope of their authority, provides an appropriate nexus for the corporation to be considered to have engaged in insider trading.

It is not considered appropriate that the new provisions should require an officer, employee or agent to have come into possession of the inside information in the course of performing their duties, or otherwise as a result of their position. Market integrity requires that those who have an informational advantage should not be able to trade in relevant financial products, and the manner in which a natural person came to possess the information has no bearing on their personal liability. Similarly, for a corporation to be taken to have engaged in insider trading, it should not be relevant how its officers, employees and agents came to possess the relevant information, if allowing them to trade (or authorise trading) on the corporation's behalf would give it an unfair advantage. Accordingly, the new provisions would apply so that information possessed by an officer, employee or agent of a corporation is taken to be possessed by the corporation, regardless of how the officer, employee or agent came to possess that information. The proposed amendments to the *Corporations Act* are set out in full in chapter 8.

# 6 The Chinese Wall defence to insider trading

There are various statutory exceptions and defences available in relation to insider trading. When the alleged insider trader is a corporation, the manner in which those exceptions and defences may apply is not always straightforward. This chapter examines the most important and relevant defence for corporations – that of the Chinese Wall. This defence purportedly exists to allow a corporation to avoid, in some circumstances, liability for insider trading that it might otherwise have as a result of the operation of various statutory mechanisms relating to the liability of corporations for insider trading. The nature of a Chinese Wall is considered, as well as the arrangements that must be put in place to establish a Chinese Wall that satisfies the statutory requirements. The problems associated with this defence are identified and analysed in order to demonstrate that there are significant flaws in the current regulatory regime which could be improved by legislative reform. In particular, the Chinese Wall defence as currently drafted does not serve the stated rationale for the prohibition of insider trading – the maintenance of market integrity – because of the significant uncertainty that exists: there is a gap in the operation of the defence because it extends only to trading and not the procuring of trading; and it does not apply where inside information is possessed by an agent of the corporation who is not an officer or employee. Additionally, the uncertainty which exists in relation to the various mechanisms for determining when a corporation possesses inside information, has knowledge that the information is inside information, and engages in the trading or procuring of trading in financial products or tipping, leads to further uncertainty in the application of the Chinese Wall defence when a corporation would otherwise have fulfilled the various elements of insider trading. Accordingly, the reforms proposed to the application of the insider trading laws to corporations necessitate amendment to the Chinese Wall defence in order to best protect and maintain market integrity and ensure the international competitiveness of Australia's securities markets.[1]

---

1 Much of the material addressed in this chapter is also discussed in detail in Juliette Overland, 'Reforming Australian Insider Trading Laws: A New Model of Corporate Criminal Liability – Part 2' (2018) 33 *Australian Journal of Corporate Law* 99.

## The nature of the Chinese Wall defence

The *Corporations Act* provides a variety of exceptions and defences to the offence of insider trading.[2] The defence most applicable to corporations is that of the Chinese Wall, which allows a corporation to avoid liability for insider trading which might otherwise arise if the corporation can demonstrate, amongst other things, that it has a sufficient Chinese Wall in place.

It is not clear whether it is more appropriate to refer to a 'Chinese Wall defence' or a 'Chinese Wall exception'. As noted by Lyon and du Plessis, the *Corporations Act* does not use either term in connection with s 1043F and appears to alternate between the terms 'defence' and 'exception' when providing for other circumstances in which a person will not be liable for insider trading.[3] Sections 1043B to 1043E, and ss 1043H to 1043J, are referred to in their titles as 'exceptions', whereas ss 1043F, 1043G[4] and 1043K do not use the term 'defence' or 'exception'. Sections 1043B to 1043E provide that each of ss 1043A(1) or 1043A(2) 'does not apply' in respect of the stated circumstances, whereas ss 1043F to 1043K instead state that a person who satisfies the requirements of the relevant section 'does not contravene' ss 1043A(1) or 1043A(2). In s 1043M(1) of the *Corporations Act* it is stated that 'it is a defence' if the 'facts or circumstances' existed which would 'preclude the act or omission from constituting a contravention' under ss 1043B to 1043K. There does not appear to be any discernible reason for the different use of the terms 'defence' and 'exception', or 'does not apply' and 'does not contravene', in these provisions. In general, an exception limits the scope of conduct which is prohibited by an offence and a defence is an excuse for conduct that would otherwise be prohibited. However, in the context of considering the liability of corporations for insider trading, there is no practical

---

2  There is an exception for withdrawal by a member from a registered scheme: s 1043B; an exception for underwriters entering into or acting under an underwriting agreement: s 1043C; an exception for an acquisition pursuant to a requirement imposed by the *Corporations Act*: s 1043D; an exception for bodies corporate entering into a transaction or agreement in relation to financial products issued by another person if the inside information is merely the body corporate's knowledge of its own intentions or activities: s 1043I; and an exception for financial service licensees entering transactions of behalf of a principal: s 1043K. Section 1043M also contains additional defences to a prosecution – defences where a person came into possession of the inside information solely as a result of it having been made known in a manner likely to bring it to the attention of people who commonly invest in financial products of a kind whose price might be affected by the information: ss 1043M(2)(a) and 1043M(3)(a); and defences where the other party knew, or ought reasonably to have known, of the information: ss 1043M(2)(b) and 1043M(3)(b).

3  Gregory Lyon and Jean J du Plessis, *The Law of Insider Trading in Australia* (Federation Press, Sydney, 2005) 71.

4  Section 1043G of the *Corporations Act* relates to Chinese Wall arrangements by partnerships.

consequence to the use of the alternative terms. Section 13.3(3) of the *Criminal Code* clearly provides that:

> A defendant who wishes to rely on any exception, exemption, excuse, quali-fication or justification provided by the law creating an offence bears an evi-dential burden in relation to that matter.

'Evidential burden' is then described in s 13.3(6) of the *Criminal Code* to mean 'the burden of adducing or pointing to evidence that suggests a reasonable pos-sibility that the matter exists or does not exist'. Thus, a defendant relying on an exception or a defence to insider trading will bear the evidential burden of proof in relation to the relevant matters. If the legal burden of proof is imposed on a defendant, the defendant must establish the existence of the exception or defence on the balance of probabilities,[5] and the prosecution must then refute the exception or defence beyond reasonable doubt. However, the legal burden of proof in relation to exceptions or defences to insider trading is not imposed on the defendant under the *Corporations Act*. Thus, the position of a person accused of insider trading is not altered by use of the term 'defence' instead of 'exception' in relation to the certain matters which may enable them to avoid liability.

In *ASIC v Citigroup*,[6] Jacobson J used the term 'Chinese Wall defence' rather than 'Chinese Wall exception' and that term appears to be favoured by the majority of aca-demic commentators.[7] Accordingly, for consistency and simplicity, the term 'Chinese Wall defence' and not 'Chinese Wall exception' is used throughout this book.

Section 1043F of the *Corporations Act* provides as follows:

> A body corporate does not contravene subsection 1043A(1) by entering into a transaction or agreement at any time merely because of information in the possession of an officer or employee of the body corporate if:
>
> (a) the decision to enter into the transaction or agreement was taken on its behalf by a person or persons other than that officer or employee; and

---

5  *Criminal Code*, s 13.5.
6  *ASIC v Citigroup Global Markets Australia Pty Ltd* (2007) 160 FCR 35, 110.
7  See, for example, Robert P Austin and Ian M Ramsay, *Ford's Principles of Corporations Law* (LexisNexis Butterworths, Sydney, 2018) 9.900.12; Roman Tomasic, Stephen Bottomley and Rob McQueen, *Corporations Law in Australia* (Federation Press, 2nd ed, Sydney, 2002) 636–638; Ashley Black, 'Insider Trading and Market Misconduct' (2011) 29 *Company and Securities Law Journal* 313; Vivien Goldwasser, 'Recent Developments in the Regulation of Chinese Walls and Business Ethics – In Search of a Remedy for a Problem that Persists' (1993) 11 *Company and Securities Law Journal* 227; Roman Tomasic, 'Chinese Walls, Legal Principle and Commercial Reality in Multi-Service Professional Firms' (1991) 14 *University of New South Wales Law Journal* 46; CAMAC, *Insider Trading Report*, 2003, 6–7.

(b) it had in operation at that time arrangements that could reasonably be expected to ensure that the information was not communicated to the person or persons who made the decision and that no advice with respect to the transaction or agreement was given to that person or any of those persons by a person in possession of the information; and

(c) the information was not so communicated and no such advice was so given.

Thus, the defence operates so that a corporation is not liable for insider trading, even if an officer or employee in the corporation possesses inside information at the time when the corporation trades in certain financial products, so long as the person who decided to trade did not possess the inside information, the corporation had a sufficient Chinese Wall in place and the inside information was not communicated to the person deciding to trade.

The 'arrangements' referred to in s 1043F(b) of the *Corporations Act* have become known as 'Chinese Walls', although in recent times such arrangements are increasingly referred to as 'information barriers'.[8] As seen below, the arrangements comprise physical, documentary and electronic barriers. Section 1043F is titled 'Chinese Wall arrangements by bodies corporate' but the term 'Chinese Wall' is not used elsewhere in the legislation.[9] There is divergence over the origin of the term Chinese Wall in this context – some consider that it is a reference to the 'Great Wall of China',[10] while others consider that it is a reference to the fact that the 'Chinese used to make walls out of paper through which you could whisper and therefore the name is a flagrant indication of what frequently goes on'.[11] Regardless of the origins of the term, in *Mallesons Stephen Jaques v KPMG Peat Marwick*,[12] Ipp J stated that:

The derivation of the nomenclature is obscure. It appears to be an attempt to clad with respectable antiquity and impenetrability something that is relatively novel and potentially porous.[13]

## The origins of Chinese Walls

The first documented use of a Chinese Wall in relation to insider trading occurred in the United States, as a settlement device in the case of *Re Merrill Lynch, Pierce,*

---

8  *Asia Pacific Telecommunications Limited v Optus Networks Pty Limited* [2007] NSWSC 350 [4]; *ASIC v Citigroup Global Markets Australia Pty Ltd* (2007) 160 FCR 35, 43.
9  Other than in the title of s 1043G of the *Corporations Act*, which contains a similar exception for partnerships.
10  See, for example, Charles Hollander and Simon Salzedo, *Conflicts of Interest and Chinese Walls* (Sweet & Maxwell, London, 2000) 96.
11  John Quarrell, 'Modern Trusts in Legal Education' (1991) 5 *Trust Law International* 99, 103.
12  *Mallesons Stephen Jaques v KPMG Peat Marwick* [1990] WAR 357.
13  Ibid 371–372.

*Fenner and Smith, Inc.*[14] Merrill Lynch, a large multinational financial institution, became the subject of an insider trading claim in connection with its dual role as underwriter and retail broker to a client, Douglas Aircraft. As a result of the underwriting activities, a number of Merrill Lynch employees obtained information about a severe reduction in projected future earnings for Douglas Aircraft and, before the market was properly informed, trading on the basis of this inside information occurred through Merrill Lynch's retail brokerage division. The SEC alleged that Merrill Lynch had engaged in insider trading but the case was ultimately settled, with a term of the settlement being an undertaking given by Merrill Lynch to impose stricter policies and procedures on its business operations in an effort to limit the sharing of inside information within the corporation in the future – effectively amounting to a Chinese Wall.[15]

This type of structure was then adopted by other investment banks and multiservice organisations to try to limit any potential liability for insider trading and avoid conflicts of interest.[16] Chinese Wall arrangements have since become common and accepted practice in investment banking.[17] Australian law first provided for these types of structures as a statutory defence to insider trading under s 128(7) of the former *Securities Industry Code*.[18] Using language that is similar, but not identical, to that in the current s 1043F of the *Corporations Act*, s 128(7) of the *Securities Industry Code* then provided that:

> A body corporate is not precluded . . . from entering into a transaction at any time by reason only of information in the possession of an officer of that body corporate if:
>
> (a) the decision to enter into the transaction was taken on its behalf by a person other than the officer;
> (b) it had in operation at that time arrangements to ensure that the information was not communicated to that person and that no advice with respect to the transaction was given to him by a person in possession of the information; and
> (c) the information was not so communicated and such advice was not so given.

---

14  *Re Merrill Lynch, Pierce, Fenner and Smith, Inc.* 43 S.E.C. 933 (1968); Tomasic, above n 7, 53; Goldwasser, above n 7, 232.

15  Stanislav Dolgopolov, 'Insider Trading, Chinese Walls, and Brokerage Commissions: The Origins of Modern Regulation of Information Flows in Securities Markets' (2008) 4 *Journal of Law, Economics and Policy* 311, 347; Norman Poser, 'Chinese Wall or Emperor's New Clothes? Regulating Conflicts of Interest of Securities Firms in the U.S. and the U.K.' (1988) 9 *Michigan Yearbook International Legal Studies* 91, 106.

16  Martin Lipton and Robert B Mazur, 'The Chinese Wall Solution to the Conflicts Problems of Securities Firms' (1975) 50 *New York University Law Review* 459, 461.

17  Norman Poser, *International Securities Regulation* (Little Brown & Co, New York, 1991) 207.

18  And then under s 1002(7) of the *Corporations Law*, as noted by Goldwasser, above n 7, 230.

The two primary differences between s 128(7) of the *Securities Industry Code* and s 1043F of the *Corporations Act* are that s 128(7) referred only to information in possession of an officer of the corporation, whereas s 1043F also refers to information in the possession of an employee. Section 128(7) also required arrangements 'to ensure' information was not communicated to the person deciding to enter the relevant transaction, whereas s 1043F more leniently requires arrangements 'that could reasonably be expected to ensure' that the information was not communicated. These concepts are discussed in detail later in this chapter.

Chinese Wall arrangements have been described as a form of 'procedural architecture'[19] whose primary purpose is to separate areas of conflict of interest and prevent the transfer of information.[20] In general, Chinese Walls aim to prevent officers and employees of a corporation from sharing confidential information by separating those parts of a corporation that are most likely to receive inside information, such as corporate advisory, research and analysis departments (the 'private' side of a corporation) from those which are most likely to engage in securities trading (the 'public' side of a corporation).[21]

The most common types of corporations which utilise Chinese Walls are investment banks – large organisations providing a wide range of financial intermediary services. Such services include issuing, buying and selling of securities and giving of related financial advice, securities underwriting and financial advisory services in connection with mergers and acquisitions, divestitures, restructurings, joint ventures and privatisations. A wide range of additional services are also commonly provided, such as securities trading, investment research, financing asset management and foreign exchange dealings.[22]

Apart from being utilised as a defence to insider trading, Chinese Walls are also frequently created to avoid more general conflicts of interest. There are a wide variety of cases involving Chinese Walls in other contexts, particularly those concerning conflicts of interests in accounting and law firms. In these situations, Chinese Walls may be established in an effort to ensure there is no breach of fiduciary and contractual duties to act in the best interests of clients and avoid a conflict of interest, and to avoid the sharing of information between lawyers and accountants acting for different parties, or each side of a dispute or set of proceedings. Chinese Walls are also utilised by organisations which carry on a business of providing financial services, due to a requirement under s 912A(1)(aa) of the *Corporations Act* that a person licensed to carry on such a business must maintain Chinese Wall arrangements in order to manage conflicts.[23]

---

19  Roman Tomasic, *Casino Capitalism? Insider Trading in Australia* (Australian Institute of Criminology, Canberra, 1991) 89.
20  Goldwasser, above n 7, 228.
21  CAMAC, *Insider Trading Discussion Paper*, 2001, [2.190].
22  Andrew Tuch, 'Investment Banks as Fiduciaries: Implications for Conflicts of Interest' (2005) 29 *Melbourne University Law Review* 15.
23  Section 912A(1) of the *Corporations Act* provides that:

A financial services licensee must:

## The necessity for Chinese Walls

For the purposes of insider trading, the Chinese Wall defence is considered to be necessary due to the operation of the mechanisms which set out when a corporation will possess information, have the requisite knowledge that information is inside information, and engage in the trading or procuring of trading in financial products. Theoretically, it may be possible for one person in a corporation to possess inside information (which is information that the corporation may be regarded as possessing) and for another person elsewhere in the corporation to engage in trading or the procuring of trading in relevant financial products (which is conduct that the corporation may be considered to have engaged in). Therefore, the corporation could potentially be regarded as having engaged in trading in relevant financial products while in possession of inside information and therefore be potentially liable for insider trading,[24] even if neither of the relevant individuals would have any such liability themselves. The varying operation of different statutory and general law mechanisms for determining when a corporation is considered to possess inside information, have the requisite knowledge that the information is inside information, and to have engaged in the relevant trading conduct, has been discussed in detail in chapter 5.

In certain circumstances, in order to avoid the cumulative effect of these various mechanisms, the Chinese Wall defence provides, in essence, that there will be no liability for insider trading just because an officer or employee of a corporation possesses inside information, so long as any trading in affected financial products is undertaken by or at the direction of another officer or employee to whom the inside information or related advice has not been communicated, and so long as the corporation has arrangements in place that could 'reasonably be expected to ensure' that the inside information would not be communicated.

In addition to operating as a means of avoiding liability for insider trading, Chinese Walls may also prevent insider trading from occurring, by restricting access to inside information to employees on the 'public side' of organisations. As stated by Poser:

> a Chinese wall can have two very different regulatory purposes. Its purpose may be merely prophylactic: to prevent inside information in the possession of persons in one part of a firm from being misused by persons in another part of the firm. Its purpose may also, however, be legal: to provide a defence to the firm against liability for insider trading or breach of duty to a customer

---

(aa) have in place adequate arrangements for the management of conflicts of interest that may arise wholly, or partially, in relation to activities undertaken by the licensee or a representative of the licensee in the provision of financial services as part of the financial services business of the licensee or the representative.

24 Christopher M Gorman, 'Are Chinese Walls the Best Solution to the Problems of Insider Trading and Conflicts of Interests in Broker-Dealers?' (2004) 9 *Fordham Journal of Corporate and Financial Law* 475, 476; Lyon and du Plessis, above n 3, 80.

that would normally arise as a result of the imputation of knowledge of an employee to the employer.[25]

## Requirements for reliance on the Chinese Wall defence

Section 1043F of the *Corporations Act* has three distinct elements which must be satisfied before a corporation can rely on the Chinese Wall defence to insider trading, which can be summarised as follows: (i) the person deciding to trade in the relevant financial products did not possess the inside information; (ii) the corporation had a sufficient Chinese Wall in place; and (iii) the person deciding to trade did not receive the inside information or advice from a person in possession of the inside information.

### *The person deciding to trade in relevant financial products did not possess inside information*

Section 1043F(a) of the *Corporations Act* requires that the decision to enter a transaction or agreement – effectively, the decision to trade in certain financial products – must have been made by a person who did not possess inside information. To repeat the precise language of the section, the first element requires that:

> the decision to enter into the transaction or agreement was taken on its [the body corporate's] behalf by a person or person other than that officer or employee [in possession of inside information].

This gives rise to three issues to consider: (i) is making 'the decision to enter' a transaction or agreement different from the prohibited conduct for insider trading? (ii) What occurs if inside information is possessed by an agent of the corporation who is not also an officer or employee? (iii) As the defence refers to a decision to enter into a transaction or agreement 'on its behalf', does it extend to liability for procuring trading, or only to actual trading in financial products by a corporation?

As discussed earlier, insider trading occurs where a person trades, or procures trading, in relevant financial products, or engages in tipping while in possession of inside information, and with knowledge that the information is inside information (or where the person ought reasonably to have known that the information was inside information). The act or trading, or procuring of trading, or tipping, is the conduct which prohibited and is referred to in this book as the 'trading element'. The manner in which a corporation engages in the trading element has been discussed in detail earlier.

The person who actually made 'the decision to enter' the transaction or agreement might not be the same person who actually engaged in the trading element

---

25 Poser, above n 15, 189–190.

on the corporation's behalf. Once again, the specific conduct prohibited by s 1043A(1) is to:

(c)  apply for, acquire, or dispose of, relevant Division 3 financial products, or enter into an agreement to apply for, acquire, or dispose of, relevant Division 3 financial products; or
(d)  procure another person to apply for, acquire, or dispose of, relevant Division 3 financial products, or enter into an agreement to apply for, acquire, or dispose of, relevant Division 3 financial products.

It is also prohibited conduct under s 1043A(2) for an insider to:

directly or indirectly, communicate the information, or cause the information to be communicated, to another person if the insider knows, or ought reasonably to know, that the other person would or would be likely to:

(c)  apply for, acquire, or dispose of, relevant Division 3 financial products, or enter into an agreement to apply for, acquire, or dispose of, relevant Division 3 financial products; or
(d)  procure another person to apply for, acquire, or dispose of, relevant Division 3 financial products, or enter into an agreement to apply for, acquire, or dispose of, relevant Division 3 financial products.

Clearly, a 'decision to enter' into a 'transaction or agreement' is not necessarily the same as the prohibited conduct set out in s 1043A(1) (c) and (d). It is certainly possible that a person may 'apply for, acquire, or dispose of, relevant Division 3 financial products, or enter into an agreement to apply for, acquire, or dispose of, relevant Division 3 financial products' without being a person who made 'the decision to enter' the relevant transaction or agreement. For example, a trader in a merchant bank may possess inside information and may be directed by a more senior employee to purchase certain shares in a corporation to which the inside information relates. If the trader buys the shares on behalf of the corporation, he or she has caused the corporation to acquire the financial products while he or she is in possession of inside information. As a result of the application of s 769B(1) of the *Corporations Act*, the trader has acquired financial products on behalf of the merchant bank, satisfying s 1043A(1)(c) of the *Corporations Act*. However, since the decision to buy the shares was actually made by a more senior employee who did not possess the inside information, the more senior employee has actually made 'the decision to enter' the transaction. As that more senior employee did not possess the inside information, s 1043F(a) of the *Corporations Act* can be applied, and the defence can operate, so long as the other requirements of s 1043F are met.

Insider trading laws should be framed to reflect the underlying legislative rationale and intent, which is to protect and maintain market integrity. Therefore, it is not necessary or appropriate to prohibit conduct where the party who has engaged in the trading conduct has not obtained, and does not appear to have obtained, an advantage for themselves at the expense of other market participants. However, the other difficulties and uncertainties which arise in relation to Chinese Walls, which are explored throughout this chapter, result in a need to reform this defence.

The availability of the defence is restricted due to the use of the terms 'officer or employee' in s 1043F of the *Corporations Act*. As demonstrated earlier, s 769B(3) of the *Corporations Act* or the general law may apply so that a corporation will be considered to possess information which is in the possession of an agent, who is not necessarily an officer or employee of the corporation. However, the Chinese Wall defence will not be available if the information was possessed by an agent who was not also an officer or employee, as s 1043F quite clearly states that:

> A body corporate does not contravene subsection 1043A(1) by entering into a transaction or agreement at any time merely because of information in the possession of any *officer or employee* of the body corporate. . .[26]

This creates a gap in the operation of the Chinese Wall defence, limiting its application to the possession of information by some persons associated with a corporation and not others. If the inside information was possessed by an agent of the corporation, such that s 769B(3) of the *Corporations Act* or the general law could apply and the corporation would be taken to possess the information, the Chinese Wall defence in s 1043F of the *Corporations Act* would not be applicable, even though it could apply if the inside information were possessed by an officer or employee. There is an absence of any available explanation, in either legislative history or commentary, for the different treatment of agents as opposed to officers and employees in this respect. This issue is addressed in the proposals for reform described later in this chapter and set out in full in chapter 8.

Some commentators have noted that the Chinese Wall defence only operates in relation to the trading limb of insider trading, and not the procuring limb.[27] This is because the defence only applies where 'the decision to enter' a transaction or agreement (being the decision to trade in relevant financial products) was taken 'on its behalf' by a person other than the person in possession of the inside information. The words 'on its behalf' make it clear that the decision must be made for the person or entity that is actually trading. A person who procures trading by another will not ordinarily be the person who makes the ultimate 'decision to enter a transaction or agreement' unless they are also a decision-maker for that other person (for example, if the other person is a corporation controlled

---

26  Emphasis added.
27  Austin and Ramsay, above n 7, [9.880.6]; Michael Ziegelaar, 'Insider Trading Law in Australia', in Gordon Walker, Brent Fisse and Ian Ramsay (eds), *Securities Regulation in Australia and New Zealand* (Lawbook, 2nd ed, Sydney, 1998) 554, 585; Goldwasser, above n 7, 242; Lyon and du Plessis, above n 3, 82; Robert Baxt, Ashley Black and Pamela Hanrahan, *Securities and Financial Services Law* (Lexis Nexis, 8th ed, Sydney, 2012) 710.

by that person). A person who merely 'encourages' another person to trade in securities may be regarded as procuring that other person to trade,[28] but the ultimate decision is still made by that other person. Thus, the requirement that the relevant person makes a 'decision to enter' a transaction or agreement on a corporation's 'behalf' prevents the defence from applying where the corporation procures another person to trade.

This is obviously a significant anomaly in the law as it applies to corporations, many of which operate in circumstances where trading recommendations may be made to clients by employees in one part of the organisation (which may amount to procuring) at times when others in the organisation possess inside information. Technically, such conduct is not protected by the existence of a sufficient Chinese Wall and may amount to insider trading. Why should a corporation be liable for insider trading for recommending that a client buy or sell certain securities when there would not be any such liability if it bought or sold the same securities itself?

A corporation with a sufficient Chinese Wall will be protected from claims of insider trading where, for example, it engages in proprietary trading on its own behalf even though inside information is possessed elsewhere in the organisation, but not where it procures others to trade. Section 1043K of the *Corporations Act* provides a version of the Chinese Wall defence for the holders of financial services licences,[29] but it only operates where the holder of the licence or their representative acts as the agent of another party and where the other party gives specific instructions to the agent to trade on their behalf, rather than where the agent

---

28 Section 1042F of the *Corporations Act* defines 'procure' as follows:

For the purposes of this Division, but without limiting the meaning that the expression procure has apart from this section, if a person incites, induces, or encourages an act or omission by another person, the first-mentioned person is taken to procure the act or omission by the other person.

29 Section 1043K of the *Corporations Act* provides that:

A person (the agent) does not contravene subsection 1043A(1) by applying for, acquiring, or disposing of, or entering into an agreement to apply for, acquire, or dispose of, financial products that are able to be traded on a licensed market if:

(a) the agent is a financial services licensee or a representative of a financial services licensee; and
(b) the agent entered into the transaction or agreement concerned on behalf of another person (the principal) under a specific instruction by the principal to enter into that transaction or agreement; and
(c) the licensee had in operation, at the time when that transaction or agreement was entered into, arrangements that could reasonably be expected to ensure that any information in the possession of the licensee, or of any representative of the licensee, as a result of which the person in possession of the information would be prohibited by subsection 1043A(1) from entering into that transaction or agreement was not communicated to the agent and that no advice with respect to the transaction or agreement was given to the principal or to the agent by a person in possession of the information; and
(d) the information was not so communicated and no such advice was so given; and
(e) the principal is not an associate of the licensee or of any representative of the licensee; but nothing in this section affects the application of subsection 1043A(1) in relation to the principal.

procures the other party to trade. The defence in s 1043K does not fill this gap within the Chinese Wall defence in s 1043F of the *Corporations Act*.

When CAMAC undertook its review of Australian insider trading laws, this gap in the legislation was noted[30] and in 2003 CAMAC recommended that the Chinese Wall defence be extended to include procuring as well as trading, as this omission was considered to be 'the result of a legislative oversight'.[31] While this recommendation was accepted by the Commonwealth Treasury in 2007 as an appropriate amendment to be made to Australian insider trading laws,[32] despite the passing of a number of years, no action has yet been taken to give formal effect to this proposed reform. As there appears to be no sound basis for the exclusion of procuring of trading from the operation of the Chinese Wall defence, the reforms proposed in this book would amend the Chinese Wall defence to insider trading, and operate so that such gap would no longer exist.

### A sufficient Chinese Wall was in place

Section 1043F(b) of the *Corporations Act* requires that a sufficient Chinese Wall be in place, as for a corporation to rely on the defence it must be shown that:

> it had in operation at that time arrangements that could reasonably be expected to ensure that the information was not communicated to the person or persons who made the decision [to enter the transaction or agreement] and that no advice with respect to the transaction or agreement was given to that person or any of those persons by a person in possession of the information.

Despite describing the nature of the arrangements that must be in place as arrangements 'that could reasonably be expected to ensure' that information is not communicated or advice given by those who possess the inside information, the *Corporations Act* does not specify what is required to establish a sufficient Chinese Wall.

The phrase 'could reasonably be expected to ensure' was first used in connection with the Chinese Wall defence in s 1002M of the former *Corporations Law*, due to amendments resulting from the *Corporations Legislation Amendment Act 1991* (Cth). This language was used instead of the previously proposed phrase, which would require arrangements 'reasonably designed to *ensure*'[33] that information was not communicated,[34] which would have appeared to have created a

---

30  CAMAC, *Insider Trading Discussion Paper*, above n 21, [2.190]-[2.195]; CAMAC, *Insider Trading Proposals Paper*, 2002, [3.58]-[3.62].

31  CAMAC, *Insider Trading Report*, above n 7, 2 and 7.

32  Commonwealth Treasury, *Insider Trading Position and Consultation Paper*, 2007, 5.

33  Emphasis added.

34  Explanatory Memorandum, Corporations Legislation Amendment Bill 1991 (Cth), [355].

higher standard.[35] In *Attorney-General's Department and Australian Iron and Steel Pty Ltd v Cockcroft*,[36] it was determined that:

> the correct approach to the interpretation of the phrase 'could reasonably be expected to' . . . is that the words should be given their ordinary and natural meaning. They require a judgment to be made as to whether something is reasonable, as distinct from something that is irrational, absurd or ridiculous.[37]

Finding an objective and appropriate yardstick for measuring the sufficiency of Chinese Walls, and whether they can be reasonably expected to ensure that information is not communicated and advice is not given, is challenging because the detection of insider trading is notoriously difficult.[38] Without accurate empirical evidence, it is difficult to determine objectively whether Chinese Walls actually work, particularly as Chinese Walls are only likely to come under scrutiny if and when claims of insider trading, or other forms of misconduct or conflict, are brought.

However, in order to avoid liability for insider trading where appropriate, corporations must have confidence that their internal arrangements would withstand scrutiny to be considered sufficient. It is therefore necessary to look at other sources to determine what is needed to establish and maintain a sufficient Chinese Wall to protect a corporation from liability for insider trading, including: (i) cases interpreting s 1043F of the *Corporations Act*; (ii) market rules and accepted industry practices in relation to Chinese Walls; and (iii) cases considering Chinese Walls in other contexts.

### Cases concerning Chinese Walls and insider trading

Although the Chinese Wall defence to insider trading is set out in the *Corporations Act*, and has existed in legislative form in the former *Companies Code* and the *Corporations Law*, the requirements for a sufficient Chinese Wall as a defence to insider trading were untested judicially until the case of *ASIC v Citigroup*.[39] In this case, ASIC made two separate claims of insider trading against

---

35 Austin and Ramsay, above n 7, [9.990.12].
36 *Attorney-General's Department and Australian Iron and Steel Pty Ltd v Cockcroft* (1986) 10 FCR 180.
37 Ibid 190.
38 Simon Rubenstein, 'The Regulation and Prosecution of Insider Trading in Australia: Towards Civil Penalty Sanctions for Insider Trading' (2002) 20 *Company and Securities Law Journal* 89; Roman Tomasic and Brendan Pentony, 'The Prosecution of Insider Trading: Obstacles to Enforcement' (1989) 22 *Australian and New Zealand Journal of Criminology* 65; Explanatory Memorandum, Financial Services Bill 2001 (Cth) [2.78]-[2.79]; Lyon and du Plessis, above n 3, 163–168.
39 *ASIC v Citigroup Global Markets Australia Pty Ltd* (2007) 160 FCR 35.

Citigroup: (i) ASIC alleged that the sale of Patrick shares by the proprietary trader, Mr Manchee, which occurred after he was told by his manager, Mr Darvall, to stop *buying* Patrick shares, amounted to insider trading attributable to Citigroup; and (ii) ASIC alleged that there was not a sufficient Chinese Wall in place, so that *all* buying and selling of Patrick shares by the proprietary trader amounted to insider trading, as at all relevant times executives in the Investment Banking Division of Citigroup possessed inside information about the proposed takeover of Patrick by Toll. The case also gave rise to claims that Citigroup had failed to properly manage conflicts of interest and that it breached fiduciary duties it owed to its client, Toll.[40]

As discussed in chapter 5, the first insider trading claim brought against Citigroup ultimately failed because the proprietary trader, Mr Manchee, was not found to be an 'officer' of Citigroup and Jacobson J determined that this meant that any information he possessed was not to be taken to be information possessed by Citigroup. Additionally, as a matter of fact, it was found that Mr Manchee had not made the necessary supposition alleged by ASIC – that Citigroup was acting for Toll on an imminent takeover of Patrick[41] – and that such a supposition had not been conveyed to him by his manager.[42]

Most relevant in the context of a review of the Chinese Wall defence, the second insider trading claim brought against Citigroup also failed, because Citigroup's Chinese Wall was found to satisfy the necessary requirements. Although officers in the Investment Banking Division of Citigroup, who were advising Toll, were aware of relevant inside information concerning Patrick shares at a time when trading in those shares was occurring in another part of the organisation (that is, at the time the proprietary trader was trading in those shares on Citigroup's behalf), the Chinese Wall in place between the Investment Banking Division (which was on the 'private' side of the Chinese Wall) and the proprietary trading group (which was on the 'public' side of the Chinese Wall) was found to be sufficient.[43]

The existence of a sufficient Chinese Wall meant that there was no contravention of the prohibition of insider trading. In this context, the most pertinent statements made by the Court are those which describe the requirements for a sufficient Chinese Wall. Jacobson J described the type of organisational arrangements which would ordinarily be sufficient as:

a    the physical separation of departments to isolate them from each other;
b    an educational programme, normally recurring to emphasise the importance of not improperly or inadvertently divulging confidential information;

---

40 Jacobson J ultimately determined that there was no duty to avoid a conflict of interest because of the absence of a fiduciary relationship between Citigroup and Toll, but a discussion of those issues is unrelated to the topic of insider trading and beyond the scope of this book.
41 *ASIC v Citigroup Global Markets Australia Pty Ltd* (2007) 160 FCR 35, 101–102.
42 Ibid 103–104.
43 Ibid 110–112.

c    strict and carefully designed procedures for dealing with situations where it is thought the Chinese Wall should be crossed, and the maintaining of proper records where this occurs;

d    monitoring of the effectiveness of the Chinese Wall by compliance officers; and

e    disciplinary sanctions where there has been a breach of the Chinese Wall.[44]

It is clear from his judgment that Jacobson J considered that these characteristics would usually be considered to give rise to a sufficient Chinese Wall, but also that each situation is to be determined on its own merits, and he did not attempt to exhaustively describe how a Chinese Wall should be established.

It was noted by Jacobson J that a Chinese Wall arrangement '[does] not require a standard of absolute perfection. The test stated . . . is an objective one'.[45] Indeed, the 'practical impossibility of ensuring that every conceivable risk is covered by written procedures and followed by employees'[46] was also noted.

Thus, *ASIC v Citigroup* usefully describes the quite general characteristics a sufficient Chinese Wall might be expected to have, with a recognition that each case will need to be determined objectively on its facts. However, it is clearly not a detailed or exhaustive list of the ways in which a sufficient Chinese Wall can be established and maintained.

### Market rules and accepted industry practices

As noted by Lyon and du Plessis,[47] the financial sector has had significant input into the requirements for Chinese Walls, and there are a variety of industry practices and rules which relate to these sorts of arrangements. Independent of the prohibition of insider trading, s 912A(1)(aa) of the *Corporations Act* provides, as noted earlier, that a financial services licensee must have in place 'adequate arrangements for the management of conflicts of interest'. ASIC has produced *Regulatory Guide 181 Licensing: Managing Conflicts of Interest* (RG 181) to assist financial services licensees to meet their obligations under this section, which is supplemented by *Regulatory Guide 79 Managing Conflicts of Interest: A Guide for Research Report Providers* (RG 79). RG 181 set outs ASIC's 'general approach to compliance with the statutory obligation'.[48] While the regulatory guide is not prescriptive, ASIC takes the view that:

> licensees whose conflict of interest management arrangements are not consistent with the guidelines and expectations . . . are less likely to be complying with their obligations . . . and will be exposed to greater risk of regulatory action.[49]

44  Ibid 82, citing with approval statements of Lord Millett in *Prince Jefri Bolkiah v KPMG* [1999] 2 AC 222, 238.

45  Ibid 112.

46  Ibid.

47  Lyon and du Plessis, above n 3, 86–87.

48  ASIC, *Regulatory Guide 181, Licensing: Managing Conflicts of Interest*, 2004, 1.

49  Ibid 4.

RG 181 does not explicitly set out requirements for Chinese Walls (or information barriers, as they are described in the regulatory guide) but it does emphasise the role of monitoring procedures,[50] internal structures – including 'organisational structure, physical layout and reporting processes'[51] – and documentation and record-keeping.[52] It also states that:

> robust information barriers may help a licensee manage their conflicts of interest. They may allow a licensee to insulate one group of staff from the information. . . . To be effective, such barriers must actually prevent information being passed to the relevant group of staff.[53]

RG 79 contains a more definitive statement about Chinese Walls:[54]

> We expect research report providers[55] to ensure that research staff are structurally and physically separated from (and not supervised by) any staff who are performing an investment banking, corporate advisory or dealing function.[56]

The ASX previously had in place a set of Market Rules that set out requirements for Chinese Walls for market participants in connection with the provision of advice to clients. Market Rule 7.18.3 provided that:

> A Market Participant will not be regarded as having possession of inside information that is not generally available in relation to a Financial Product where that Market Participant has Chinese Walls in place and the person advising the client is not in possession of that information.

Market Rule 7.18.1 of the ASX Market Rules then defined a 'Chinese Wall' as an arrangement:

> whereby information known to persons included in one part of the business of the Market Participant is not available (directly or indirectly) to those involved in another part of the business of the Market Participant and it is accepted that in each of the parts of the business of the Market Participant so divided decisions will be taken without reference to any interest which any other such part or person in any other such part of the business of the Market Participant may have in the matter.

---

50 Ibid 10.
51 Ibid 11.
52 Ibid 14–15.
53 Ibid 11.
54 ASIC, *Regulatory Guide 79, Managing Conflicts of Interest: A Guide for Research Report Providers*, 2012, 34.
55 That is, 'public' side employees.
56 That is, 'private' side employees.

Additionally, the ASX Market Rules required further measures such as advising the ASX of the creation, alteration or removal of Chinese Walls before any action could be taken by the market participant.[57] However, ASIC has now taken over the supervision of financial markets and the ASIC Market Integrity Rules (Securities Markets) 2017 apply. Rule 3.6.3 of these rules has similar content to the ASX Market Rules in relation to Chinese Walls, but market participants are no longer required to advise ASIC of the creation of a Chinese Wall.[58]

The ASX had released a Guidance Note under the old ASX Market Rules, which set out certain procedures to be adopted by market participants in connection with Chinese Wall arrangements, but specifically stated that it did 'not deal with the provisions . . . of the Corporations Act which provides the statutory basis of the regulation of insider trading'.[59] This Guidance Note required market participants to have: (i) a written policy statement and restricted communication flows; (ii) a personal acknowledgement completed by staff on commencement of employment; (iii) physical access restrictions; (iv) separate supervision of each department or work unit; (v) physical separation; (vi) limits on transfer of staff between departments or work units; (vii) continuing education; and (viii) monitoring and detection of breaches.[60]

Although these concepts have some similarity and overlap with those outlined by the Court in *ASIC v Citigroup*, they are not identical and the ASX Guidance Note requirements were more expansive than those already identified. While the adoption of such further arrangements would not necessarily ensure that a Chinese Wall would pass judicial scrutiny when considering whether the elements of s 1043F are satisfied, the ASX Guidance Note provided helpful assistance as to how a regulator considers that Chinese Walls are to be managed and interpreted. However, these requirements were not considered by the Court in *ASIC v Citigroup* when determining what is necessary for a sufficient Chinese Wall.

As noted earlier, while Chinese Walls are maintained in order to avoid liability for offences such as insider trading, by restricting the flow of information, such arrangements also serve to minimise opportunities for insider trading which might otherwise exist within organisations – whether such trading might be undertaken on behalf of a corporation or by an officer, employee or agent of the corporation on their own account. Accordingly, while amendments are proposed to the Chinese Wall defence to remedy the various problems with the application of insider trading laws to corporations, as identified throughout this book, it is recognised that Chinese Wall arrangements serve more than one purpose, and that it would not be appropriate to remove the Chinese Wall defence in its entirety.

---

57 ASX, Market Rules, r 7.18.1–17.18.2.
58 ASIC, *Regulatory Guide 214, Guidance on ASIC Market Integrity Rule for ASX and ASX 24 Markets*, 2010, RG 214.78. This regulatory guide has now been replaced by ASIC, *Regulatory Guide 265, Guidance on ASIC Market Integrity Rules for Participants of Securities Markets*, 2018.
59 ASX, Market Rules, *Guidance Note 13, Prohibition of Advice to Clients*, 2005, 1.
60 Ibid 2–4.

## Cases concerning Chinese Walls in other contexts

Chinese Wall arrangements may be used by professional service firms, such as law firms and accounting firms, in circumstances where there is a conflict of interest – for example, if a law firm wishes to act for more than one party to a dispute or to act against a current or former client of the firm. This has resulted in much judicial consideration of the effectiveness and operation of Chinese Walls in this context.

Such arrangements commonly involve the use of a Chinese Wall to separate the relevant sections of the firm in order to avoid a breach of fiduciary duty and the inappropriate disclosure of confidential client information. Where a firm acting for one client seeks to act for another client in circumstances where a conflict of interest would arise,[61] the firm may deal with the conflict by implementing a Chinese Wall. This means that the relevant employees who act for each client are separated from each other so that an employee who acts for one of those clients cannot act for the other, or have access to information concerning the other client.[62] Where a conflict of interest arises because a firm seeks to act against a former client of the firm, the firm may also implement a Chinese Wall. This generally means that an employee who has previously acted for the former client will not be permitted to act against them, and that employees acting against the former client will not be permitted to have access to the files or confidential information concerning the former client.[63] It is also common for these arrangements to be supported by appropriate undertakings – for example, undertakings given to a court by individual employees that they will not seek or obtain access to documents, act for a particular party or discuss any relevant issues with other identified employees within the firm.[64]

An analysis of the cases which have considered what is necessary for a sufficient Chinese Wall in those circumstances reveals that courts are willing to accept such arrangements as a means of quarantining information within a firm,[65] but it will be a question of fact in each case as to whether a particular Chinese Wall is sufficient.[66] The primary issue on which a court needs to be satisfied is that the arrangements have no real risk of disclosure.[67] Mere physical segregation of particular

---

61  For example, if the firm were to take instructions from one client to act against another client of the firm.

62  See, for example, *Blackwell v Barroile Pty Limited* (1994) 51 FCR 347, 359; *Wan v McDonald* (1992) 33 FCR 491, 511; *Spincode Pty Ltd v Look Software Pty Ltd* [2001] VSC 287.

63  See, for example, *British American Tobacco Australian Services Ltd v Blanch* [2004] NSWSC 7; *Spincode Pty Ltd v Look Software Pty Ltd* [2001] VSC 287; *Asia Pacific Communications Limited v Optus Networks Pty Limited* [2007] NSWSC 350.

64  For example, undertakings of this type were given to the Court in *Photocure ASA v Queen's University at Kingston* [2002] FCA 905.

65  See *Prince Jefri Bolkiah v KPMG* [1999] 2 AC 222, 237–238 (Lord Millett), as approved by Jacobson J in *ASIC v Citigroup Global Markets Australia Pty Ltd* (2007) 160 FCR 35, 81.

66  *Prince Jefri Bolkiah v KPMG* [1999] 2 AC 222, 239, as noted by Jacobson J in *ASIC v Citigroup Global Markets Australia Pty Ltd* (2007) 160 FCR 35, 82.

67  *McDonald Estate v Martin* (1991) 77 DLR (4th) 249, 269.

employees is not enough[68] – there also need to be 'sensible and safe systems in place'.[69] Due to the fiduciary duties owed by lawyers to their clients,[70] the relevant clients must also expressly consent to the Chinese Wall arrangements.[71]

A Chinese Wall which is 'an established part of the organisational' structure, rather than one created 'ad hoc' to deal with a particular conflict, is likely to be preferred by the courts.[72] Additionally, a consideration of the adequacy of Chinese Walls in law firms requires an appreciation that 'it is not part of everyday legal practice for a lawyer to have his or her knowledge from a case quarantined from another lawyer within the same section of the firm'.[73] It is considered unrealistic:

> to place reliance on such arrangements in relation to people with opportunities for daily contact over long periods, as wordless communication can take place inadvertently and without explicit expressions, by attitudes, facial expression or even by avoiding people one is accustomed to see, even by people who sincerely intend to conform to control.[74]

Accordingly, there needs to be awareness that:

> there will always be an element of some risk of disclosure where its prevention depends upon human contact because people make mistakes. The lack of a real risk of disclosure or misuse will depend on the design of the information barrier.[75]

Thus, the key principles relevant to the sufficiency of Chinese Walls within law firms can be summarised as follows: (i) each case must be assessed on an independent basis to determine if there is a real risk of disclosure of confidential information; (ii) the physical separation of relevant employees must also be supported by appropriate systems and practices as well as undertakings; and

---

68  *Prince Jefri Bolkiah v KPMG* [1999] 2 AC 222, 239; Lee Aitkin, 'Chinese Walls, Fiduciary Duties and Intra-Firm Conflicts – A Pan-Australian Conspectus' (2000) 19 *Australian Bar Review* 116, 122.

69  *Asia Pacific Communications Limited v Optus Networks Pty Limited* [2007] NSWSC 350, [5] (Bergin J).

70  Fiduciary duties are not ordinarily owed by investment banks to their clients, and are customarily excluded by contract, as noted in *ASIC v Citigroup Global Markets Australia Pty Ltd* (2007) 160 FCR 35, 75.

71  Hollander and Salzedo, above n 10, 98.

72  As noted by Jacobson J in *ASIC v Citigroup Global Markets Australia Pty Ltd* (2007) 160 FCR 35, 82, citing *Prince Jefri Bolkiah v KPMG* [1999] 2 AC 222, 239.

73  *Asia Pacific Communications Limited v Optus Networks Pty Limited* [2007] NSWSC 350, [35].

74  As stated by Bryson J in *D & J Constructions Pty Limited v Head & Ors Trading as Clayton Utz* (1987) 9 NSWLR 118, 123.

75  *Asia Pacific Communications Limited v Optus Networks Pty Limited* [2007] NSWSC 350 [14].

(iii) established structures will be preferred to 'ad hoc' arrangements because they are more likely to be effective.

Tomasic has suggested that the problems identified in relation to the use of Chinese Walls within law firms could apply equally to the securities industry and that therefore 'the Chinese Wall defence to insider trading should logically also be abandoned'.[76] However, when comparing investment banks and financial services organisations to law firms and accounting firms, it is worth noting that Chinese Walls in corporations such as investment banks are more likely to be well-established structures. As noted earlier, lawyers are not generally accustomed to being quarantined from sharing knowledge with other lawyers within the same firm, but corporate organisations such as investment banks with established Chinese Walls have employees who are used to working within a section of the organisation where information sharing with others in other parts of the organisation is prohibited. Employees within those organisations will always be on either the 'public' or 'private' side of the Chinese Wall and become used to that position. In law firms, employees may be on one side of a Chinese Wall in respect of certain cases and not others, on a true 'case by case' basis. As the arrangements have differing functions, purposes and degrees of permanence in the various forms of organisations, those in corporations such as investment banks or financial services organisations are more likely to have the degree of permanence necessary to be regarded as sufficient structures for the purposes of s 1043F of the *Corporations Act*. Thus, it can be argued that Chinese Wall structures within corporations in the securities industry are less likely to suffer from the same problems as those within law firms.

Although there are certain basic characteristics which would generally need to be present in order for a Chinese Wall to be regarded as sufficient to provide a defence against a claim of insider trading, there is an absence of a clear objective measure against which such sufficiency can be measured. This does create an inherent lack of certainty in connection with the Chinese Wall defence.

Since insider trading is prohibited in Australia in order to protect market integrity, the available exceptions and defences to the prohibition should also be grounded in the same rationale. The principles of market fairness, market efficiency and maintenance of investor confidence are fundamental pillars of the legislation, pursuant to which the securities markets are intended to operate 'freely and fairly, with all participants having equal access to relevant information'.[77] While Chinese Walls themselves may not always prevent insider trading, the presence of such a mechanism should nevertheless provide a degree of security, as their existence can serve to reassure market participants that all parties are

---

76 Roman Tomasic, 'Insider Trading Law Reform in Australia' (1991) 9 *Company and Securities Law Journal* 121, 134.
77 Standing Committee on Legal and Constitutional Affairs, House of Representatives, *Fair Shares for All: Insider Trading in Australia* (Australian Government Publishing Service, Canberra, 1989) 3.34–3.36.

'playing by the same rules'.[78] However, in order for market participants, investors, regulators and the corporations that maintain Chinese Walls to have confidence that those walls are both likely to prevent confidential information from being communicated and that they can be relied upon as a potential defence to a claim of insider trading, there must be a clear understanding by all parties as to the basic requirements that will generally be necessary for these arrangements to be considered sufficient.

### *The inside information was not communicated and no advice was given*

Section 1043F(c) of the *Corporations Act* requires that the relevant inside information must not have been communicated to the person or persons who made the decision to enter a transaction or agreement – that is, to the person who made the decision to trade in certain financial products – and that no advice relating to the transaction or agreement was given to them by a person in possession of inside information.

In *ASIC v Citigroup*, when determining whether any inside information was communicated or 'advice given with regard to the transaction', the Court recognised that the communications which took place between the Investment Banking Division executives and the proprietary trader's manager did 'reveal the potential fragility of Chinese Walls'.[79] However, those particular discussions, because of their equivocal nature, did not amount to the communication of any inside information or advice, primarily because the proprietary trader's manager was 'astute to ensure that confidential information should remain quarantined',[80] but the Court did note that, due to the pressured nature of the investment banking environment, such a result might not always prevail.[81]

It is widely recognised that there is a risk that Chinese Walls are not effective at preventing the transfer of information and that they can be porous or 'leak'.[82] Anecdotal evidence suggests that many who work within the securities industry may doubt the effectiveness of Chinese Walls. Indeed, Tomasic quotes market participants who have such a view, with one stating that 'I've never seen a Chinese Wall without a grapevine growing over it'.[83] In *ASIC v Citigroup*, Jacobson J noted the 'practical impossibility of ensuring that every conceivable risk is

---

78  Raymond Gozzi, 'The Chinese Wall Metaphor' (2003) 60 *ETC: A Review of General Semantics* 171; Goldwasser, above n 7, 249.

79  *ASIC v Citigroup Global Markets Australia Pty Ltd* (2007) 160 FCR 35, 104.

80  Ibid.

81  Ibid.

82  See, for example, Philip Anisman, *Insider Trading Legislation for Australia: An Outline of the Issues and Alternatives* (National Companies and Securities Commission, Australian Government Publishing Service, Canberra, 1986) 85–86.

83  Tomasic, above n 19, 79.

covered by written procedures and followed by employees',[84] and in *Asia Pacific Communications Limited v Optus Networks Pty Limited*, Bergin J stated that 'there will always be an element of some risk of disclosure where its prevention depends upon human contact because people make mistakes'.[85] It is also recognised that Chinese Walls are more difficult to utilise within small corporations,[86] so that there may then be an increased risk of disclosure.[87]

This element of the Chinese Wall defence requires a consideration as to whether advice was given to a person who made a decision to trade in financial products ('the decision-maker') by a person who was in possession of inside information ('the insider') rather than merely whether the insider communicated the inside information to the decision-maker. This is necessary to ensure that the insider does not indicate, either expressly or impliedly, to the decision-maker matters that might influence their decision to trade, even if they do not actually pass on the inside information. Such matters might include a suggestion or intimation that the trade is a 'good idea' (or a 'bad idea') or that it might be better to wait to conduct the trading at a future time. In such circumstances, the Chinese Wall defence would be unlikely to apply. This would be the case regardless of whether the decision-maker was aware that the insider possessed inside information. This is an appropriate restriction as, for market integrity to be protected and maintained, those who possess inside information must not be able to benefit from it at the expense of other investors and participants in the market. If those who make decisions to trade in securities on behalf of corporations are able to do so with the advice of those who possess inside information, the corporation does receive an unfair advantage and should be unable to avoid any resulting liability for insider trading. This principle is reflected in the proposals for reform described in this chapter and set out in full in chapter 8.

### International comparisons

Several jurisdictions specifically provide for a Chinese Wall defence under statute: the United Kingdom, New Zealand, Hong Kong, Singapore and the United States. However, a number of jurisdictions have no specific provision for a Chinese Wall defence for insider trading: the European Union and Germany.

In Germany, the *Securities Trading Act (WpHG)* does not specifically provide for a Chinese Wall defence to insider trading. However, it seems that it is still

---

84 *ASIC v Citigroup Global Markets Australia Pty Ltd* (2007) 160 FCR 35, 112.
85 *Asia Pacific Communications Limited v Optus Networks Pty Limited* [2007] NSW SC 350, [14].
86 Goldwasser, above n 7, 237.
87 B E Brown and C M Herringes, 'Dovetailing the "Chinese Wall" Defence Within the Rules of Professional Conduct – Washington Should Finish What It Has Started' (1990/91) 26 *Gonzaga Law Review* 569, 583.

common practice for merchant banks in Germany to utilise Chinese Walls to quarantine information.[88] There is no specific Chinese Wall defence[89] provided for in the Market Abuse Directive[90] or the Market Abuse Regulation[91] of the European Union.[92] In the absence of any guidance in the Market Abuse Directive, or related legislative instruments, the availability of a Chinese Wall defence for insider trading will depend on the content of local laws of each Member State

88 See, for example, Alfred Lehar and Otto Randl, 'Chinese Walls in German Banks' (2006) 10 *Review of Finance* 301. Indeed, Part 6 of the *Securities Trading Act (WpHG)* provides for the 'Rules of Conduct for Investment Enterprises' which include obligations on organisations providing 'investment services' to: endeavour to avoid conflicts of interest (s 31(1)2); be organised in such a way that, in the provision of investment services, conflicts of interest are kept to an unavoidable minimum (s 33(1)2); and have adequate internal control procedures capable of countering infringements (s 33(1)3). While these provisions are not specifically related to the prohibition of insider trading, and there is no specific reference to Chinese Walls, these obligations indicate that merchant banks have the option to determine their own methods for managing conflicts of interest, which could include the use of information barriers such as Chinese Walls: European Commission, 'Best Practices in an Integrated European Financial Market – Recommendations from the Forum Group to the European Commission Services', Annexure 3 (2003) 21.

89 In the superseded *Directive 2003/6/EC of the European Parliament and of the Council of 28 January 2003 on Insider Dealing and Market Abuse*, OJ 2003 1 96/16, Chinese Walls were referred to in recital (24) as a measure to 'contribute to market integrity', and there was an obligation in Article 6(6) to ensure that 'market operators adopt structural provisions aimed at preventing and detecting market manipulation practices'. However, such provisions have not been incorporated into the current Market Abuse Directive or Market Abuse Regulation, and no reason has been proffered for the removal of these provisions.

90 *Directive 2014/57/EU of the European Parliament and of the Council of 16 April 2014 on Criminal Sanctions for Market Abuse*, OJ 2014 L 173.179.

91 *Regulation (EU) 596/2014 of the European Parliament and of the Council of 16 April 2014 on Market Abuse.*

92 *Directive 2004/39/EC of the European Parliament and of the Council of 21 April 2004 on Markets in Financial Instruments*, OJ 2004 L 145 (the Markets in Financial Instruments Directive) does set out, amongst other things, organisational requirements for 'investments firms'. It provides, in Article 13(3), that 'an investment firm must maintain and operate effective organisational and administrative arrangements with a view to taking all reasonable steps designed to prevent conflicts of interest . . . from adversely affecting the interests of its clients'. While not explicitly referred to, information barriers such as Chinese Walls could certainly form part of such arrangements. However, the Markets in Financial Instruments Directive primarily requires such arrangements for the protection of clients, rather than to protect the market generally or to prevent market abuse such as insider trading, as evidenced by the recitals to this Directive. It is also clear that the use of arrangements such as Chinese Walls is considered necessary under applicable codes of conduct. For example, the *Market Conduct Standards* developed by the Forum of European Securities Commissions require participants in an offering to have Chinese Walls in place to restrict the flow of information between business areas to prevent the misuse of material information: The Forum of European Securities Commissions, 'Market Conduct Standards' 99-FESCO-B (1999) 14–18.

of the European Union, which does give rise to the potential for inconsistent positions in the different Member States.

In those jurisdictions which do specifically provide for a statutory Chinese Wall defence to insider trading, there are certain similarities with the Australian position but, as is shown below, there are two primary differences – not all jurisdictions require that the relevant Chinese Wall arrangements must be 'reasonably expected to ensure' that inside information is not communicated, and not all jurisdictions expressly provide that, for the defence to apply, advice must not be given by a person in possession of inside information to a person making the relevant decision to trade. Unlike Australia, some jurisdictions also apply the Chinese Wall defence to the procuring of trading, as well as trading, in relevant financial products.

In the United Kingdom, which applies civil liability for insider trading to corporations under the *Financial Services and Markets Act 2000* (UK) c 8, there is no specific provision for a Chinese Wall defence in that Act. However, s 147 gives the Financial Conduct Authority (formerly the Financial Services Authority) the power to make rules about the disclosure and use of information,[93] and it does so in the *Financial Conduct Authority Handbook*, which provides in SYSC 10.2.2R that a Chinese Wall is:

> an arrangement that requires information held by a person, in the course of carrying on one part of the business, to be withheld from, or not to be used for, persons with or for whom it acts in the course of carrying on another part of its business.[94]

SYSC 10.2.3R of the *Financial Conduct Authority Handbook* then provides that acting in conformity with SYSC 10.2.2R does not amount to market abuse, thereby providing a defence to a civil action against a corporation for insider trading. Additionally, SYSC 10.2.4R of the *Financial Conduct Authority Handbook* specifically provides that where an organisation has in place such arrangements, it 'will not be taken to act with knowledge . . . if none of the relevant individuals involved on behalf of the firm acts with that knowledge'. SYSC 10.2.5R of the *Financial Conduct Authority Handbook* then provides that 'Individuals on the other side of the wall will not be regarded as being in possession of knowledge denied to them as a result of [a] Chinese Wall.'

Unlike the Australian Chinese Wall defence, the Chinese Wall defence available in the United Kingdom does not require that the relevant arrangements be 'reasonably expected to ensure' that the relevant inside information was not communicated. Additionally, there is no express requirement in the United Kingdom

---

93 Known as 'control of information rules': *Financial Services and Market Act 2000* (UK), s 147.
94 SYSC 10.2.2R is specifically stated to be a 'control of information rule' made under s 147 of the *Financial Services and Markets Act* (UK) c 8.

that no advice be given by a person in possession of the inside information to the person making the decision to trade.

As noted earlier, the use of Chinese Walls as a defence to insider trading claims made against corporations first occurred in the United States. This defence is now contained in statutory form in SEC Rule 10b5–1(c)(2) made pursuant to the *Securities Exchange Act of 1934*, 15 USC § 78a (1934) and it provides that:

> A person other than a natural person also may demonstrate that a purchase or sale of securities is not 'on the basis of' material nonpublic information if the person demonstrates that:
>
> (i)　The individual making the investment decision on behalf of the person to purchase or sell the securities was not aware of the information; and
> (ii)　The person had implemented reasonable policies and procedures, taking into consideration the nature of the person's business, to ensure that individuals making investment decisions would not violate the laws prohibiting trading on the basis of material nonpublic information. These policies and procedures may include those that restrict any purchase, sale, and causing any purchase or sale of any security as to which the person has material nonpublic information, or those that prevent such individuals from becoming aware of such information.

While this defence is similar in substance to the Australian Chinese Wall defence found in s 1043F of the *Corporations Act*, it does not require that the relevant arrangements be 'reasonably expected to ensure' that inside information was not communicated, instead mandating that the corporation must have 'implemented reasonable policies and procedures . . . to ensure that' the prohibition of insider trading is not violated, and there is no express requirement that advice not be given by a person in possession of the inside information to the person making the decision to trade in relevant financial products.

In New Zealand, a Chinese Wall defence is contained in s 261 of the *Financial Markets Conduct Act 2013* (NZ), which is in very similar terms to the Australian Chinese Wall defence. It provides that it is a defence to any proceedings for insider trading if:

(a)　A [the relevant corporation] had in place arrangements that could reasonably be expected to ensure that no individual who took part in the decision to trade the financial products or to advise or encourage (as the case may be) received or had access to, the inside information or was influenced, in relation to that decision, by an individual who had the information; and
(b)　no individual who took part in the decision received, or had access to, the inside information, or was influenced, in relation to that decision, by an individual who had the information; and

(c) every individual who had the information and every individual who took part in that decision acted in accordance with the arrangements referred to in paragraph (a).

The Chinese Wall defence in New Zealand expressly covers both trading and the procuring of trading – being 'advising or encouraging'. As in Australia, the arrangements must be 'reasonably expected to ensure' that the relevant inside information is not communicated and while there is no prohibition of the 'giving of advice' by a person in possession of inside information, such persons must not 'influence' any individual making a trading decision.

In Hong Kong, s 271(2) of the *Securities and Futures Ordinance* (Hong Kong) cap 571 provides for a Chinese Wall defence for corporations – it is also very similar to that contained in s 1043F of the *Corporations Act*. It provides that a corporation shall not be regarded as having engaged in insider dealing if it establishes that:

(a) although one or more of its directors or employees had the inside information in relation to the corporation the listed securities of which were, or the derivatives of the listed securities of which were, the listed securities or derivatives in question, each person who took the decision for it to deal in or counsel or procure the other person to deal in such listed securities or derivatives (as the case may be) did not have the inside information up to (and including) the time when it dealt in or counseled or procured the other person to deal in such listed securities or derivatives (as the case may be);

(b) arrangements then existed to secure that –

(i) the inside information was up to (and including) the time when it dealt in or counseled or procured the other person to deal in listed securities or derivatives (as the case may be), not communicated to any person who took the decision; and

(ii) none of its directors or employees who had the inside information gave advice concerning the decision to any person who took the decision at any time before it dealt in counseled or procured the other person to deal in such listed securities or derivatives (as the case may be); and

(c) the inside information was in fact not so communicated to any person who took the decision and none of its directors or employees who had the inside information in fact so gave advice to any person who took the decision.

Rather than being 'reasonably expected to ensure' that inside information was not communicated, the laws of Hong Kong require instead that 'arrangements then existed to secure that' inside information was not communicated. There is an express prohibition of the giving of advice by a person in possession of inside information and this Chinese Wall defence does apply to both trading and the procuring of trading.

In Singapore, s 226(2) of the *Securities and Futures Act 2001* sets out a Chinese Wall defence, in almost identical terms to that contained in s 1043F of the *Corporations Act*. It provides that a corporation does not contravene the prohibition of insider trading in s 218(2) of the Act (which prohibits both trading and the procuring of trading) by entering into a transaction or agreement at any time merely because of information in the possession of an officer of the corporation if:

(a) the decision to enter into the transaction or agreement was taken on its behalf by a person other than that officer;
(b) it had in operation at that time arrangements that could reasonably be expected to ensure that the information was not communicated to the person who made the decision and that no advice with respect to the transaction or agreement was given to that person by a person in possession of the information; and
(c) the information was not so communicated and no such advice was so given.

This defence does require that the arrangements be 'reasonably expected to ensure' that inside information was not communicated and there is an express prohibition of the giving of advice by a person in possession of inside information to the person making the relevant trading decision. However, unlike the position in Australia, the Chinese Wall defence in Singapore expressly applies to both trading and the procuring of trading in relevant financial products.

Thus it can be seen that some jurisdictions have no statutory Chinese Wall defence for insider trading – such as Germany and the European Union – and in those jurisdictions in which there is a statutory Chinese Wall defence, it is generally similar to the Australian Chinese Wall defence, but with a few significant points of departure. The Chinese Wall defences available in the United Kingdom and the United States do not require that the relevant arrangements be 'reasonably expected to ensure' that inside information is not communicated, focusing instead upon whether the information is actually communicated to those who make trading decisions, whereas in Hong Kong the arrangements must exist to 'secure' that inside information is not communicated. In the United Kingdom and the United States, the inside information must not be communicated to a person making a trading decision but there is no express requirement that no advice be given by a person in possession of inside information, whereas such a prohibition of the giving of advice or exerting 'influence' applies in New Zealand, Hong Kong and Singapore. The Chinese Wall defence also specifically applies to the procuring of trading as well as trading in New Zealand, Hong Kong and Singapore.

Looking at the differences between the positions adopted in these jurisdictions in relation to the Chinese Wall defence to insider trading, the only point of difference with Australian law which is recommended for adoption, is to extend the operation of the Chinese Wall defence to the procuring of trading in relevant financial products as well as trading. As noted earlier, s 1043F of the *Corporations Act* only extends the Chinese Wall defence to the trading limb of insider trading and not the procuring limb, since it only applies where 'the decision to enter' a transaction or agreement (being the decision to trade in relevant financial products) was taken 'on [a corporation's] behalf' by a person other than a person in possession of the inside information. As has previously been recommended by CAMAC[95] and accepted by the Commonwealth Treasury,[96] without a sound basis for excluding the procuring of trading from the operation of the Chinese Wall defence, it is proposed, along with other amendments to the Chinese Wall defence, to also extend it to the procuring of trading.

It is not recommended that the next point of difference be adopted – the absence of a requirement that the Chinese Wall arrangements be 'reasonably expected to ensure' that information is not communicated. The existence of such a requirement is more likely to lead to corporations maintaining appropriate arrangements at all times, thereby limiting opportunities for insider trading to occur within the corporation, which might not exist if corporations merely had to prove that a particular person did not possess inside information at a certain point in time. If opportunities for insider trading within corporations are limited, there is less likely to be any impact on market integrity, which is consistent with the rationale for the prohibition of insider trading in Australia.

The absence of an express requirement in some jurisdictions for there to be no advice given to persons making trading decisions by those who possess inside information is also not a position that is recommended for adoption in Australia. If this were to occur, advice about a transaction could be given without the need to actually communicate the relevant inside information to those making trading decisions. As noted earlier, it is appropriate to restrict the giving of advice by persons in possession of inside information as, if those who make decisions to trade in securities on behalf of corporations are able to do so with the advice of those who possess inside information, the corporation receives an unfair advantage and thus should be subject to possible liability for insider trading. To allow otherwise would enable those within corporations to circumvent the operation of the prohibition of insider trading in a manner inconsistent with the need to maintain and protect market integrity.

## Preliminary conclusions and recommended reforms

As a potential defence to a claim of insider trading against a corporation, the greatest limitation of the Chinese Wall defence is the absence of certainty. There is a lack of clarity as to the requirements for a sufficient Chinese Wall, as the only real guidance is contained in fairly general judicial comments supplemented by regulatory guidelines and market practice principles. As a result, there is a lack of certainty as to whether insider trading is actually occurring and whether corporations are exposed to liability for insider trading. This uncertainty is compounded

---

95  CAMAC, *Insider Trading Report*, above n 7, 2 and 7.
96  Commonwealth Treasury, *Insider Trading Position and Consultation Paper*, above n 32, 5.

by the application of the differing general law and statutory mechanisms which can be used to determine when a corporation engages in certain conduct, possesses information and has relevant knowledge. In its current form, the Chinese Wall defence is not available where information is possessed by an agent who is not also an officer or employee of the corporation. Additionally, the defence applies only where the corporation itself engages in trading, and not where it procures trading, although there is no logical explanation for this gap in its application. In order to respond to the limitations and uncertainty in the application of the Chinese Wall defence, legislative reform is clearly needed. The interests of market integrity are not served by statutory exceptions and defences which are unclear, imprecise and uncertain, and which may operate in limited but vague circumstances.

The reforms that are recommended in this book would remedy the difficulties identified in this chapter. As has been noted, it is proposed that the operation of the general law be expressly excluded from the statutory regime applying insider trading laws to corporations, and that a new set of provisions be adopted to provide for a model of direct liability as the exclusive means for determining when a corporation possesses inside information, has knowledge that the information is inside information and engages in the necessary trading conduct in relation to relevant financial products, and an amended version of the Chinese Wall defence for corporations would be incorporated into the *Corporations Act*.

The proposed reforms would specifically provide that the only means by which a body corporate would be liable for the insider trading prohibitions in s 1043A are those set out in what would be a new s 1042G of the *Corporations Act*, to be entitled 'Liability of Bodies Corporate'. As well as excluding the operation of the general law, and the operation of s 769B of the *Corporations Act* and Part 2.5 of the *Criminal Code*, a new s 1042G would specifically provide that a corporation would only be regarded as having engaged in insider trading if the person who possessed the information also had the requisite knowledge that it was inside information and engaged in or authorised the prohibited trading conduct within the actual or apparent scope of their authority, or received advice from a person in possession of inside information. However, there should be no liability for insider trading where a person who possesses inside information engages in the trading conduct if another person who did not possess the inside information was the person who made the decision that the trading should occur, so long as a person possessing the inside information did not pass on that information or give advice about the transaction. The new provisions would apply where an officer, employee or agent of a corporation possesses information, has the requisite knowledge and engages in the trading conduct on behalf of a corporation. Accordingly, the amended Chinese Wall defence would extend to agents, as well as to officers and employees, and would be a defence to all the forms of the prohibited conduct, not just trading in relevant financial products.

# 7 Insider trading and business obligations

While corporations are clearly caught by the prohibition of insider trading, there are a variety of additional business obligations which supplement the operation of insider trading laws. These additional obligations exist to ensure that relevant information is appropriately and efficiently disclosed to the market through a continuous disclosure regime; to minimise opportunities for insider trading through securities trading policies of public listed corporations; to ensure trading by insiders can be monitored through requirements for the notification of trading by directors of public listed corporations; and to require certain market participants to notify ASIC of suspected insider trading. In this context, the overlap between directors' duties and insider trading laws is also relevant.

## Continuous disclosure regime

As discussed in Chapters 2 and 5, continuous disclosure obligations exist under the ASX Listing Rules, which require listed public corporations to immediately notify the ASX:

> once an entity is or becomes aware of any information concerning it that a reasonable person would expect to have a material impact on the price or value of the entity's securities.[1]

The continuous disclosure regime operates to reduce opportunities for insider trading, by compelling corporations to disclose information that may materially influence the price or value of its securities, thus making that information 'generally available'. There is judicial recognition that the purpose of the continuous disclosure regime is to:

> enhance the integrity and efficiency of the Australian capital markets by ensuring that the market is fully informed. The timely disclosure of market

---

1   ASX, Listing Rules, LR 3.1.

sensitive information is essential to maintaining and increasing the confidence of investors in Australian markets, and to improving the accountability of company management. It is also integral to minimizing incidences of insider trading and other market distortions.[2]

Importantly, if corporations disclose information promptly to the market, there is less opportunity for insiders to trade on that information before it becomes publicly available. Thus, there is an interrelationship between the continuous disclosure regime and the prohibition of insider trading, and many of the relevant provisions are extremely similar.

Examples of the types of information which might require disclosure under the ASX Listing Rules include:

- a transaction that will lead to a significant change in the nature or scale of the entity's activities;
- a material mineral or hydrocarbon discovery;
- a material acquisition or disposal;
- the granting or withdrawal of a material licence;
- the entry into, variation or termination of a material agreement;
- becoming a plaintiff or defendant in a material law suit;
- the fact that the entity's earnings will be materially different from market expectations;
- the appointment of a liquidator, administrator or receiver;
- the commission of an event of default under, or other event entitling a financier to terminate, a material financing facility;
- undersubscriptions or oversubscriptions to an issue of securities;
- giving or receiving a notice of intention to make a takeover; and
- any rating applied by a rating agency to an entity or its securities and any change to such a rating.[3]

However, information does not need to be disclosed to the ASX if the exception in Listing Rule 3.1A applies, which is available where:

i    One or more of the following five situations apply:

- It would be a breach of a law to disclose the information;
- The information concerns an incomplete proposal or negotiation;
- The information comprises matters of supposition or is insufficiently definite to warrant disclosure;

---

2   *James Hardie Industries NV v ASIC* [2010] NSWSC 332 at [355], as noted by the ASX in ASX, Listing Rules, *Guidance Note 8, Continuous Disclosure: Listing Rules 3.1–3.1B*, 2018, 6.
3   ASX, Listing Rules, *Guidance Note 8, Continuous Disclosure: Listing Rules 3.1–3.1B*, 2018, 8.

- The information is generated for the internal management purposes of the entity; or
- The information is a trade secret; and

ii    The information is confidential and ASX has not formed the view that the information has ceased to be confidential; and

iii    A reasonable person would not expect the information to be disclosed.

Section 674(2) of the *Corporations Act* gives statutory effect to the continuous disclosure obligations under the ASX Listing Rules, by providing, as discussed in chapter 2, that if:

(a)  this subsection applies to a listed disclosing entity;
(b)  the entity has information that those provisions require the entity to notify to the market operator; and
(c)  that information:

    (i)  is not generally available; and
    (ii)  is information that a reasonable person would expect, if it were generally available, to have a material effect on the price or value of ED securities of the entity;

the entity must notify the market operator of that information in accordance with those provisions.

As a result, s 1311 of the *Corporations Act* applies, so that a failure to comply with the obligations in s 674 is an offence, punishable by a fine of up to 200 penalty units or imprisonment for five years, or both, in the case of a natural person,[4] and a fine of up to 1,000 penalty units for a body corporate.[5] As s 674 is also a civil penalty provision under s 1317E of the *Corporations Act*, civil penalty proceedings may be brought as an alternative to criminal proceedings, as is the case for insider trading, with a maximum fine of $200,000 for a natural person and $1,000,000 for a body corporate.[6]

As noted earlier in chapter 5, an entity is considered to be 'aware' of information concerning it:

> if, and as soon as, an officer of the entity . . . has, or ought reasonably to have, come into possession of the information in the course of the performance of their duties as an officer of that entity.[7]

---

4    *Corporations Act*, schedule 3, item 229A. As noted earlier, a fine of 200 penalty units amounts to $42,000, as a penalty unit currently amounts to $210: *Crimes Act 1914* (Cth), s 4AA.
5    *Corporations Act*, s 1312. A fine of 1,000 penalty units currently amounts to $210,000.
6    *Corporations Act*, s 1317G.
7    ASX, Listing Rules, Chapter 19.

This differs from the position relating to the possession of 'inside information' by corporations under s 1042G of the *Corporations Act*, as well as other mechanisms that might be used to attribute the possession of information to a corporation, where actual awareness of the relevant information will be required, not just information that a person 'ought reasonably to know'.

The continuous disclosure obligations under the ASX Listing Rules apply regardless of whether or not the relevant information is 'generally available', although there will be no breach of s 674 of the *Corporations Act* if the information has already become generally available. However, the test as to whether or not information is 'generally available' is the same as that which applies to 'inside information' under s 1042C of the *Corporations Act*. Similarly, the test for the 'materiality' of the relevant information is almost identical to that for 'inside information' under s 1042D of the *Corporations Act*.[8]

## Securities trading policies

Public listed corporations are required to adopt securities trading policies which regulate trading in the corporation's securities by key management personnel, pursuant to ASX Listing Rule 12.9. ASX Listing Rule 12.12 sets out the minimum requirements for these securities trading policies, which must provide for:

(i)   The corporation's closed periods.[9]
(ii)  The trading restrictions that apply to the corporation's key management personnel.[10]
(iii) Any trading which is not subject to the corporation's securities trading policy.
(iv)  Any exceptional circumstances which may permit the corporation's key management personnel to trade during a prohibited period[11] with prior written clearance.
(v)   The procedures for obtaining prior written clearance to trade during a prohibited period.

---

8  Robert P Austin and Ian M Ramsay, *Ford's Principles of Corporations Law* (LexisNexis Butterworths, Sydney, 2018) 11.300.3.
9  Closed periods are fixed periods when key management personnel are prohibited from trading in the entity's securities: ASX, Listing Rules, LR 19.12.
10 ASX Listing Rule 19.12 uses the definition of 'key management personnel' in *AASB 124 Related Party Disclosure*, which provides that 'Key management personnel are those persons having authority and responsibility for planning, directing and controlling the activities of the entity, directly or indirectly, including any director (whether executive or otherwise) of that entity': Australian Accounting Standards Board, *AASB 124 Related Party Disclosure*, 2015.
11 A prohibited period is defined to mean:

i.  any closed period; or
ii. additional periods when an entity's key management personnel are prohibited from trading, which are imposed by the entity from time to time when the company is considering matters which are subject to Listing Rule 3.1A: ASX, Listing Rules, LR 19.12.

While it is generally considered to be desirable for key management personnel of listed corporations – such as directors, executives and senior employees – to hold shares or other securities in those corporations in order that their interests are aligned with those of the corporation's shareholders, they will often have access to inside information as a result of their position. Accordingly, any perception that key management personnel may have engaged in insider trading or otherwise dealt inappropriately with confidential information not available to other shareholders may have a significant impact on their own reputation, the corporation's standing with investors and the integrity of the ASX.[12] Thus the regulation of trading by key management personnel under securities trading policies operates for the dual purposes of reducing the likelihood of insider trading and reducing market perceptions that those who might be considered to be true insiders are able to unfairly benefit from inside information, at times when inside information is most likely to be available to them.

While a corporation's securities trading policy must specify the times of the year which are closed periods, during which trading in the corporation's securities by key management personnel is generally prohibited, a corporation is free to choose whether to use 'black-out periods' or 'trading windows'.[13] Where black-out periods are used, trading in the corporation's securities is not restricted, other than during the specified black-out periods. Where trading windows are used, trading in the corporation's securities is prohibited at all times, other than during the specified trading windows. Regardless of which type of closed periods are utilised by corporations, the ASX has indicated that it expects trading in the corporation's securities to be prohibited, at a minimum, from the close of the corporation's books at half-year and full-year until the release of the corporation's half-year and full-year results.[14]

Importantly, trading in the corporation's securities is not permitted if a person possesses inside information, even during a period which is not a 'closed period' under the securities trading policy. Similarly, the application of a securities trading policy does not operate as a defence to conduct that would otherwise breach the prohibition of insider trading.

## Insider trading notifications

There is no general obligation to notify a regulator or enforcement agency of suspected insider trading. However, market participants [15] have an obliga-

---

12 ASX, Listing Rules, *Guidance Note 27, Trading Policies*, 2017, 3–4.
13 Ibid 7.
14 Ibid 8.
15 A 'Participant' in a 'Market' is defined in rule 1.4.3 of the ASIC, Market Integrity Rules (Securities Markets) 2017 as 'a person who is allowed to directly participate in the Market under the Operating Rules of the Market'. Market Participants generally include trading participants, clearing participants and settlement participants.

tion to notify ASIC of certain suspicious trading activities.[16] In particular, rule 5.11.1(1)(a) provides that if a market participant has reasonable grounds to suspect that a person has entered into a transaction on a market while in possession of inside information, the market participant must notify ASIC in writing as soon as practicable. The market participant is obliged to provide ASIC with the details of the transaction and the reasons for its suspicion. The market participant is then prohibited from disclosing both the fact that it is made a notification of suspicious trading, and the information contained in the notification, other than for the purpose of obtaining legal advice, or as required by law.[17] The maximum penalty for failing to comply with these obligations is a fine of $20,000.[18]

The obligation placed on the market participant is only to report the suspicious trading activity and the details known to it, not to investigate the suspicious trading activity or to put in place mechanisms to detect it.[19] The reporting should occur as soon as possible but certainly within three business days of determining that a report should be made.[20] ASIC has also indicated that it expects market participants to have a 'clear, well-understood and documented process' in place for complying with this obligation, which should include:

(a) identifying indicators of reportable matters;
(b) ensuring that employees escalate potentially reportable matters to compliance staff, who are made aware of the indicators identified;
(c) determining whether indicators of reportable matters give rise to an obligation to report; and
(d) notifying ASIC in writing of reportable matters.[21]

## Notification of directors' securities trading

A corporation listed on the ASX must notify the exchange of any change to a director's interests in its securities within five business days of the change occurring.[22] The corporation is responsible for making and enforcing any necessary arrangements with its directors to ensure that it is able to comply with this

---

16 This obligation arises under Part 5.11 of the ASIC, Market Integrity Rules (Securities Markets) 2017.
17 ASIC, Market Integrity Rules (Securities Markets) 2017, rule 5.11.2.
18 ASIC, Market Integrity Rules (Securities Markets) 2017, rules 5.11.1 and 5.11.2.
19 ASIC, *Regulatory Guide 265, Guidance on ASIC Market Integrity Rules for Participants of Securities Markets*, 2018, RG 265.245.
20 ASIC, *Regulatory Guide 265, Guidance on ASIC Market Integrity Rules for Participants of Securities Markets*, 2018, RG 265.286.
21 ASIC, *Regulatory Guide 265, Guidance on ASIC Market Integrity Rules for Participants of Securities Markets*, 2018, RG 265.271.
22 ASX, Listing Rules, LR 3.19A.2. Appendix 3Y to the Listing Rules is to be used to make the notification.

obligation.[23] Additionally, a director of an Australian listed corporation must notify the relevant exchange of any change to their interests in the corporation's securities within 14 business days.[24] It is an offence of strict liability for a director to breach this obligation,[25] which means that there is no 'fault element' or mens rea for the offence.[26] However, if the corporation has already notified the ASX as required under Listing Rule 3.19A.2, the director need not make an additional notification.[27] These obligations clearly apply to the sale or purchase of any securities in the relevant public corporation. While these provisions are aimed at ensuring that the market is generally aware of trading by directors of listed corporations, they also enable consideration to be given as to whether directors are trading are at appropriate times and whether there should be any suspicion that there has been insider trading by directors – particularly as the corporation is obliged by the ASX Listing Rules to state whether the trading occurred during a 'closed period' under the corporation's securities trading policy and whether any prior written clearance was necessary or obtained.[28]

## Directors' duties and conflicts of interest

There is an overlap between the statutory and general law fiduciary obligations placed on directors to avoid conflicts of interest, and the prohibition of insider trading. At general law, directors have an obligation to avoid conflicts of interest,[29] including those which result from the use of confidential information belonging to the corporation.[30] Under the *Corporations Act*, s 183(1) provides that:

> A person who obtains information because they are, or have been, a director or other officer or employee of a corporation must not improperly use the information to:
>
> (a) gain an advantage for themselves or someone else;
> (b) cause detriment to the corporation.

Dishonest use of the information can also amount to a criminal breach of the duty under s 184(3) of the *Corporations Act*.

---

23  ASX, Listing Rules, LR 3.19A.3. A suggested pro forma agreement is contained in ASX, Listing Rules, *Guidance Note 22, Director Disclosure of Interests and Transactions in Securities – Obligations of Listed Entities*, 2002.
24  *Corporations Act*, s 205G(4).
25  *Corporations Act*, s 205G(9).
26  *Criminal Code*, s 6.1.
27  ASIC, *Regulatory Guide 193*, '*Notification of Directors' Interests in Securities – Listed Companies*', 2008, RG 193.8.
28  ASX, Listing Rules, LR 3.19.A.2
29  See, for example, *Aberdeen Railway v Blaikie* (1854) 1 Macl 461; *Phipps v Boardman* [1967] 2 AC 46.
30  See, for example, *Artedomus v Del Casale* [2006] NSWSC 146.

Clearly, if a director obtains inside information as a result of their position within a corporation, and they trade on that information in order to make a profit or avoid a loss, as well as having potential liability for insider trading, the director may also breach the duties imposed on directors to avoid a conflict of interest and not to improperly use information acquired from their position. The relevance of directors' duties in a trading context was highlighted in the case of *ASIC v Vizard*,[31] in which a non-executive director of Telstra Corporation Ltd admitted liability for breaches of s 183(1) of the *Corporations Act* in civil penalty proceedings. It appeared that the director had access to information about Telstra's proposed investments in certain technology companies and that shares in those technology companies were then purchased through investment vehicles controlled by the director's accountant. While it has been suggested that this could potentially have amounted to insider trading, the Commonwealth Department of Public Prosecutions indicated that it had declined to bring a prosecution due to insufficient evidence of criminality.[32] The relevant conduct took place prior to the introduction of civil penalty proceedings for insider trading, so such proceedings would not have been available to consider as a potential alternative, and ASIC elected to bring civil penalty proceedings for a breach of directors' duties.

## Concluding comments on business obligations

In addition to complying with the prohibition of insider trading, which may necessitate the maintenance of an appropriate 'Chinese Wall', it can be seen that many corporations have a variety of complementary business obligations which must be met. Listed public corporations must ensure that information is appropriately and efficiently disclosed through a continuous disclosure regime, that a securities trading policy is adopted and complied with and that trading by directors is notified to the exchange. Market participants must also notify ASIC of any suspected insider trading. The potential liability of directors for breaches of directors' duties does not of itself directly impact on the criminal or civil liability of a corporation for an offence. However, due to the overlap between individual and corporate liability, and the fact that the rules of attribution may operate to impute the fault elements and physical elements of an offence to the corporation as a result of the knowledge and intentions of directors and others, directors must clearly be mindful of the corporation's position when considering their own actions and, in particular, when dealing with confidential information which might also amount to 'inside information'.

---

31  *ASIC v Vizard* [2005] FCA 1037. Mr Vizard was ordered to pay pecuniary penalties totalling $390,000, to pay ASIC's costs, and was disqualified from managing a corporation for a period of ten years pursuant to s 206G of the *Corporations Act*.
32  Ian Ramsay, 'Steve Vizard, Insider Trading and Directors' Duties', University of Melbourne Centre for Corporate Law and Securities Regulation, Research Reports and Research Papers (2005), available at https://law.unimelb.edu.au/centres/cclsr/research/research-reports-and-research-papers.

# 8 Corporate liability for insider trading

## Reform proposals

In this book, the current system of the regulation of insider trading in Australia, including the rationale for the prohibition of insider trading, has been reviewed, with a thorough consideration of the relevant principles of corporate liability, and the application of insider trading laws to corporations. The manner in which the elements of insider trading are attributed to corporations has been evaluated in detail, as well as the availability of the Chinese Wall defence for corporations, and the resulting difficulties and problems have been carefully analysed. This chapter sets out in full the resulting recommendations and proposals for the reform of Australian insider trading laws.

Throughout this book, it has been demonstrated that Australia's current insider trading laws are significantly flawed due to the uncertainty of their application to corporations which arises in a number of ways – there is uncertainty as to which mechanisms, statutory and general law, are to be applied to determine when corporations possess information, have knowledge and engage in the relevant conduct; the potential availability of several different attribution mechanisms applying a variety of tests results in significant uncertainty as to when the elements of insider trading will be satisfied in relation to corporations; and there is also uncertainty in the manner and extent of the application of the Chinese Wall defence for corporations. Since insider trading laws are intended to maintain and protect market integrity, which clearly requires certainty in the application of insider trading laws to corporations, the law should be reformed in order to give better effect to this aim.

As a result of the identified flaws in the current system of regulation, three key reforms to Australian insider trading laws are proposed: that the operation of the general law be expressly excluded from the statutory regime applying insider trading laws to corporations; that a revised set of provisions be adopted to provide for a new model of direct liability as the exclusive means for determining when the elements of insider trading apply to a corporation; and that an amended version of the Chinese Wall defence for corporations be adopted. The new statutory provisions would provide greater clarity, be more consistent with the market integrity rationale for the prohibition of insider trading and offer increased certainty for all affected and interested parties as to the intended operation of the law.

In this chapter, the flaws in the current legislative regime which have been analysed and discussed in detail throughout this book are summarised. The proposed legislative amendments aimed at overcoming the identified flaws are then set out in full, followed by a detailed description of the suggested amendments to the law and the ways in which they will address the identified problems with the current regime.[1]

## Flaws in the current regime

As noted earlier, throughout this book three significant flaws in the application of Australian insider trading laws to corporations have been identified: (i) there is confusion as to which mechanisms are to be used to determine how the elements of insider trading are applied to corporations; (ii) the different mechanisms which are available to apply the elements of insider trading to corporations have conflicting and varying tests; and (iii) there are uncertainties and difficulties associated with the application of the Chinese Wall defence for corporations to insider trading.

In chapter 5, there was a discussion of the manner in which the key elements of insider trading – the possession of information, the requisite knowledge and the necessary conduct – are applied to corporations. One of the main flaws identified was the confusion as to the manner in which these elements are actually to be applied to corporations. A careful review of these elements leads to the necessary conclusion that both the statutory provisions and general law rules operate concurrently to provide a variety of mechanisms which can be used to establish that a corporation possesses inside information, has knowledge that the information is not generally available and is likely to be material and has traded or procured trading in relevant financial products, or tipped. The *Corporations Act* is silent on the application of the general law to the statutory offence of insider trading, but the operation of the general law is not excluded when determining how the insider trading laws apply to corporations. Cases interpreting other pieces of legislation which use the same or very similar provisions make it clear that the general law is not intended to be excluded and, in order to make sense of other provisions of the *Corporations Act*, it is necessary to infer that the general law is also intended to apply. However, there is widespread confusion as to whether and how this is to occur. In *ASIC v Citigroup*, Jacobson J considered only one of the potentially applicable statutory provisions of the *Corporations Act* when determining whether the information allegedly possessed by a proprietary trader acting on behalf of Citigroup was possessed by the corporation, and did not consider the potential application of the general law at all.[2] Meanwhile, some

---

1   The material addressed in this chapter is also discussed in Juliette Overland, 'Reforming Australian Insider Trading Laws: A New Model of Corporate Criminal Liability – Part 2' (2018) 33 *Australian Journal of Corporate Law* 99.

2   *ASIC v Citigroup Global Markets Australia Pty Ltd* (2007) 160 FCR 35, 99. Similarly, no other mechanisms were considered in *ASIC v Hochtief* [2016] FCA 1489.

commentators do regard the general law as relevant, but suggest that it is to be used to rebut statutory presumptions which might otherwise apply elements of the offence to a corporation.[3]

Even when considering the statutory tests alone, there is confusion as to which of those tests relate to the possession of information and which relate to the requisite knowledge. Some commentators[4] consider s 1042G(1)(b) of the *Corporations Act* to apply when attempting to determine whether a corporation had the requisite knowledge rather than the possession of information, whereas others[5] regard it as applicable to both the possession of information *and* the requisite knowledge. This uncertainty needs to be resolved.

It has been demonstrated in this book that a wide variety of mechanisms, both statutory and general law, are potentially available to apply the elements of insider trading to a corporation. As discussed in chapter 5, each of the various available statutory mechanisms applies a different set of tests – some require that, for the possession of information, knowledge or conduct of a natural person to be applied to a corporation, the natural person must be an officer of that corporation,[6] whereas others will operate in respect of any employee or agent who is able to act on the corporation's behalf.[7] Some require that there be a link or nexus with the person's role within the corporation.[8] Some require that the possession of information or knowledge must be linked to the relevant conduct,[9] while others do not.[10] Significant uncertainty is created by having many overlapping statutory mechanisms with a variety of different requirements. This uncertainty is further compounded when the general law mechanisms are also considered, as the principles of the identification doctrine require only that the relevant person who possesses the information, has the requisite knowledge and engages in the relevant conduct be the 'directing mind and will' of the corporation, with no necessary connection with their role or other elements of the offence. This gives rise to additional uncertainty as to the circumstances in which

---

3 See, for example, Charles Zhen Qu, 'How Statutory Civil Liability is Attributed to a Company: An Australian Perspective Focusing on Civil Liability for Insider Trading by Corporations' (2006) 32 *Monash Law Review* 177, 191.

4 See, for example, Gregory Lyon and Jean J du Plessis, *The Law of Insider Trading in Australia* (Federation Press, Sydney, 2005) 57; Ashley Black, 'The Reform of Insider Trading Law in Australia' (1992) 15 *University of New South Wales Law Journal* 214, 255.

5 See, for example, Robert P Austin and Ian M Ramsay, *Ford's Principles of Corporations Law* (LexisNexis Butterworths, Sydney, 2018) 9.870.21; J P Hambrook, 'Market Misconduct and Offences', in *Australian Corporations Law Principles and Practice* (LexisNexis Butterworths, Sydney, 2018) 7.13.0145.

6 See, for example, *Corporations Act*, ss 1042G(1)(b) and 1042G(1)(c).

7 See, for example, *Corporations Act*, ss 769B(1) and 769B(3).

8 See, for example, *Corporations Act*, ss 1042G(1)(b) and 1042G(1)(c); *Corporations Act*, ss 769B(3) and 769B(1).

9 See, for example, *Corporations Act*, s 769B(3).

10 See, for example, *Corporations Act*, ss 1042G(1)(b), 1042G(1)(c) and 769B(1).

the elements of insider trading are to be applied to a corporation, and that uncertainty needs to be resolved.

The adoption of a new set of provisions, which would provide the only mechanism for applying insider trading laws to corporations, would resolve the existing uncertainties and would also implement the following changes to the application of those trading laws: (i) there would no longer be any requirement for a nexus between a natural person's role or position for information they come to possess or knowledge they have to be attributed to a corporation; (ii) a corporation could have liability for insider trading as a result of information possessed, knowledge held and conduct engaged in by any officer, employee or agent of the corporation; (iii) the trading element would continue to require that the conduct occur within the scope of a person's authority, or was undertaken with the authorisation of a person with authority, on behalf of the corporation; and (iv) there would be a new requirement for a link between the possession of information, knowledge and conduct, as it would be necessary that the same natural person possess the inside information, have the requisite knowledge and engage in the relevant conduct for it to be attributed to a corporation, removing the possibility of aggregation.

The uncertainties concerning the manner in which the elements of insider trading are applied to corporations are further exacerbated by the fact that the primary defence to insider trading for corporations – the Chinese Wall defence – is expressed in vague terms which appear to have inconsistencies with the statutory provisions. As discussed in chapter 6, s 1043F of the *Corporations Act*, which sets out the Chinese Wall defence for corporations, refers to 'information in the possession of an *officer or an employee*' even though s 1042G(1)(a) of the *Corporations Act*, which sets out the circumstances in which a corporation is taken to possess information, refers only to information in possession of an *officer* of a body corporate. Although this inconsistency may be overcome by either inferring that s 1042G does not provide an exclusive mechanism for attributing the possession of information, and that other statutory provisions and the general law might apply where an employee and not an officer of a corporation possesses information, or by assuming that the discrepancy results from a drafting error, the uncertainty created requires clarification and resolution.

The reference to 'an officer or an employee' in s 1043F of the *Corporations Act* also creates a further gap in the application of the defence, because, though s 769B(3) of the *Corporations Act* can apply so that a corporation may have liability for insider trading where information is possessed by an agent, the Chinese Wall defence will not be available if that agent is not also an officer or employee of the corporation.

There is additional uncertainty created by the fact that the Chinese Wall defence does not extend to the procuring of trading, but only the actual act of trading. This occurs because the Chinese Wall defence only applies to a corporation's 'decision to enter a transaction or agreement' made 'on its behalf' by an employee or officer. A person who procures trading by another is not necessarily the person who makes the ultimate 'decision to enter a transaction or agreement' on that other person's behalf unless they are also the ultimate decision-maker for that other person (for example, if the other person is a corporation controlled by that person). A person who merely 'encourages' another person to trade in securities will be regarded as procuring that other person to trade,[11] but the ultimate decision is still made by that other person. As there appears to be no rationale for applying the Chinese Wall defence to trading only, and not the procuring of trading, and the gap appears to be 'the result of a legislative oversight',[12] this inconsistency, along with the other uncertainties in the application of the Chinese Wall defence, needs to be corrected.

The uncertainty resulting from the confusion as to which mechanisms are to be used to apply the elements of insider trading to corporations, the differing nature of the tests applied by those various mechanisms, and the lack of clarity as to the application and availability of the Chinese Wall defence, is detrimental to the accepted rationale for the prohibition of insider trading, being the protection and maintenance of market integrity. The uncertainty that these various factors create is problematic, not only for those corporations which may be accused of having engaged in insider trading, but also for regulators responsible for supervising securities markets and taking action against market misconduct, as well as the many participants in the securities market who are entitled to have confidence in the integrity of that market. As noted earlier in this book, insider trading damages market integrity because it prevents the market from operating freely and fairly, with 'all participants having equal access to relevant information'.[13] A belief by potential investors and market participants that insiders have an informational advantage and unfair opportunities to trade in securities reduces investor confidence in market integrity, and therefore may also reduce investor participation in securities markets.[14] Thus, the particular statutory provisions which regulate insider trading and apply the prohibition to corporations should also be directed to the aim of protecting and maintaining market integrity. This requires that there be certainty for all affected and interested parties as to the manner in which

---

11 *Corporations Act*, s 1042F of the *Corporations Act*.

12 CAMAC, *Insider Trading Report*, 2003, 2 and 7.

13 Committee of Inquiry into the Australian Financial System, *Australian Financial System: Final Report* (Australian Government Publishing Service, Canberra, 1981) 382, approved by the Standing Committee on Legal and Constitutional Affairs, House of Representatives, *Fair Shares for All: Insider Trading in Australia* (Australian Government Publishing Service, Canberra, 1989) 17 and confirmed by the majority of the High Court in *Mansfield and Kizon v R* (2012) 87 ALJR 20, [45] (Hayne, Crennan, Kiefel and Bell JJ).

14 See, for example, ASIC, *Consultation Paper 68, Competition for Market Services – Trading in Listed Securities and Related Data*, 2007; Utpal Bhattacharya and Hazem Daouk, 'The World Price of Insider Trading' (2002) 57 *Journal of Finance* 75; Laura Nyantung Beny, 'Insider Trading Laws and Stock Markets Around the World: An Empirical Contribution to the Theoretical Law and Economics Debate' (2007) 32 *Journal of Corporation Law* 237.

insider trading laws apply to corporations. Unfortunately, this is not currently the case. As has been noted by CAMAC:

> Insider trading laws also need to be clear and workable, so that all parties know where they stand. For instance, corporate managers, financial services providers and legal advisers should not be subject to undue uncertainty in their ability to deal in securities in conformity with the law, or advise on that law. Lack of clarity may result in reduced compliance as well as unproductive uncertainty for the market.[15]

While CAMAC was referring to the general operation of Australian insider trading laws, these comments are particularly relevant to the application of those laws to corporations, which has been demonstrated to be unclear and uncertain. Additionally, in order for there to be appropriate oversight of securities markets, and to enable the detection and prosecution of unlawful conduct, regulators must also have certainty as to the application of insider trading laws to corporations. The protection and maintenance of market integrity will also ensure that Australia's securities markets remain internationally competitive.

Accordingly, it is proposed that the current regulatory regime prohibiting insider trading be amended so that it applies to corporations in the following ways: (i) the operation of the general law should be expressly excluded; (ii) new statutory provisions which apply the elements of insider trading – the possession of information, the requisite knowledge and the necessary conduct – to corporations are to replace the current provisions of the *Corporations Act*; and (iii) the Chinese Wall defence to insider trading should be redrafted.

## Proposed new provisions

In order to address the identified flaws in the current regulatory regime relating to corporate criminal liability for insider trading, it is proposed that the following amendments be made to the *Corporations Act*:

1   Section 1042G of the *Corporations Act*, entitled 'Information in possession of a body corporate', should be amended by deleting paragraphs (a), (b) and (c). Paragraph (d) relates only to s 1043M(2)(b), so this paragraph should be moved to become a new paragraph (4) of s 1043M, with some amendments.[16]

---

15 CAMAC, *Insider Trading Discussion Paper*, 2001, [0.5].
16 As noted earlier in this book, s 1043M of the *Corporations Act* sets out several defences to a prosecution for insider trading and s 1043M(2) provides that:

> In a prosecution brought against a person for an offence based on subsection 1043A(1) because the person entered into, or procured another person to enter into, a transaction or agreement at a time when certain information was in the first mentioned person's possession:

2   Section 1042G of the *Corporations Act* should be renamed 'Liability of Bodies Corporate', the existing paragraphs should be deleted, and new paragraphs should be inserted.
3   Section 1043F of the *Corporations Act*, entitled 'Chinese Wall arrangements by bodies corporate' should be amended by deleting the existing paragraphs and inserting new paragraphs.

To the maximum extent possible, for the purposes of consistency and ease of reference, language has been used which is similar to that already employed within the *Corporations Act*. It is proposed that the new amendments would read as follows:

## Section 1042G:

### LIABILITY OF BODIES CORPORATE

(1)   This section sets out the only means by which a body corporate will be liable for the purposes of the prohibitions in section 1043A. For the avoidance of doubt, section 769B of this Act and Part 2.5 of the Criminal Code do not apply in relation to the prohibitions in section 1043A.

(2)   A body corporate is taken to possess information for the purposes of section 1043A(1) and (2) if an officer, employee or agent of the body corporate possesses the information.

(3)   A body corporate is taken to know, or to ought reasonably to know, that the matters specified in paragraphs (a) and (b) of the definition of inside information in section 1042A are satisfied in relation to the information if an officer, employee or agent of the body corporate knows, or ought reasonably to know, those matters.

(4)   A body corporate is taken to engage in the conduct set out in section 1043A(1)(c) or (d), or section 1043A(2)(c) or (d), if:

(a)   an officer, employee or agent of the body corporate engages in the conduct on behalf of the body corporate within the scope of his or her actual or apparent authority; or

(b)   any person engages in the conduct on behalf of the body corporate with the authorisation of an officer, employee or agent of the body corporate.

(5)   For the purposes of paragraph (4), conduct is taken to be authorised by an officer, employee or agent of a body corporate if the conduct is undertaken at that person's direction, or with that person's consent or agreement (whether express or implied) where the giving of the direction, consent or agreement is within the scope of the actual or apparent authority of that person.

---

. . . (b)   it is a defence if the other party to the transaction or agreement knew, or ought reasonably to have known, of the information before entering into the transaction or agreement.

(6) A body corporate will only be in breach of a prohibition in section 1043A if a person who possesses inside information which the body corporate is taken to possess pursuant to paragraph (2) also:

(a) knows, or ought reasonably to know, that the matters specified in paragraphs (a) and (b) of the definition of inside information in section 1042A are satisfied in relation to the information so that the body corporate would be taken to know, or to ought reasonably to know, those matters in accordance with paragraph (3); and

(b) either:

    (i) engages in the conduct on behalf of the body corporate in accordance with paragraph (4)(a);

    (ii) authorises another person to engage in the conduct on behalf of the body corporate in accordance with paragraph (4)(b); or

    (iii) gives advice about the conduct to a person:

        (A) who engages in the conduct on behalf of the body corporate in accordance with paragraph (4)(a); or

        (B) authorises another person to engage in the conduct on behalf of the body corporate in accordance with paragraph (4)(b).

## Section 1043F

### CHINESE WALL ARRANGEMENTS BY BODIES CORPORATE

A body corporate does not contravene subsection 1043A(1) or (2) by engaging in the conduct set out in section 1043A(1)(c) or (d), or section 1043A(2)(c) or (d) at a time when inside information is possessed by an officer, employee or agent of the body corporate if:

(a) the decision to engage in the conduct was made by a person who did not possess the inside information;

(b) it had in operation at the time arrangements that could reasonably be expected to ensure that the inside information was not communicated to the person who decided to engage in the conduct; and

(c) no advice about the conduct was given to the person who decided to engage in the conduct by a person who possessed the inside information.

## Section 1043M:

(4) For the purposes of subsection (2)(b), a body corporate is taken to have known, or to ought reasonably to have known, of the relevant information if an officer, employee or agent of the body corporate who was aware of the body corporate's entry into the transaction or agreement knew or ought reasonably to have known of the relevant information.

# Nature of the proposed reforms

A detailed explanation of the nature of each of the proposed amendments follows, including a description of the relevant statutory provision, the ways in which it will change the state of the current law and the reasons why the amendment is necessary.

### *Exclusion of the general law*

Some of the current confusion regarding which mechanisms are to be used to apply the elements of insider trading to corporations would be alleviated by excluding the application of the general law. This would be done by codifying insider trading in relation to its application to corporations, to make it clear that only the particular statutory provisions of the *Corporations Act* apply. While this might initially appear to narrow the scope of the application of the insider trading laws, it is also proposed to redraft the statutory provisions to widen their current application. Thus, greater certainty would be provided without reducing the potential to apply the law to corporations where appropriate. In particular, it would be clear that general law principles of agency and the identification doctrine would not be available to be utilised as separate mechanisms for determining when a corporation has engaged in insider trading, and the demonstrated difficulties in attempting to apply those general law rules would therefore be avoided.

Even though there may be other areas of the law which do not exclude the general law and allow statutory and general law rules to operate concurrently, this does not mean that the insider trading regime must continue to allow the general law to apply. The use of clear language would avoid any difficulties of interpretation and, in the interests of clarity and certainty, a more definitive regime is required for corporate criminal and civil liability for insider trading. Additionally, other parts of the *Corporations Act* exclude the general law when appropriate.[17]

The proposed amendments would result in only one set of statutory provisions to be used to apply the elements of insider trading to corporations. Currently there are multiple statutory provisions which may apply, which causes significant confusion and uncertainty. The general principles of corporate criminal responsibility contained in the *Criminal Code* are currently excluded and therefore do not apply to the operation of the present insider trading provisions. Under the proposed new provisions, the *Criminal Code* provisions relating to corporate criminal liability would continue to be excluded and the provisions in s 769B of the *Corporations Act* would also be excluded.

---

17  For example, s 133 of the *Corporations Act* excludes the operation of the general law in relation to preregistration contracts and s 236(3) of the *Corporations Act* abolishes the general law derivative action.

## Continued exclusion of the Criminal Code

Part 2.5 of the *Criminal Code* relating to corporate criminal liability is currently excluded from the insider trading regime,[18] and it is proposed that this would continue. It is not appropriate to apply these provisions to corporate criminal liability for insider trading. As noted earlier in this book, in relation to physical elements – with the physical element for insider trading being the possession of information[19] – the *Criminal Code* provides that:

> If a physical element of an offence is committed by an employee, agent or officer of a body corporate acting within the actual or apparent scope of his or her employment, or within his or her actual or apparent authority, the physical element must also be attributed to the body corporate.[20]

This provision, while it differs from the other mechanisms available to determine when a corporation is in possession of inside information, would still import some concepts which have been identified as causing uncertainty – for example, that the relevant employee, agent or officer must come into possession of the information within the scope of his or her employment or within his or her actual authority.

In relation to fault elements – with the fault element for insider trading being the knowledge that certain information is inside information[21] – the *Criminal Code* provides that:

> If intention, knowledge or recklessness is a fault element in relation to a physical element of an offence, that fault element must be attributed to a body corporate that expressly, tacitly or impliedly authorised or permitted the commission of the offence.[22]

A variety of ways in which such authorisation or permission might occur are then provided for:

(a) proving that the body corporate's board of directors intentionally, knowingly or recklessly carried out the relevant conduct, or expressly, tacitly or impliedly authorised or permitted the commission of the offence; or

(b) proving that a high managerial agent of the body corporate intentionally, knowingly or recklessly engaged in the relevant conduct, or expressly, tacitly or impliedly authorised or permitted the commission of the offence; or

---

18 *Corporations Act*, s 769A.
19 *Corporations Act*, s 1043A(3).
20 *Criminal Code*, s 12.2.
21 *Corporations Act*, s 1043A(3).
22 *Criminal Code*, s 12.3(1).

(c) proving that a corporate culture existed within the body corporate that directed, encouraged, tolerated or led to non-compliance with the relevant provision; or

(d) proving that the body corporate failed to create and maintain a corporate culture that required compliance with the relevant provision.[23]

However, as with the physical element, the adoption of such provisions for insider trading would not improve the position of uncertainty which currently exists, as it is not clear how it would be demonstrated, for example, that a corporate culture existed that 'directed, encouraged, tolerated or led to' insider trading. Instead, the proposed model specifically sets out the way in which the fault element would be proved for insider trading. As the insider trading laws are intended to maintain and protect market integrity, it is most appropriate to utilise a particular set of provisions focused on achieving that rationale, rather than relying on the general statutory provisions applicable to the majority of Commonwealth offences, which do not necessarily have similar aims or appropriate application to insider trading.

### *Exclusion of section 769B of the Corporations Act*

Under the proposed reforms, the provisions of s 769B will be excluded in order to allow for a single set of mechanisms within the *Corporations Act* to apply liability for insider trading to corporations. It has been noted throughout this book that the operation of multiple different mechanisms for attributing liability for insider trading liability to corporations causes significant uncertainty and confusion. Instead of continuing to allow the provisions in s 769B to operate in addition to those contained in the current s 1042G of the *Corporations Act*, relevant aspects of s 769B would be incorporated into the new provisions to be contained in the new amended s 1042G.

### *No requirement for nexus with role or position for information or knowledge*

A link or nexus with the relevant person's role within the corporation would not be required in relation to the possession of information or knowledge. It is consistent with the protection and maintenance of market integrity that the new statutory provisions for corporate liability for insider trading should not contain any requirement for a link or nexus with the role or responsibilities of the natural person within a corporation whose information or knowledge is being attributed to the corporation. If an officer, employee or agent of a corporation possesses inside information, the corporation should not be able to benefit from the use of that information, regardless of the manner in which they came to possess it. It is irrelevant whether they acquired the information in a private or professional

---

23 *Criminal Code*, s 12.3(2).

capacity if the corporation is to potentially receive an advantage. Natural persons who come to possess inside information cannot use it for their own benefit, or that of another person, if they came to possess the information in a personal rather than professional capacity, and corporations should be placed in the same position for consistency and clarity.

### *Attribution is possible for all officers, employees and agents of a corporation*

The new rules would apply to all officers, employees and agents of a corporation, and would not be limited to executives or senior management within a corporation. This is a significant extension from the existing provisions of s 1042G of the *Corporations Act*, which currently only provide that a corporation will possess information if it is possessed by an officer. However, s 769B of the *Corporations Act* attributes a 'state of mind' to a corporation under s 769B(3) if an officer, employee or agent had the state of mind and engaged in the relevant conduct. Similarly, s 769B(1) applies the conduct of an officer, employee or agent acting with authority or authorisation to a corporation.

The new statutory provisions would make no distinction between the different positions that a person might hold within an organisation. This is to ensure that the operation of the law is not avoided by ensuring that certain activities are only carried out by junior employees or agents of a corporation, or by the altering of position descriptions or job titles. Since the intent of the law is to maintain and protect market integrity, the relevant consideration is whether a corporation obtains an informational advantage, to which the position that a person within the organisation might hold is irrelevant. Corporations would be protected from liability for the actions of 'rogue' employees, or those who might carry out activities beyond their limits of authority, by a requirement that the relevant trading conduct occur within the scope of a person's authority (regardless of whether they are an officer, employee or agent of the corporation) or with the authorisation of another person who is acting with appropriate authority.

### *Conduct must occur within the scope of authority or with authorisation of a person with authority, on behalf of corporation*

Although information possessed by an officer, employee or agent of a corporation would no longer need to have been acquired in circumstances which have a nexus with the position or role of that person, the trading element would maintain a requirement that the conduct occurred within the scope of the authority of the relevant officer, employee or agent (or was undertaken with the authorisation of a person with authority) on behalf of the corporation. This mirrors the conduct requirements which currently exist in s 769B(1) of the *Corporations Act* which, for the sake of clarity and certainty, will be excluded from the operation of the insider trading provisions as a result of the proposed reforms. As noted earlier, this requirement would ensure that corporations would be protected from liability for the actions of 'rogue' employees, or those acting without authority or authorisation, while still ensuring that a corporation has liability where it would obtain an unfair informational advantage. As with the other proposed amendments, this requirement is consistent with the maintenance and protection of market integrity.

### Link between the possession of information, knowledge and conduct

The new provisions would require a link between the possession of information, knowledge and conduct – there would only be liability for insider trading by a corporation where the same officer, employee or agent who possesses inside information also knows, or ought reasonably to know, that it is inside information and either carries out or authorises the relevant conduct. If one person within a corporation possesses inside information but does not use it, and another person elsewhere in the corporation does not possess or know about the inside information but does trade in affected securities on the corporation's behalf, neither person has sought to obtain an unfair advantage for the corporation, and the corporation cannot be said to have obtained such an advantage. If a natural person who trades (or decides to trade) on a corporation's behalf has no inside information, and therefore no unfair informational advantage, the rationale for the prohibition of insider trading is not infringed. However, if a person who possesses inside information gives advice to a person who trades (or decides to trade) on a corporation's behalf, the corporation receives the benefit of the information and there is a loss of market fairness – accordingly, this would also be regarded as conduct which should be caught by the application of insider trading laws to corporations.

### Direct model of corporate liability for insider trading

The codified and clearer tests described earlier, which would be used to attribute the possession of information, knowledge and conduct to corporations under the proposed amendments, would make it easier to determine when that attribution is likely to occur and therefore when a corporation would be in breach of the insider trading prohibition. A direct model of corporate liability would be utilised, so that the possession of information, knowledge and conduct of the relevant officer, employee or agent would be taken to be that of the corporation. A direct model of liability has been chosen because it is consistent with the underlying rationale for the insider trading prohibition, being the protection and maintenance of market integrity, rather than a model reliant on principles of vicarious liability or aggregation.

Under the direct model proposed, a corporation would have liability for insider trading where it is regarded as having engaged in the prohibited conduct itself through the information, knowledge and conduct of an authorised officer, employee or agent. It is only in these circumstances that a corporation can be considered to obtain an unfair advantage over other participants in securities markets. The resulting amendments would give much greater certainty in the application of the insider trading laws to corporations.

### Redrafting of the Chinese Wall defence

The identified problems with the Chinese Wall defence in s 1043F of the *Corporations Act* require a redrafting of this provision.

The redrafted s 1043F would apply as a defence to both trading and the procuring of trading, if the relevant requirements are satisfied, closing the previous loophole which did not extend the application of the defence to the procuring of trading. Having proposed amendments to s 1042G of the *Corporations Act* in relation to the liability of bodies corporate for insider trading, the previous problem of s 1042G referring to information in the possession of 'officers and employees' and s 1043F referring only to information in the possession of 'officers' would be resolved, as the new provisions will apply to information in the possession of officers, employees or agents, so long as they also have the requisite knowledge and are carrying out the relevant conduct within his or her authority, or with authorisation from a person with authority.

The Chinese Wall defence would apply so long as the person who made the decision to engage in the conduct (that is, the decision that the corporation engage in the relevant trading conduct) did not possess inside information; sufficient Chinese Wall arrangements were in place; and no advice about the conduct was given to the person who made that decision by a person who possessed inside information. The defence provides an additional protection to corporations where a person within a corporation may possess information which they know to be inside information and may trade or procure trading in relevant financial products on a corporation's behalf, but do so only at the direction of another person who does not possess the information. Even if they engage in trading at the direction of another person who does not possess the inside information, there would be no liability for the corporation if appropriate Chinese Wall arrangements are in place and no advice is given by the person who possesses the inside information. This is consistent with the market integrity rationale for the prohibition of insider trading, because the corporation is receiving no benefit or unfair advantage as a result of the person possessing the information.

### Amendments concerning section 1043M of the Corporations Act

A final amendment is needed in relation to s 1043M of the *Corporations Act*, which provides a defence to insider trading where the other party to a trade was also aware of the relevant inside information. It has been noted in this book that it is very difficult to demonstrate that a person 'ought reasonably to know' something because of their position. Consistent with the amendments already described, it should not be relevant how a person comes to know certain inside information, but the person who knows or ought reasonably to know of the inside information should also have to be aware of the corporation's entry into the relevant transaction or agreement, in order for such a defence to apply. Accordingly, it is proposed that the new s 1043M(2) be adopted to incorporate the concepts previously contained in s 1042G(1)(d) but to provide that a corporation will be taken to know or to ought reasonably to know of the relevant inside information if an officer, employee or agent who was aware of the corporation's entry into the relevant transaction or agreement knew or ought reasonably to have known of the relevant information. This will make the various statutory provisions relating to corporate liability for insider trading and the applicable defences consistent.

# 9   Conclusions

The detailed study of the application of Australian insider trading laws to corporations undertaken throughout this book has revealed a number of flaws in the current regime, in the form of inconsistencies, issues of uncertainty, difficulties of interpretation and unnecessary complexities. Australia's insider trading laws are generally considered to be overly complex and legalistic, and the application of those laws to corporations is equally difficult, if not more so. It has been demonstrated that the insider trading laws of Australia, and those of a number of other jurisdictions, are intended to safeguard market integrity, but the uncertainty which exists under the current application of insider trading laws to corporations makes it difficult to have the necessary confidence that such laws are serving their purpose, particularly in light of the absence of a successful set of contested insider trading proceedings against a corporation.

The primary flaws of the current regime have been shown to be the uncertainty as to which of the various statutory and general law mechanisms are to be applied in respect of the various elements of insider trading, and the widely varying tests which are used for each of the different mechanisms, making it difficult to determine when a corporation engages in insider trading, compounded by the lack of clarity as to the availability of the Chinese Wall defence for corporations. The proposed reforms of Australia's insider trading laws are intended to improve their application to corporations in a manner that is consistent with the market integrity rationale for the prohibition of insider trading. The three key reforms which have been proposed – the exclusion of the general law, the implementation of a new set of exclusive statutory mechanisms for applying insider trading laws to corporations and the adoption of an amended Chinese Wall defence – would remove the existing uncertainty and create a new model of applying insider trading laws that is more certain, but less complex, than the current provisions.

As well as applying the elements of insider trading to corporations more effectively and appropriately, the proposed reforms have the potential to bring additional benefits. While there may be various reasons for a lack of enforcement action being taken against corporations for insider trading, it is unlikely that it is due to a lack of any misconduct by or within corporations. It is more likely that uncertainties as to the operation and effect of insider trading laws deter prosecutors and regulators from bringing such actions, and they instead choose to focus their enforcement activities on individual offenders. While the proposed reforms are not intended to lead to a greater number of insider trading prosecutions against corporations for their own sake, the resulting improvements in the clarity and certainty of the content of insider trading laws as they apply to corporations will better enable regulators to contemplate bringing enforcement action against corporations where appropriate. If corporations are seen to be the subject of insider trading enforcement action, the deterrent effect for all potential offenders, whether natural persons or legal persons, is more likely to be increased.

If the reforms proposed in this book were adopted, it would also result in Australia having a model system of insider trading laws for corporations of international significance and relevance which would demonstrate 'best practice' in insider trading regulation. In an increasingly globalised world, in which transnational corporations are able to conduct businesses across many countries, insider trading is not necessarily limited to national borders or conducted locally. As almost all jurisdictions with established securities exchanges prohibit insider trading, and apply that prohibition to corporations, Australia's new regime could serve as a best practice example for other jurisdictions. Additionally, as the new laws have been developed with the objective of maintaining and protecting market integrity, Australia's securities markets would be better safeguarded, enabling Australia to remain competitive in the global economy.

The impact of the possible adoption of the proposed reforms on corporations themselves should not be forgotten. All who operate within our securities markets are entitled to the benefit of market integrity and certainty as to the operation and application of the relevant laws, including corporate participants. Corporations will be better placed to take action to ensure that their officers, employees and agents comply with the law, and do not engage in any conduct which would result in the corporation committing an offence, if the operation and application of the law is made more certain.

It is hoped that the ideas expounded in this book will lead to a renewed interest in corporate liability for insider trading, and the regulation of insider trading in general, and stimulate further academic discussion and research on a significant, but challenging and complex, topic.

# Appendix

Some of the material included in this book has previously been published in journal articles, and the publishers of those journals have generously granted permission for that material to be included in this book, as set out below.

1   Material from the following journal articles which were published in the *Australian Journal of Corporate Law* has been included in this book and is reproduced with the permission of LexisNexis, lexisnexis.com

   (a) Overland, Juliette, 'Reforming Australian Insider Trading Laws: A New Model of Corporate Criminal Liability – Part 2' (2018) 33 *Australian Journal of Corporate Law* 99;

   (b) Overland, Juliette, 'Reforming Australian Insider Trading Laws: A New Model of Corporate Criminal Liability – Part 1' (2018) 32 *Australian Journal of Corporate Law* 314; and

   (c) Overland, Juliette, 'Corporate Liability for Insider Trading: How Does a Company Have the Necessary "Mens Rea"?' (2010) 24 *Australian Journal of Corporate Law* 266.

   These articles were first published by LexisNexis in the *Australian Journal of Corporate Law* and should be cited as described above. For all subscription inquiries please phone, from Australia: 1800 772 772, from overseas: +61 2 9422 2174 or online at lexisnexis.com

   The official PDF version of these articles can also be purchased separately from LexisNexis.

2   Material from the following journal articles which were published in the *Company and Securities Law Journal* has been included in this book and is reproduced with the permission of Thomson Reuters (Professional) Australia Limited, legal.thomsonreturners.com.au

   (a) Overland, Juliette, 'Recent Developments in Corporate Liability for Insider Trading: ASIC v Hochtief' (2017) 35 *Company and Securities Law Journal* 204;

   (b) Overland, Juliette, 'Insider Trading, General Deterrence and the Penalties for Corporate Crime' (2015) 33 *Company and Securities Law Journal* 317;

(c) Overland, Juliette, 'The Possession and Materiality of Information in Insider Trading Cases' (2014) 32 *Company and Securities Law Journal* 353; and

(d) Overland, Juliette, 'What Is Inside "Information"? Clarifying the Ambit of Insider Trading Laws' (2013) 31 *Company and Securities Law Journal* 189.

These articles were first published by Thomson Reuters in the *Company and Securities Law Journal* and should be cited as described above. For all subscription inquiries please phone, from Australia: 1300 304 195, from overseas: +61 2 8587 7980 or online at legal.thomsonreuters.com.au/search

The official PDF version of these articles can also be purchased separately from Thomson Reuters.

3  Material from the following journal articles which were published in the Australian Business Law Review has been included in this book and is reproduced with the permission of Thomson Reuters (Professional) Australia Limited, legal.thomsonreturners.com.au

(a) Overland, Juliette, 'Insider Trading, Materiality and the Reasonable Person: Who Must Be Influenced for Information to Have a "Material Effect"?' (2017) 45 *Australian Business Law Review* 213;

(b) Overland, Juliette, 'Re-Evaluating the Elements of the Insider Trading Offence: Should There Be a Requirement for the Possession of Inside Information?' (2016) 44 *Australian Business Law Review* 256; and

(c) Overland, Juliette and Katrina Li, 'Room for Improvement: Insider Trading and Chinese Walls' (2012) 40 *Australian Business Law Review* 22

These articles were first published by Thomson Reuters in the *Australian Business Law Review* and should be cited as described above. For all subscription inquiries please phone, from Australia: 1300 304 195, from overseas: +61 2 8587 7980 or online at legal.thomsonreuters.com.au/search

The official PDF version of these articles can also be purchased separately from Thomson Reuters.

# Bibliography

## Articles/books/reports

Aitkin, Lee, 'Chinese Walls, Fiduciary Duties and Intra-Firm Conflicts – A Pan-Australian Conspectus' (2000) 19 *Australian Bar Review* 116

Alexander, Kern, 'UK Insider Dealing and Market Abuse Law: Strengthening Regulatory Law to Combat Market Misconduct', in Stephen M Bainbridge (ed), *Research Handbook on Insider Trading* (Edward Elgar, Cheltenham, 2013) 407

Anisman, Philip, *Insider Trading Legislation for Australia: An Outline of the Issues and Alternatives* (National Companies and Securities Commission, Australian Government Publishing Service, Canberra, 1986)

ASIC, *Consultation Paper 68, Competition for Market Services – Trading in Listed Securities and Related Data*, 2007

ASIC, *Consultation Paper 118, The Responsible Handling of Rumours*, 2009

ASIC, Market Integrity Rules (Securities Markets) 2017

ASIC, *Regulatory Guide 79, Managing Conflicts of Interest: A Guide for Research Report Providers*, 2012

ASIC, *Regulatory Guide 181, Licensing: Managing Conflicts of Interest*, 2004

ASIC, *Regulatory Guide 193, 'Notification of Directors' Interests in Securities – Listed Companies'*, 2008

ASIC, *Regulatory Guide 214, Guidance on ASIC Market Integrity Rules for ASX and ASX 24 Markets*, 2010

ASIC, *Regulatory Guide 265, Guidance on ASIC Market Integrity Rules for Participants of Securities Markets*, 2018

ASIC, *Report 387, Penalties for Corporate Wrongdoing*, 2014

ASX, Listing Rules

ASX, Listing Rules, *Guidance Note 8, Continuous Disclosure: Listing Rules 3.1–3.1B*, 2018

ASX, Listing Rules, *Guidance Note 22, Director Disclosure of Interests and Transactions in Securities – Obligations of Listed Entities*, 2002

ASX, Listing Rules, *Guidance Note 27, Trading Policies*, 2017

ASX, Market Rules

ASX, Market Rules, *Guidance Note 13, Prohibition of Advice to Clients*, 2005

Austin, Robert P and Ian M Ramsay, *Ford's Principles of Corporations Law* (LexisNexis Butterworths, Sydney, 2018)

Australian Accounting Standards Board, *AASB 124 Related Party Disclosure*, 2015

Ayres, Ian and John Brathwaite, *Responsive Regulation: Transcending the Deregulation Debate* (Oxford University Press, Oxford, 1992)

Bainbridge, Stephen M, 'Insider Trading Regulation: The Path Dependent Choice Between Property Rights and Securities Fraud' (1999) 52 *Southern Methodist University Law Review* 1589

Bainbridge, Stephen M, 'An Overview of Insider Trading Law and Policy: An Introduction to the Research Handbook on Insider Trading', in Stephen M Bainbridge (ed), *Research Handbook on Insider Trading* (Edward Elgar, Cheltenham, 2013) 1

Bainbridge, Stephen M, 'Regulating Insider Trading in the Post-Fiduciary Duty Era: Equal Access or Property Rights?', in Stephen M Bainbridge (ed), *Research Handbook on Insider Trading* (Edward Elgar, Cheltenham, 2013) 80

Balkin, R P and J L R Davies, *Law of Torts* (LexisNexis Butterworths, 4th ed, Sydney, 2009)

Baxt, Robert, Ashley Black and Pamela Hanrahan, *Securities and Financial Services Law* (LexisNexis, 8th ed, Sydney, 2012)

Beny, Laura Nyantung, 'Do Insider Trading Laws Matter? Some Preliminary Comparative Evidence' (2005) 7 *American Law and Economics Review* 144

Beny, Laura Nyantung, 'Insider Trading Laws and Stock Markets Around the World: An Empirical Contribution to the Theoretical Law and Economics Debate' (2007) 32 *Journal of Corporation Law* 237

Beny, Laura Nyantung, 'The Political Economy of Insider Trading Laws and Enforcement: Law vs. Politics? International Evidence', in Stephen M Bainbridge (ed), *Research Handbook on Insider Trading* (Edward Elgar, Cheltenham, 2013) 266

Beny, Laura Nyantung and H Nejat Seyhun, 'Has Illegal Insider Trading Become More Rampant in the United States? Empirical Evidence from Takeovers', in Stephen M Bainbridge (ed), *Research Handbook on Insider Trading* (Edward Elgar, Cheltenham, 2013) 211

Bhattacharya, Utpal and Hazem Daouk, 'The World Price of Insider Trading' (2002) 57 *Journal of Finance* 75

Black, Ashley, 'Insider Trading and Market Misconduct' (2011) 29 *Company and Securities Law Journal* 313

Black, Ashley, 'The Reform of Insider Trading Law in Australia' (1992) 15 *University of New South Wales Law Journal* 214

Bris, Arturo, 'Do Insider Trading Laws Work' (2005) 11 *European Financial Management* 267

British Institute of International and Comparative Law, *Comparative Implementation of EU Directives (I) – Insider Dealing and Market Abuse*, 2005

Brown, B E and C M Herringes, 'Dovetailing the "Chinese Wall" Defence Within the Rules of Professional Conduct – Washington Should Finish What It Has Started' (1990/91) 26 *Gonzaga Law Review* 569

Brown, David, David Farrier, Luke McNamara, Alex Steel, Michael Grewcock, Julia Quilter and Melanie Schwartz, *Criminal Laws: Materials and Commentary on Criminal Law and Process in New South Wales* (Federation Press, 6th ed, Sydney, 2015)

Brown, Philip, Mark Foo and Iain Watson, 'Trading by Insiders in Australia: Evidence on the Profitability of Directors' Trades' (2003) 21 *Company and Securities Law Journal* 248

Brudney, Victor, 'Insiders, Outsiders and Informational Advantages under the Federal Securities Laws' (1979) 93 *Harvard Law Review* 322

Burrow, Vanessa, 'ASIC on Insider Trading Hunt', *The Age* (Melbourne), 21 March 2008

CAMAC, *Aspects of Market Integrity Report*, 2009

CAMAC, *Insider Trading Discussion Paper*, 2001

CAMAC, *Insider Trading Proposals Paper*, 2002

CAMAC, *Insider Trading Report*, 2003

Chesterman, Simon, 'The Corporate Veil, Crime and Punishment' (1994) 19 *Melbourne University Law Review* 1064

Chiu, Hse-Yu, 'Australian Influence on the Insider Trading Laws in Singapore' (2002) *Singapore Journal of Legal Studies* 574

Clough, Jonathan and Carmel Mulhern, *The Prosecution of Corporations* (Oxford University Press, Melbourne, 2002)

Coffee, John C, 'Corporate Crime and Punishment: A Non-Chicago View of the Economics of Criminal Sanctions' (1980) *American Criminal Law Review* 419

Coffee, John C, 'No Soul to Damn, No Body to Kick: An Unscandalized Inquiry into the Problem of Corporate Punishment' (1981) 79 *Michigan Law Review* 386

Colvin, Eric, 'Corporate Personality and Criminal Liability' (1995) 6 *Criminal Law Forum* 1

Committee of Inquiry into the Australian Financial System, *Australian Financial System: Final Report of the Committee of Inquiry* (Australian Government Publishing Service, Canberra, 1981)

Commonwealth Attorney-General's Department, Criminal Justice Division, *A Guide to Framing Commonwealth Offences, Infringement Notices and Enforcement Powers*, 2011

Commonwealth Treasury, *Insider Trading Position and Consultation Paper*, 2007

Criminal Law Officers Committee of the Standing Committee of Attorneys-General, *Model Criminal Code*, Final Report (1992)

D'Aloisio, Tony, *ASIC's Approach to Market Integrity* (speech delivered at the Monash Centre for Regulatory Studies and Clayton Utz Luncheon Lecture, Melbourne, 11 March 2010)

D'Aloisio, Tony, *Insider Trading and Market Manipulation* (speech delivered at the Supreme Court of Victoria Law Conference, Melbourne, 13 August 2010)

Davies, Paul, *Gower & Davies: Principles of Modern Company Law* (Sweet & Maxwell, London, 2012)

Deans, Alan, 'The Fetter of the Law', *The Bulletin* (Sydney), 28 November 2000, 52

DeMott, Deborah A, 'When Is a Principal Charged with an Agent's Knowledge?' (2003) *Duke Journal of Comparative and International Law* 291

Dolgopolov, Stanislav, 'Insider Trading, Chinese Walls, and Brokerage Commissions: The Origins of Modern Regulation of Information Flows in Securities Markets' (2008) 4 *Journal of Law, Economics and Policy* 311

Dolgopolov, Stanislav, 'Risks and Hedges of Providing Liquidity in Complex Securities: The Impact of Insider Trading on Options Market Makers' (2010) 15 *Fordham Journal of Corporate and Financial Law* 387

Earp, Martin K and Gai M McGrath, *Listed Companies – Law and Market Practice* (Lawbook, Sydney, 1996)

Estrada, Javier, 'Insider Trading: Regulation, Deregulation and Taxation' (1994) 5 *Swiss Review of Business Law* 209

European Commission, *Best Practices in an Integrated European Financial Market – Recommendations from the Forum Group to the European Commission Services*, 2003

Fama, Eugene F, 'Efficient Capital Markets: A Review of Theory and Empirical Work' (1970) 25 *Journal of Finance* 383

Ferran, Eilis, 'Corporate Attribution and the Directing Mind and Will' (2011) 127 *Law Quarterly Review* 239

*Financial Conduct Authority Handbook* (UK)

Fisse, Brent, 'The Attribution of Criminal Liability to Corporations: A Statutory Model' (1991) 13 *Sydney Law Review* 277

Fisse, Brent and John Braithwaite, 'The Allocation of Responsibility for Corporate Crime: Individualism, Collectivism and Accountability' (1988) 11 *Sydney Law Review* 468

Forum of European Securities Commissions, *Market Conduct Standards*, 99-FESCO-B, 1999

Freeman, Mark A and Michael A Adams, 'Australian Insiders' Views on Insider Trading' (1999) 10 *Australian Journal of Corporate Law* 148

German Federal Ministry of Finance, *Our Stock Exchange and Securities System*, 2000

Gething, Michael, 'Insider Trading Enforcement: Where Are We Now and Where Do We Go from Here?' (1998) 16 *Company and Securities Law Journal* 607

Gevurtz, Franklin A, 'The Globalisation of Insider Trading Prohibitions' (2002) 15 *Transnational Lawyer* 63

Gobert, James, 'Corporate Criminality: Four Models of Fault' (1994) 14 *Legal Studies* 393

Gobert, James, 'Corporate Criminality: New Crimes for the Times' (1994) *Criminal Law Review* 722

Goldwasser, Vivien, 'Recent Developments in the Regulation of Chinese Walls and Business Ethics – In Search of a Remedy for a Problem That Persists' (1993) 11 *Company and Securities Law Journal* 227

Goode, Matthew, 'Corporate Criminal Liability', in Neil Gunningham, Jennifer Norberry and Sandra McKillop (eds), *Environmental Crime* (Australian Institute of Criminology, Canberra, 1995)

Gorman, Christopher M, 'Are Chinese Walls the Best Solution to the Problems of Insider Trading and Conflicts of Interests in Broker-Dealers?' (2004) 9 *Fordham Journal of Corporate and Financial Law* 475

Gozzi, Raymond, 'The Chinese Wall Metaphor' (2003) 60 *ETC: A Review of General Semantics* 171

Grantham, Ross, 'Attributing Responsibility to Corporate Entities: A Doctrinal Approach' (2001) 19 *Company and Securities Law Journal* 168

Grantham, Ross, 'Corporate Knowledge: Identification or Attribution' (1996) 59 *Modern Law Review* 732

Green, Stuart P, *Lying, Cheating and Stealing: A Moral Theory of White-Collar Crime* (Oxford University Press, Oxford, 2006)

Hambrook, J P, 'Market Misconduct and Offences', in *Australian Corporations Law Principles and Practice* (LexisNexis Butterworths, Sydney, 2018)

Herzel, Leo and Leo Katz, 'Insider Trading: Who Loses?' (1987) *Lloyds Bank Review* 15

Hill, Jennifer and Ronald Harmer, 'Criminal Liability of Corporations – Australia', in H De Doelder and K Tiedemann (eds), *Criminal Liability of Corporations* (Kluwer Law International, The Hague, 1994) 71

Hollander, Charles and Simon Salzedo, *Conflicts of Interest and Chinese Walls* (Sweet & Maxwell, London, 2000)

International Organisations of Securities Commissions, *Objectives and Principles of Securities Regulation*, 2010

Jacobs, Adam, 'Time is Money: Insider Trading from a Globalisation Perspective' (2005) 23 *Company and Securities Law Journal* 231

Kendall, Keith, 'The Need to Prohibit Insider Trading' (2008) 25 *Law in Context* 106

Kendall, Keith and Gordon Walker, 'Insider Trading in Australia', in Stephen M Bainbridge (ed), *Research Handbook on Insider Trading* (Edward Elgar, Cheltenham, 2013) 365

Kendall, Keith and Gordon Walker, 'Insider Trading in Australia and New Zealand: Information that is Generally Available' (2006) 24 *Company and Securities Law Journal* 343

Langenbucher, Katja, 'The "Use or Possession" Debate Revisited – Spector Photo Group and Insider Trading in Europe' (2010) 5 *Capital Markets Law Journal* 452

Latimer, Paul and Philipp Maume, *Promoting Information in the Marketplace for Financial Services – Financial Market Regulation and International Standards* (Springer, Cham, 2014)

Law Reform Commission of New South Wales, *Sentencing: Corporate Offenders*, Report No 10, 2003

Lehar, Alfred and Otto Randl, 'Chinese Walls in German Banks' (2006) 10 *Review of Finance* 301

Leland, Hayne E, 'Insider Trading: Should It Be Prohibited?' (1992) 100 *Journal of Political Economy* 859

Lewis, Kevin A, 'A Decade On: Reforming the Financial Services Law Reforms' (Paper presented at Sixth Annual Supreme Court Corporate Law Conference, Sydney, 23 August 2011)

Lipton, Martin and Robert B Mazur, 'The Chinese Wall Solution to the Conflicts Problems of Securities Firms' (1975) 50 *New York University Law Review* 459

Lyon, Gregory and Jean J du Plessis, *The Law of Insider Trading in Australia* (Federation Press, Sydney, 2005)

Manne, Henry G, 'Entrepreneurship, Compensation, and the Corporation', in Stephen M Bainbridge (ed), *Research Handbook on Insider Trading* (Edward Elgar, Cheltenham, 2013) 67

Manne, Henry G, 'In Defence of Insider Trading' (1966) 43 *Harvard Business Review* 113

Manne, Henry G, *Insider Trading and the Stock Market* (The Free Press, New York, 1966)

Manne, Henry G, 'Insider Trading: Hayek, Virtual Markets, and the Dog that Did Not Bark' (2005) 31 *Journal of Corporation Law* 167

Mannolini, Justin J, 'Insider Trading – The Need for Conceptual Clarity' (1996) 14 *Company and Securities Law Journal* 151

Mitchell, Lawrence E, 'The Jurisprudence of the Misappropriation Theory and the New Insider Trading Legislation: From Fairness to Efficiency and Back' (1988) 52 *Albany Law Review* 775

Monetary Authority of Singapore, *Insider Trading: Consultation Document*, 2001

Moore, Jennifer, 'What is Really Unethical About Insider Trading?' (1990) 9 *Journal of Business Ethics* 171

North, Gil, 'The Australian Insider Trading Regime: Workable or Hopelessly Complex?' (2009) 27 *Company and Securities Law Journal* 310

North, Gil, 'The Insider Trading Generally Available and Materiality Carve-Outs: Are They Achieving Their Aims?' (2009) 27 *Company and Securities Law Journal* 234

O'Hara, Phillip Anthony, 'Insider Trading in Financial Markets: Legality, Ethics, Efficiency' (2001) 28 *International Journal of Social Economics* 1046

Overland, Juliette, 'Corporate Liability for Insider Trading: How Does a Company Have the Necessary "Mens Rea"?' (2010) 24 *Australian Journal of Corporate Law* 266

Overland, Juliette, 'Insider Trading, Materiality and the Reasonable Person: Who Must Be Influenced for Information to have a "Material Effect"?' (2017) 45 *Australian Business Law Review* 213

Overland, Juliette, 'Making the Most of a Lost Opportunity: Do Civil Penalty Proceedings for Insider Trading need to be Reformed?' (2018) 33 *Australian Journal of Corporate Law* 364

Overland, Juliette, 'Recent Developments in Corporate Liability for Insider Trading: ASIC v Hochtief' (2017) 35 *Company and Securities Law Journal* 204

Overland, Juliette, 'Re-Evaluating the Elements of the Insider Trading Offence: Should There Be a Requirement for the Possession of Inside Information?' (2016) 44 *Australian Business Law Review* 256

Overland, Juliette, 'Reforming Australian Insider Trading Laws: A New Model of Corporate Criminal Liability – Part 1' (2017) 32 *Australian Journal of Corporate Law* 314

Overland, Juliette, 'Reforming Australian Insider Trading Laws: A New Model of Corporate Criminal Liability – Part 2' (2018) 33 *Australian Journal of Corporate Law* 99

Overland, Juliette, 'The Concept of Attribution in Corporate Law: Making Corporations Liable for Criminal Conduct', in David Chaikin and Gordon Hook (eds), *Corporate and Trust Structures: Legal and Illegal Dimensions* (Australian Scholarly Publishing, Melbourne, 2018) 35

Overland, Juliette, 'The Possession and Materiality of Information in Insider Trading Cases' (2014) 32 *Company and Securities Law Journal* 353

Overland, Juliette, 'What Is Inside "Information"? Clarifying the Ambit of Insider Trading Laws' (2013) 31 *Company and Securities Law Journal* 189

Overland, Juliette and Katrina Li, 'Room for Improvement: Insider Trading and Chinese Walls' (2012) 40 *Australian Business Law Review* 223

Pearce, D C and R S Geddes, *Statutory Interpretation in Australia* (LexisNexis Butterworths, 8th ed, Sydney, 2014)

Pompilio, David, 'On the Reach of Insider Trading Law' (2007) 25 *Company and Securities Law Journal* 467

Poser, Norman, 'Chinese Wall or Emperor's New Clothes? Regulating Conflicts of Interest of Securities Firms in the U.S. and the U.K.' (1988) 9 *Michigan Journal of International Law* 91

Poser, Norman, *International Securities Regulation* (Little Brown & Co, New York, 1991)

Qu, Charles Zhen, 'How Statutory Civil Liability is Attributed to a Company: An Australian Perspective Focusing on Civil Liability for Insider Trading by Companies' (2006) 32 *Monash Law Review* 177

Quarrell, John, 'Modern Trusts in Legal Education' (1991) 5 *Trust Law International* 99

Ramsay, Ian, 'Steve Vizard, Insider Trading and Directors' Duties', University of Melbourne Centre for Corporate Law and Securities Regulation, Research Reports and Research Papers (2005), available at https://law.unimelb.edu.au/centres/cclsr/research/research-reports-and-research-papers

Rubenstein, Simon, 'The Regulation and Prosecution of Insider Trading in Australia: Towards Civil Penalty Sanctions for Insider Trading' (2002) 20 *Company and Securities Law Journal* 89

Sainsbury, Michael, 'Insider Trading Rife in Australia', *The Australian* (Sydney), 20 February 2008

SEC, *Final Rule: Selective Disclosure and Insider Trading*, SEC Release No 33–7881, 23 October 2000

Semaan, Lori, Mark Freeman and Michael Adams, 'Is Insider Trading a Necessary Evil for Efficient Markets? An International Comparative Analysis' (1999) 17 *Company and Securities Law Journal* 220

Seyhun, H Negat, 'Insider Profits, Costs of Trading and Market Efficiency' (1986) 16 *Journal of Financial Economics* 189

Standing Committee on Legal and Constitutional Affairs, House of Representatives, *Fair Shares for All: Insider Trading in Australia* (Australian Government Publishing Service, Canberra, 1989)

Steel, Alex, 'The True Identity of Australian Identity Theft Offences: A Measured Response or an Unjustified Status Offence?' (2010) 33 *University of New South Wales Law Journal* 503

Steinberg, Marc I, 'Insider Trading: A Comparative Perspective' (2003) 37(1) *The International Lawyer* 153

Strudler, Alan and Eric W Orts, 'Moral Principle in the Law of Insider Trading' (1999) 78 *Texas Law Review* 375

Sullivan, G R, 'The Attribution of Culpability to Limited Companies' (1996) 55 *Cambridge Law Journal* 515

Tomasic, Roman, 'Chinese Walls, Legal Principle and Commercial Reality in Multi-Service Professional Firms' (1991) 14 *University of New South Wales Law Journal* 46

Tomasic, Roman, 'Corporate Crime: Making the Law More Credible' (1990) 8 *Company and Securities Law Journal* 369

Tomasic, Roman, 'Insider Trading Law Reform in Australia' (1991) 9 *Company and Securities Law Journal* 12

Tomasic, Roman (with the assistance of Brendan Pentony), *Casino Capitalism? Insider Trading in Australia* (Australian Institute of Criminology, Canberra, 1991)

Tomasic, Roman and Brendan Pentony, 'The Prosecution of Insider Trading: Obstacles to Enforcement' (1989) 22 *Australian and New Zealand Journal of Criminology* 65

Tomasic, Roman, Stephen Bottomley and Rob McQueen, *Corporations Law in Australia* (Federation Press, 2nd ed, Sydney, 2002)

Ts'ai, Lim Win, 'Corporations and the Devil's Dictionary: The Problem of Individual Responsibility for Corporate Crimes' (1990) 12 *Sydney Law Review* 311

Tuch, Andrew, 'Investment Banks as Fiduciaries: Implications for Conflicts of Interest' (2005) 2 *Melbourne University Law Review* 478

UK Financial Services Authority, Consultation Paper 59, *Market Abuse: A Draft Code of Market Conduct*, 2000

Walker, Gordon, 'Insider Trading in Australia: When Is Information Readily Available?' (2000) 18 *Company and Securities Law Journal* 213

Walker, Gordon R and Andrew F Simpson, 'Insider Conduct Regulation in New Zealand: Exploring the Enforcement Deficit' (2013) *New Zealand Law Review* 521

Welsh, Michelle, 'Civil Penalties and Responsive Regulation: The Gap Between Theory and Practice' (2009) 33 *Melbourne University Law Review* 908

West, Michael, 'Insider Trading Still on the Rise: Banker', *The Sydney Morning Herald* (Sydney), 20 February 2008

Whincop, Michael, 'The Political Economy of Corporate Law Reform in Australia' (1999) 27 *Federal Law Review* 77

Whincop, Michael, 'Towards a Property Rights and Market Microstructural Theory of Insider Trading Regulation – The Case of Primary Securities Markets Transactions' (1996) 7 *Journal of Banking and Finance Law and Practice* 212

Wilkinson, Meaghan, 'Corporate Criminal Liability – The Move Towards Recognising Genuine Corporate Fault' (2003) 9 *Canterbury Law Review* 142

Winn, C R N, 'The Criminal Responsibility of Corporations' (1929) 3 *Cambridge Law Journal* 398

Wolff, Martin, 'On the Nature of Legal Persons' (1938) 54 *Law Quarterly Review* 494

Ziegelaar, Michael, 'Insider Trading Law in Australia', in Gordon Walker, Brent Fisse and Ian Ramsay (eds), *Securities Regulation in Australia and New Zealand* (Lawbook, 2nd ed, Sydney, 1998) 554

## Cases

*AAPT Ltd v Cable & Wireless Optus Ltd and Others* (1999) 32 ACSR 63

*ABC Developmental Learning Centres Pty Ltd v Wallace* [2006] VSC 171 (3 May 2006)

*Aberdeen Railway v Blaikie* (1854) 1 Macl 461

*Ampolex Ltd v Perpetual Trustee Trading Co (Canberra) Ltd* (1996) 20 ACSR 649; (1996) 14 ACLC 1514

*Ansari v The Queen* [2010] HCA 18

*Artedomus v Del Casale* [2006] NSWSC 146

*Asia Pacific Telecommunications Limited v Optus Networks Pty Limited* [2007] NSWSC 350

*ASIC v Citigroup Global Markets Australia* Pty Ltd (2007) 160 FCR 35

*ASIC v Fortescue Metals Group Ltd* (2009) 264 ALR 201

*ASIC v Fortescue Metals Group Ltd* [2011] FCAFC 19

*ASIC v Hochtief Aktiengesellschaft* [2016] FCA 1489

*ASIC v Macdonald (No 11)* (2009) 256 ALR 365

*ASIC v Petsas and Miot* [2005] FCA 88; [2005] 23 ACLC 269

*ASIC v Vizard* [2005] FCA 1037

*Attorney-General's Department and Australian Iron and Steel Pty Ltd v Cockcroft* (1986) 10 FCR 180

*Attorney-Generals' Reference (No 2 of 1999)* [2000] QB 796

*Australasian Brokerage Ltd v Australia and New Zealand Banking Corporation Ltd* (1934) 52 CLR 430

*Australian Competition and Consumer Commission v Australian Safeway Stores Pty Ltd and Another* (2003) 129 FCR 339

*Australian Competition and Consumer Commission v J McPhee & Son (Australia) Pty Ltd* [1997] 469 FCA (19 May 1997)

*Australian Competition and Consumer Commission v Simsmetal Limited and Ors* [2000] FCA 818 (20 June 2000)

*Ballard v Sperry Rand Aust Ltd* (1975) 8 ALR 696

*Beach Petroleum NL and Claremont Petroleum NL v Johnson* (1993) 115 ALR 411

*Beckwith v R* (1976) 135 CLR 569

*Bell Group Ltd (in Liq) v Westpac Banking Corporation (No 9)* (2008) 70 ACSR 1
*Blackwell v Barroile Pty Limited* (1994) 51 FCR 347
*Boardman v Phipps* [1967] 2 AC 46
*Boughey v Queen* (1986) 161 CLR 10
*Brambles Holdings v Carey* (1976) 2 ACLR 126
*British American Tobacco Australian Services Ltd v Blanch* [2004] NSWSC 7
*Brockley Investments Ltd v Black* (1991) 9 ACLC 255
*Case C-45/08, Spector Photo Group*, 2009 ECR I-12073
*City of Perth and Ors v DL (Representing the Members of People Living with Aids (WA) (Inc) and Ors* BC960167 [1996] EOC 92–796 (27 March 1996)
*Cody v J H Nelson Pty Ltd* (1947) 74 CLR 629
*Collins v State Rail Authority (NSW)* (1986) 5 NSWLR 209
*Commissioner for Corporate Affairs v Green* [1978] VR 505
*Commonwealth v Baume* (1905) 2 CLR 405
*Crabtree-Vickers v Australian Direct Mail* (1975) 33 CLR 72
*D & J Constructions Pty Limited v Head & Ors Trading as Clayton Utz* (1987) 9 NSWLR 118
*Director of Public Prosecutions Reference No 1 of 1996* [1998] 3 VR 352
*Dirks v Securities and Exchange Commission*, 463 US 646 (1983)
*Downey v Carlson Hotels Asia Pacific Pty Ltd* [2005] QCA 199
*Duke Group Limited (in liquidation) v Pilmer and Ors* (1999) 73 SASR 64
*El Ajou v Dollar Land Holdings Plc* [1994] 2 All ER 685
*Emhill Pty Ltd v Bonsoc Pty Ltd* (2005) 55 ACSR 379
*Endresz v Whitehouse* (1997) 24 ACSR 208
*Ex Parte Sun Securities Ltd* (1990) 1 ACSR 588
*Exicom Pty Ltd v Futuris Corporation Ltd* (1995) 18 ACSR 404; 13 ACLC 1758
*Forrest v ASIC; Fortescue Metals Group Ltd v ASIC* [2012] HCA 39
*Freeman & Lockyer v Buckhurst Park Properties (Mangal) Ltd* [1964] 2 QB 480
*Fysh v R* [2013] NSWCCA 284
*G J Coles & Co Ltd v Goldsworthy* [1985] WAR 183
*Gett v Tabet* (2009) 254 ALR 504
*Grant-Taylor v Babcock & Brown Limited* [2016] FCAFC 60
*H L Bolton (Engineering) Co Ltd v T J Graham & Sons Ltd* [1957] 1 QB 159
*Hadgkiss v Sunland Constructions Pty Ltd* [2007] FCA 346 (14 March 2007)
*Hamilton v Whitehead* (1988) 166 CLR 121
*Hunley v Automotive Food, Metals, Engineering, Printing and Kindred Industries Union* (2000) 100 FCR 530; [2000] FCA 1188
*Hannes v DPP* [2006] NSW CCA 373; (2006) 165 A Crim R 151
*Hannes v R* [2008] HCA 224
*Harkness v Commonwealth Bank of Australia Ltd* (1993) 32 NSWLR 543
*He Kaw Teh v R* (1985) 157 CLR 523
*Hely-Hutchinson v Brayhead Ltd* [1968] 1 QB 549
*Herbert Adams Pty Ltd v Federal Commission for Taxation* (1932) 47 CLR 222
*Hollis v Vabu* (2001) HCA 44
*Hooker Investments Pty Ltd v Baring Bros Halkerston & Partners Securities Ltd* (1986) 10 ACLR 462
*Hooker Investments Pty Ltd v Baring Bros Halkerston & Partners Securities Ltd* (1986) 5 NSWLR 157
*Houghton and Co v Nothard, Lowe and Wills Ltd* [1928] AC 1

*ICAL Ltd v County Natwest Securities Australia Ltd* (1988) 13 ACR 129

*International Harvester Co of Australia Pty Lt v Carrigan's Hazledene Pastoral Co* (1958) 100 CLR 644

*James Hardie Industries NV v ASIC* [2010] NSWCA 332

*Jubilee Mines NL v Riley* (2009) 253 ALR 673

*Kelly v Cooper* [1993] AC 205

*Krakowski v Eurolynx Properties Ltd* (1995) 182 CLR 563; 130 ALR 1

*Lennard's Carrying Co Ltd v Asiatic Petroleum Co Ltd* [1915] AC 705

*Lisciandro v Official Trustee in Bankruptcy* (1996) 69 FCR 180

*McDonald Estate v Martin* (1991) 77 DLR (4th) 249

*Mallesons Stephen Jaques v KPMG Peat Marwick* [1990] WAR 357

*Mansfield and Kizon v R* (2012) 87 ALJR 20

*Marshall v Director-General, Department of Transport* (2001) 205 CLR 603

*Meridian Global Funds Management Asia Limited v Securities Commission* [1995] AC 500

*Minister for Environment and Heritage v Greentree and Others* (2004) 138 FCR 198

*Moors v Burke* (1919) 26 CLR 265

*Mousell Bros Ltd v London and North-Western Railway Co* [1917] 2 KB 836

*NMFM Property Pty Ltd v Citibank (No 10)* (2000) 186 ALR 442

*Peso Silver Mines v Cropper* [1966] SCR 673

*Peterson v Maloney* (1951) 84 CLR 91

*Phipps v Boardman* [1967] 2 AC 46

*Photocure ASA v Queen's University at Kingston* [2002] FCA 905

*Prince Jefri Bolkiah v KPMG* [1999] 2 AC 222

*Queen v LK* [2010] HCA 17

*R v Australasian Films Ltd* (1921) 29 CLR 195

*R v Barker* (1983) 153 CLR 338

*R v Birmingham and Gloucester Railway Co* (1842) 114 ER 492

*R v Doff* [2005] NSWSC 50; (2005) 23 ACLC 317

*R v Evans & Doyle* (Supreme Court of Victoria, McDonald J, 15 November 1999)

*R v Firns* (District Court of New South Wales, Sides J, 4 November 1999)

*R v Firns* (2001) 19 ACLC 1495; 38 ACSR 223

*R v Hannes* (2000) 158 FLR 359

*R v Kruse* (District Court of New South Wales, O'Reilly DCJ, 2 December 1999)

*R v Mansfield and Kizon* (2011) 251 FLR 286

*R v Rivkin* (2003) 198 ALR 400

*R v Rivkin* (2004) 184 FLR 365

*R v Teh* (District Court of Victoria, Kelly DCJ, 2 September 1991)

*R v The Great North of England Railway Co* (1846) 115 ER 1294

*Re Chisum Services* (1982) 7 ACLR 641

*Re David Payne & Co Ltd* [1904] 2 Ch 608

*Re Marseilles Extension Railway Company* (1971) LR 7 Ch App 161

*Re Merrill Lynch, Pierce, Fenner and Smith, Inc.* 43 S.E.C. 933 (1968)

*Re Rossfield Group Operations Pty Ltd* [1981] Qd R 372

*Regal Hastings v Gulliver* [1967] 2 AC 134

*Riley v Jubilee Mines NL* [2009] HCA Trans 168 (31 July 2009)

*Rivkin Financial Services Ltd v Sofcom Ltd* (2004) 51 ACSR 486

*Rowe v Transport Workers Union of Australia* (1998) 160 ALR 66

*Securities and Exchange Commission v Texas Gulf Sulphur Co*, 401 F 2d 833 (1968)

*Shapiro v Merrill Lynch*, 495 F 2D 228 (2d Cir 1974)
*Sherras v De Rutzen* (1895) 1 QB 918
*Societe Generale de Paris v Tramways Union Co Ltd* (1884) 14 QBD 424
*Spincode Pty Ltd v Look Software Pty Ltd* [2001] VSC 287
*Stevens v Brodribb Sawmilling Co Pty Ltd* (1986) HCA 1
*Sun Securities v National Companies and Securities Commission* (1990) 2 ACSR 796
*Sydbank Soenderjylland A/S v Bannerton Holdings Pty Ltd* (1996) ATPR 41–525
*Tesco Supermarkets Ltd v Nattrass* (1972) AC 153
*Towers & Co Ltd v Gray* [1961] 2 QB 351
*Trade Practices Commission v Queensland Aggregates Pty Ltd* (1982) 44 ALR 391
*Trade Practices Commission v Tubemakers of Australia Ltd* (1983) 47 ALR 719
*United States v Bank of England*, 821 F2d 844 (1987)
*United States v O'Hagan*, 521 US 642 (1997)
*Universal Telecasters (Qld) Ltd v Guthrie* (1978) 18 ALR 531
*Walplan Pty Ltd v Wallace* (1985) 8 FCR 27
*Wan v McDonald* (1992) 33 FCR 491
*Warner v Commissioner of Police of the Metropolis* [1969] 2 AC 256
*Westgold Resources NL v St George Bank Ltd* [1988] WASC 352

## Legislation and regulatory instruments

*Acts Interpretation Act 1901* (Cth)
*Corporate Law Economic Reform Program Act 1999* (Cth)
*Corporate Law Reform Act 1992* (Cth)
*Corporations Act 1989* (Cth)
*Corporations Act 2001* (Cth)
*Corporations Law*
*Corporations Legislation Amendment Act 1991* (Cth)
*Corporations Regulations 2001* (Cth)
*Council Directive 89/592/EEC of 13 November 1989 Coordinating Regulations on Insider Dealing*, OJ 1989 L 334/30
*Crimes Act 1914* (Cth)
*Criminal Code Act 1995* (Cth)
*Criminal Justice Act 1993* (UK) c 36
*Directive 2003/6/EC of the European Parliament and of the Council of 28 Junuary 2003 on Insider Dealing and Market Abuse*, OJ 2003 l 96/16
*Directive 2004/39/EC of the European Parliament and of the Council of 21 April 2004 on Markets in Financial Instruments*, OJ 2004 L 145
*Directive 2014/57/EU of the European Parliament and of the Council of 16 April 2014 on Criminal Sanctions for Market Abuse*, OJ 2014 L 173.179
Explanatory Memorandum, Acts Interpretation Amendment Bill 2011 (Cth)
Explanatory Memorandum, Corporate Law Economic Reform Program (Audit Reform and Corporate Disclosure) Bill 2003 (Cth)
Explanatory Memorandum, Corporate Law Reform Bill 1992 (Cth)
Explanatory Memorandum, Corporations Legislation Amendment Bill 1991 (Cth)
Explanatory Memorandum, Financial Services Reform Bill 2001 (Cth)
*Financial Markets Conduct Act 2013* (NZ)
*Financial Services and Markets Acts 2000* (UK) c 8

*Financial Services Reform Act 2001* (Cth)

*Insider Trading and Securities Fraud Enforcement Act of 1988*, P.L. No 100–704 (1988)

*Insider Trading Sanctions Act of 1984*, P.L. No 98–376 (1984)

*Interpretation Act 1965* (Singapore)

*Interpretation Act 1978* (UK) c 30

*Interpretation Act 1999* (NZ)

*Interpretation and General Clauses Ordinance* (Hong Kong) cap 1

*Regulation (EU) 596/2014 of the European Parliament and of the Council of 16 April 2014 on Market Abuse*

*Securities Amendment Act 1988* (NZ)

*Securities and Futures Act 2001* (Singapore)

*Securities and Futures Ordinance (Hong Kong)* cap 571

*Securities Exchange Act of 1934*, 15 USC § 78a (1934)

*Securities Industry Act 1970* (NSW)

*Securities Industry Act 1970* (Qld)

*Securities Industry Act 1970* (Vic)

*Securities Industry Act 1970* (WA)

*Securities Industry (NSW) Code*

*Securities Industry (WA) Code*

*Trade Descriptions Act 1968* (UK)

*Trade Practices Act 1974* (Cth)

*Wertpapierhandelsgesetz (Securities Trading Act) (WpHG)* (Germany)

*Workplace Relations Act 1996* (Cth)

# Index

*ABC Developmental Learning Centres Pty Ltd v Wallace* 63, 64
*Acts Interpretation Act 1901* 40
actus reus 55–56, 58, 64–67, 92
agency 73, 117; actual and apparant authority and 114; common law 86, 97; defined 88; general law 79, 89, 90–91, 95, 102; principles of 105–106; proposed reforms to 164; rules of 63
aggregation doctrine 64–65
*Ampolex Ltd v Perpetual Trustee Company (Canberra) Ltd (No 2)* 49
*Ampolex Ltd v Perpetual Trustee Trading Co (Canberra) Ltd* 14
*Asia Pacific Communications Limited v Optus Networks Pty Limited* 140
*ASIC v Citigroup Global Markets Australia Pty Ltd* 4–5, 13, 17–18, 32, 50, 70, 71; Chinese Wall defence and 121, 131–133, 139–140; different mechanisms for determining when a corporation possess information and 98; element of possession and 75, 79; flaws in current regime and 157; identification doctrine and 104; insider trader notifications and 152–153; statutory mechanisms and 82–84, 90, 114
*ASIC v Hochtief* 50–51, 70–71; different mechanisms for determining when a corporation possess information 98; element of possession and 76, 79
*ASIC v Petsas & Miot* 31–32, 70
*ASIC v Vizard* 155
'Aspects of Market Integrity' report 19
ASX Listing Rules 94–95, 133–135; continuous disclosure obligations 148–151; notification of directors' securities trading 156–157; securities trading policies 151–152

*Attorney-General's Department and Australian Iron and Steel Pty Ltd v Cockcroft* 131
authority: agency and 88; Chinese Wall defence and 147; conduct of corporations and 116, 162, 165, 167–169; corporate liability and 68–69, 159, 167–168; general law agency rules and 90–91; identification doctrine and 91–94, 115–116; knowledge of corporations and 105–106; to receive and disclose information 96, 105; scope of 88–90, 102, 113–114; state of mind and 81, 87; vicarious liability and 57, 59, 62
awareness 20–23, 40, 75, 81, 87, 105, 137, 151
Ayres, Ian 70

Bainbridge, Stephen M. 8
*Bell Group Ltd (in Liq) v Westpac Banking Corporation (No 9)* 93
*Boardman v Phipps* 84
Braithwaite, John 70
*Brockley Investments Ltd v Black* 46
business obligations: concluding comments on 155; continuous disclosure regime in 94–95, 148–151; directors' duties and conflicts of interest 154–155; insider trader notifications 152–153; notification of directors' securities trading 153–154; securities trading policies 151–152

CAMAC (Corporations and Markets Advisory Committee) 38; on application of insider trading laws limited to natural persons 51–52; 'Aspects of Market Integrity' report 19; on Chinese Wall defence 130,

146; flaws in current regime and 161; on 'use' requirement 24

'Campbell Inquiry' 9

Chinese Wall defence 40, 41, 43–44, 50, 52, 54, 78, 119, 159–160; cases concerning, in other contexts 136–139; cases concerning insider trading and 131–133; inside information not communicated and no advice given in 139–140; international comparisons of 140–146; market rules and accepted industry practices in 133–135; nature of 120–122; necessity of 125–126; origins of 122–124; person deciding to trade in relevant financial products did not possess inside information condition in 126–130; preliminary conclusions and recommended reforms 146–147; proposed new provisions for 163, 169; requirements for reliance on 126–146; sufficient Chinese Wall was in place condition in 130–131

Citigroup 4, 13, 17–18

civil liability 69–71; model of 71–72; reasons for 51–54; *see also* criminal liability

civil penalty proceedings 1, 4; application of insider trading laws to corporations and 40, 50–51, 54; attributing the elements of insider trading to corporations and 100; business obligations and 150, 155; corporate liability 70–71; regulation of insider trading and 17, 36

collective knowledge 93–94

collectivism 53

*Companies Code* 131

conduct, proposed reforms to 168

confidential information 7–8, 18, 52, 124, 132, 136–139, 152–155

conflicts of interest 43, 84; Chinese Wall defence and 123–124, 132–134, 141n88, 141n92; directors' duties and 154–155

continuous disclosure obligations 94–95, 148–151

convictions for insider trading 4, 18, 22, 26, 30

corporate liability for insider trading 156–157; flaws in current regime for 157–161; nature of proposed reforms to 164–170; proposed new provisions for 161–163, 168–169

corporations, application of insider trading laws to: corporation as a 'person' caught by the prohibition of insider trading 39–41; history and theory of 44–51; reasons for 51–54; *see also* civil liability; criminal liability; elements of insider trading attributed to corporations

*Corporations Act* 14–15, 117–119; aggregation doctrine and 65; Chinese Wall defence and (*see* Chinese Wall defence); on contentious aspects of insider trading 38; continuous disclosure obligations 94–95, 148–151; corporate criminal liability and 55–56; on corporation as a 'person' 39–41; on demonstrating that a corporation 'ought reasonably' to have certain knowledge 107–108; different mechanisms for determining when a corporation possess information 95–99; different mechanisms for establishing conduct of corporations 116–117; different mechanisms for establishing knowledge of corporations 105–106; on directors' duties and conflicts of interest 154–155; flaws in current regime and 157–159; general law agency rules 90–91; general law principles 103–104; identification doctrine 91–93; on information not generally available 24–28; on knowledge that information is inside information 34–36; on material information 28–34; on possession of information 16–24, 75–82; proposal for attribution possible for all officers, employees and agents of corporation in 167; proposal that conduct must occur within scope of authority or with authorisation of person with authority, on behalf of corporation in 167–168; proposed amendments concerning section 1043M of 169–170; proposed exclusion of section 769B of 166; proposed new provisions for 161–163; statutory mechanisms 82–90, 100–102, 111–115; on trading, procuring and tipping in relevant financial products 37–38; on trading element 110–117

*Corporations Law* 9, 107–108; Chinese Wall defence and 131

*Corporations Legislation Amendment Act 1991* 9, 130

*Criminal Code* 117; aggregation doctrine and 65; Chinese Wall defence and 147; on evidential burden 121; on organisational fault 66; proposal for continued exclusion of 165–166; statutory principles of corporate criminal liability 66–69

*Criminal Justice Act 1993* (UK) 42

criminal liability: aggregation doctrine and 64–65; direct liability 58–64; models of 55–57; organisational fault and 66; reasons for 51–54; statutory principles of corporate criminal liability in 66–69; vicarious liability in 57–58; *see also* civil liability

deductions, conclusions and inferences 28

detection of insider trading 131, 135, 161

deterrents 5, 36, 52–53, 71, 172

directing mind and will 61–64, 66, 158; attributing the possession element to corporations and 86, 90–92, 96, 104–106, 115–116; direct liability and 58–59

direct liability 58–64

direct model of corporate liability for insider trading 168–169

directors' duties and conflicts of interest 154–155

directors' securities trading notifications 153–154

efficient markets hypothesis 8

elements of insider trading attributed to corporations: agency principles 105; collective knowledge 93–94; demonstrating that a corporation 'ought reasonably' to have certain knowledge 107–108; different mechanisms for determining when a corporation possess information 95–99; different mechanisms for establishing conduct of corporations 116–117; different mechanisms for establishing knowledge of corporations and 105–106; general law agency rules 90–91; general law principles 103–104; identification doctrine 91–93, 104, 115–116; international comparisons of 108–110; knowledge 99–110; possession 75–99; preliminary

conclusions and recommended reforms 117–118; relationship with continuous disclosure obligations 94–95; relevant 73–75; statutory mechanisms 82–90, 100–102, 111–115; trading 110–117

European Council 2

evidential burden 121

executives 1, 17–20, 90, 92, 101, 114–115, 152, 167

*Exicom Pty Ltd v Futuris Corporation Ltd* 10, 48

*Ex Parte Sun Securities Ld.* 47

fault elements 56, 66

fiduciary duty rationale for prohibition of insider trading 7–8

*Financial Conduct Authority Handbook* 142

*Financial Markets Conduct Act 2013* (NZ) 143–144

financial products 1, 7, 14–16, 157, 169; information not generally available on 24–25; material information on 28–29; publishable information on 26–28; trading, procuring and tipping in relevant 37–38

*Financial Services and Markets Act 2000* (UK) 43, 142

*Financial Services Reform Act 2001* 27, 36

*Fysh v R* 22–23, 31

general law agency rules 90–91; proposed reforms to 164

generally available information 24–28

*Grant-Taylor v Babcock & Brown* 33–34

'Griffiths Committee' 9

*Hamilton v Whitehead* 61–62

*Hanley v. Automotive, Food, Metals, Engineering, Printing & Kindred Industries Union* 113, 115

Hannes, S. 22

*Hannes v. DPP* 29

*He Kaw Teh v R* 20–21

High Court of Australia 10, 15, 18, 20, 61, 64–65, 67

*H L Bolton (Engineering) Co Ltd v T J Graham & Sons Ltd* 59–61

Hochtief Actiengesellschaft 4

*Hooker Investments Pty Ltd v Baring Bros Halkerston & Partners Securities Ltd* 10, 45, 46

identification doctrine 91–93, 104, 115–116
indirect liability *see* vicarious liability
individualism 53
information: confidential 7–8, 18, 52, 124, 132, 136–139, 152–155; deductions, conclusions and inferences 28; different mechanisms for determining when a corporation possess 95–99; general availability of 24–28; knowledge that information is inside 34–36; material 28–34; materiality of 29–35, 151; nature of 16–20; not communicated and no advice given in Chinese Wall defence 139–140; person deciding to trade in relevant financial products did not possess inside, in Chinese Wall defence 126–130; possession of 16–24; price-sensitive 6–7; proposal for no requirement for nexus with role or position for knowledge or 166–167; publishable 26–28; readily observable 25–26
inside information: knowledge that information is 34–36; not communicated and no advice given, in Chinese Wall defence 139–140; person deciding to trade in relevant financial products did not possess, in Chinese Wall defence 126–130
insider trading: background to prohibition of 2–6; business obligations and (*see* business obligations); cases concerning Chinese Wall defence and 131–133; conclusions from study of Australian 171–172; contentious aspects of 38; convictions for 4, 18, 22, 26, 30; corporate liability for (*See* corporate liability for insider trading); defining 1; detection of 131, 135, 161; first conviction for 4; laws (*See* laws, Australian insider trading); rationale for prohibition of 6–12; regulation of (*see* regulation of insider trading); trading, procuring and tipping in 37–38; *see also* elements of insider trading attributed to corporations
international comparisons: of Chinese Wall defence 140–146; of insider trading laws 41–44, 43n14, 108–110
International Organisation of Securities Commissions 3

investors 1, 6–7, 18, 30, 48–49, 152, 160; confidence of 9, 138–139; materiality and 29; publishable information and 26–28; reasonable 32–33

*Jubilee Mines v Riley* 32–34

knowledge element applied to corporations 99–110; proposed reforms to 166–167, 168

laws, Australian insider trading 13–16; corporation as a 'person' caught by the prohibition of insider trading and 39–41; history and theory of application of 44–51; international comparisons of 41–44, 43n14; reasons for corporate application of 51–54; *see also* civil liability; criminal liability
*Lennard's Carrying Co Ltd v Asiatic Petroleum Co Ltd* 58–61
liability: corporate (*See* corporate liability for insider trading) *see* civil liability; criminal liability

*Mallesons Stephen Jaques v KPMG Peat Marwick* 122
*Mansfield and Kizon v R* 15, 16–17, 18
'Market Abuse Directive' 11
market efficiency rationale for prohibition of insider trading 7, 11
market fairness rationale for prohibition of insider trading 6–7, 11
market integrity 1, 5–6, 48, 69, 71, 85–86, 95, 160–161; Chinese Wall defence and 119, 127, 135, 140, 146–147; criminal liability and 53; direct liability model and 118; as rationale for prohibition on insider trading 9–11, 138
market rules and accepted industry practices with Chinese Wall defence 133–135
material effects 15, 24, 28–30, 32–34; ASX Listing Rules on 150; contentious aspects of insider trading and 38; inside information 35
material information 28–34
materiality 29–35, 151
mens rea 55, 56, 66, 67, 92
*Meridian Global Funds Management Asia Limited v Securities Commission* 62, 63–64

misappropriation rationale for prohibition of insider trading 8, 11–12
*Mousell Bros Ltd v London and North-Western Railway Co* 57

obligations *see* business obligations
officers, corporate 1, 40, 44–45, 47, 50, 69, 72, 167; attributing the possession element to corporations and 75–80, 82–87; authority and 113; board of directors and 92; business obligations and 150, 154; Chinese Wall defence and 121–126, 128, 132–133, 145, 147; collective knowledge of 93–94; continuous disclosure obligations and 94–95; corporate liability and 158–159, 162–163, 165; different mechanisms for determining when corporation possesses information and 95–101, 105–106; direct liability and 58–62; general law agency rules and 90–91; international comparisons of 108–109; 'ought reasonably to know' 107–108; proposals for 117–118; vicarious liability and 57
organisational fault 66

penalties: civil 36, 70–71; criminal 40
person deciding to trade in relevant financial products did not possess inside information in Chinese Wall defence 126–130
*Peso Silver Mines v Cropper* 84
physical elements 56, 66–68, 67n84, 74–75, 102, 111, 116, 155, 165
possession of information 16–24; attributed to corporations 75–99; different mechanisms for determining when a corporation is in 95–99; nature of information in 16–20; nature of possession in 20–24; proposed reforms to 168
price-sensitive information 6–7
primary insiders 12, 44–45, 51
procuring 37–38, 89–90, 96, 102, 113; Chinese Walls defence and 125–126, 128–130; of persons 75, 110–111; proposed reforms for 117–118
prohibition of insider trading 20–21, 27, 34; applied to corporations 51–54, 85–86; applying only to natural persons 46–51; background to 2–6; Chinese Wall defence and

132–133, 143–147; civil penalty proceedings and 70; corporation as 'person' caught by 39–41; rationale for 6–12
proprietary trader(s): *ASIC v Citizgroup* and 17, 32, 76, 79, 82–83, 90, 104, 112, 114, 132, 157; Chinese Wall defence and 132, 139; knowledge of 101
prosecution 1, 4–5, 34, 155, 161, 172; criminal 49, 70–71, 100; evidential burden in 121
prosecutors 4–5, 171
publishable information 26–28

*Queen v LK, The* 67

rationale for prohibiting insider trading 1, 6–12
readily observable information 25–26
reasonable person 35
*Re Chisum Services* 93
reforms 156–157; attributing the elements of insider trading to corporations 117–118; Chinese Wall defence 146–147; flaws in current regime and 157–161; nature of proposed corporate liability 164–170; proposed new provisions for corporate liability and 161–163, 168–169
*Regal Hastings v Gulliver* 84
regulation of insider trading: contentious aspects of insider trading and 38; key features of Australian laws for 13–16; knowledge that information is inside information and 34–36; material information and 28–34; possession of information and 16–24; trading, procuring and tipping in relevant financial products and 37–38
regulators 1, 4–6, 117, 139, 160–161, 171
*Regulatory Guide 79 Managing Conflicts of Interest: A Guide for Research Report Providers* (RG 79) 133–134
*Regulatory Guide 181 Licensing: Managing Conflicts of Interest* (RG 181) 133–134
*Re Merrill Lynch, Pierce, Fenner and Smith, Inc.* 122–123
*Rivkin Financial Services Ltd v Sofcom Ltd* 49–50, 79

*Rowe v Transport Workes Union of Australia* 77
rumours and speculation 16, 19
*R v Australasian Films Ltd* 65
*R v Evans and Doyle* 37
*R v Firns* 10, 25–26
*R v Hannes* 31, 75
*R v Kruse* 25–26
*R v Mansfield and Kizon* 10, 14
*R v Rivkin* 18–20, 30–31, 35

secondary insiders 12, 45–47
*Securities Amendment Act 1988* (NZ) 62
*Securities and Futures Act 2001* (Singapore) 97, 108–109, 145
*Securities and Futures Ordinance* (Hong Kong) 144
*Securities Exchange Act of 1934* (US) 143
*Securities Industry Acts* 13
*Securities Industry (NSW) Code* 45–47, 123–124
securities markets 1–3
*Securities Trading Act (WpHG)* 140–142
securities trading policies 148, 151–152
share prices 3, 8, 30–32, 51

shares, information regarding 3, 18, 25–26, 33, 48–51
state of mind 81
*State Securities Industry Acts* 44
statutory principles of corporate criminal liability 66–69

*Tesco Supermarkets Ltd v Nattrass* 61, 62, 115
tipping 1, 15, 37–38, 74, 89, 96, 102, 110–115; Chinese Wall defence and 119, 126
*Trade Descriptions Act 1968* (UK) 59–60, 62–63
*Trade Practices Act 1974* (Cth) 103
trading, procuring and tipping 37–38

value: continuous disclosure obligations and 94, 148; information not generally available and 24; material information and 28–29; maximum penalties and 40; price-sensitive information and 7–8; regulation of insider trading and 15, 19
vicarious liability 57–58

*Westgold Resources NL v St George Bank Ltd* 48–49
*Workplace Relations Act 1996* (Cth) 115

For Product Safety Concerns and Information please contact our EU
representative GPSR@taylorandfrancis.com
Taylor & Francis Verlag GmbH, Kaufingerstraße 24, 80331 München, Germany